Advanced Spanish
STEP-BY-STEP

Master Accelerated Grammar
to Take Your Spanish to the Next Level

Barbara Bregstein

Mc
Graw
Hill

New York   Chicago   San Francisco   Lisbon   London   Madrid   Mexico City
Milan   New Delhi   San Juan   Seoul   Singapore   Sydney   Toronto

9 10   QFR/QFR   21 20 19 18 17 16

ISBN   978-0-07-176873-3
MHID   0-07-176873-4

e-ISBN   978-0-07-176874-0
e-MHID   0-07-176874-2

Library of Congress Control Number 2011937084

McGraw-Hill products are available at special quantity discounts to use as premiums
and sales promotions or for use in corporate training programs. To contact a
representative, please e-mail us at bulksales@mcgraw-hill.com.

This book is printed on acid-free paper.

Contents

Preface   vii

I   *Ser* and *Estar*; Present, Preterit, and Imperfect Tenses; Progressive Tenses; Present Subjunctive; Commands

1   *Ser* and *Estar* and the Present Tense

Estar (to be)   3
Ser (to be)   8
Reading Comprehension   **Machu Picchu**   19

2   *Ser* and *Estar* in the Preterit and Imperfect Tenses

Preterit Tense   21
Imperfect Tense   25
Regular Verbs in the Preterit   29
Irregular Verbs in the Preterit   31
Regular Verbs in the Imperfect   33
Irregular Verbs in the Imperfect   35
Comparison of Preterit and Imperfect   35
Reading Comprehension   **Marianela**   38

3 The Present Progressive Tense

Gerund Formation   41
Formation of the Present Progressive Tense   45
Use of the Present Progressive Tense   45
Placement of Object Pronouns   48
Uses of the Gerund with Verbs Other Than *estar*   52
Reading Comprehension   **La parada del bus**   56

4 The Past Progressive Tenses

The Imperfect Progressive Tense   58
The Preterit Progressive Tense   61
Reading Comprehension   **El hospital**   67

5 The Present Subjunctive

Formation of the Present Subjunctive   70
Uses of the Present Subjunctive   77
Other Tenses That Cause the Present Subjunctive   91
Reading Comprehension   **El juicio**   94

6 Commands

Affirmative *tú* Commands   98
Negative *tú* Commands   102
Ud. and *Uds.* Commands   107
Other Ways of Asking People to Do Things   110
Reading Comprehension   **Perdida en Nicaragua**   113
The *nosotros* Command: "Let us . . ."   115
Affirmative *vosotros* Commands   118
Negative *vosotros* Commands   118
Reading Comprehension   **La Noche de Brujas**   121

II   Nouns, Articles, Adjectives, Pronouns; Present and Past Perfect Tenses

7 Nouns, Articles, Adjectives, and Pronouns

Nouns and Articles   125
Possessive Adjectives   130
Possessive Pronouns   135
Relative Pronouns   139
Demonstrative Adjectives and Pronouns   144
Reading Comprehension   **Mi viaje**   146

The Neuter *lo* + Adjective Used as a Noun   147
Adjectives Used as Nouns   149
Pronouns Used as Nouns   150
Pronunciation Practice   **Los maderos de San Juan**   151
Reading Comprehension   **Lo fatal**   152

8   The Present Perfect Tense

Formation of the Past Participle   154
Formation of the Present Perfect Tense   157
Uses of the Present Perfect Tense   159
Placement of Object Pronouns with the Present Perfect Tense   160
Use of the Infinitive *haber* and the Past Participle   161
Reading Comprehension   **El apartamento**   165

9   The Past Perfect Tense

Formation of the Past Perfect Tense   167
Uses of the Past Perfect Tense   167
Reading Comprehension   **El sueño**   170
Reading Comprehension   **Recordando Nicaragua**   171
The Past Participle as an Adjective   172
The Past Participle with *ser* and the Passive Voice   176
Reading Comprehension   **El conde Lucanor**   178

III   Future and Conditional Tenses; Past Subjunctive; Idioms

10   The Future Tense

Formation of the Future Tense   181
Uses of the Future Tense   188
The Future Progressive Tense   195
The Future Perfect Tense   196
Reading Comprehension   **El porvenir**   197

11   The Conditional Tense

Formation of the Conditional Tense   199
Uses of the Conditional Tense   205
The Conditional Progressive Tense   209
The Conditional Perfect Tense   210
Reading Comprehension   **¿Qué haría Ud. en las siguientes situaciones?**   212

12   The Present Perfect Subjunctive

Formation of the Present Perfect Subjunctive   214
Uses of the Present Perfect Subjunctive   214
Reading Comprehension   **La isla en el Caribe**   218

13   The Imperfect Subjunctive

Formation of the Imperfect Subjunctive   221
Uses of the Imperfect Subjunctive   227
Reading Comprehension   **El barco económico**   234
Reading Comprehension   **Xochicalco**   243

14   The Past Perfect Subjunctive

Formation of the Past Perfect Subjunctive   245
Uses of the Past Perfect Subjunctive   245
Reading Comprehension   **Su punto de vista**   257

15   Idioms

Idioms with Prepositions   260
Idioms with Verbs   263
Time Expressions   267
Reading Comprehension   **La defensa de Sócrates**   270

Appendix: List of Verbs   273
Answer Key   280
Index   292

Preface

Advanced Spanish Step-by-Step is a progressive program for mastering the Spanish language, written for intermediate and advanced learners. It teaches grammar and conversation in a logical order so that you can continue to develop your language skills naturally. This book is the next step after *Easy Spanish Step-by-Step.* If you're just beginning with the language or need a review, *Easy Spanish Step-by-Step* is the place to start.

To take full advantage of the unique grammatical progression of the book, you should study each chapter, or step, one after another. Each step you take will lead you to the next. Each chapter contains clear grammar explanations; be sure you understand every concept before moving on to the next. Because there are few exceptions to rules, once you have learned a concept, it is yours.

Written and oral exercises are included to check your understanding and progress. Poems and stories by acclaimed authors, as well as original stories and poems by the author of this book, are included in every chapter. These readings become progressively more challenging in form and content. The Reading Comprehension sections will help you learn new vocabulary, give you practice in reading aloud, and serve as a source for discussions with your classmates.

Advanced Spanish Step-by-Step is divided into three parts. The first part reviews the present tense and uses of *ser* and *estar,* the preterit and imperfect tenses, the progressive tenses, the present subjunctive, and commands. The second part is an in-depth explanation of nouns, articles, adjectives, pronouns, and the present and past perfect tenses. The third part covers the future and conditional tenses, the past subjunctive, and idioms.

If you studied *Easy Spanish Step-by-Step,* you'll notice a brief review of *ser* and *estar* at the beginning of the first chapter. Go over it so that you refresh the basics of these two verbs. In the second chapter, devoted mostly to the past tenses of *ser* and *estar*, there is included a review of the preterit and imperfect tenses of all verbs. The present subjunctive is included in *Advanced Spanish Step-by-Step* so that you can review it before continuing to the command form, which has many of the same conjugations. All of the rest is completely new and will complete your knowledge of Spanish grammar.

This book is written with a logical approach that makes Spanish grammar accessible, even when some individual concepts are difficult. With *Advanced Spanish Step-by-Step*, you can learn to speak fluently, using all elements of Spanish. Have fun, and enjoy speaking and understanding Spanish everywhere you need it. See you in Xochicalco!

Acknowledgments

I would like to thank John Piazza for his insights, contributions, and editing of *Advanced Spanish Step-by-Step*, and to Néstor Rodriguez, teacher of English and Spanish at City College of New York, for his expertise and editing of both *Easy Spanish Step-by-Step* and *Advanced Spanish Step-by-Step*. I would also like to thank William Bronner for his invaluable guidance.

I

Ser and *Estar*;
Present, Preterit,
and Imperfect Tenses;
Progressive Tenses;
Present Subjunctive;
Commands

1

Ser and *Estar* and the Present Tense

Estar (to be)

Spanish has two verbs that are equivalent to English *to be*. Begin with the conjugation of **estar** in the present tense.

yo **estoy**	*I am*	nosotros **estamos**	*we are*
tú **estás**	*you are*	vosotros **estáis**	*you are*
él **está**	*he is*	ellos **están**	*they are*
ella **está**	*she is*	ellas **están**	*they are*
Ud. **está**	*you are*	Uds. **están**	*you are*

There is no subject pronoun *it* in Spanish. **Él** and **ella** refer to people and sometimes to animals, but not to things.

Practice the conjugation of the verb aloud. Notice that **él**, **ella**, **Ud.** (the third-person singular) have the same form of the verb. Notice also that **ellos**, **ellas**, **Uds.** (the third-person plural) have the same form of the verb.

Estar is used to express four basic concepts: location, health, changing mood or condition, and personal opinion in terms of taste or appearance.

- **Location** (where someone or something is physically located)

Nosotros estamos en el tren.	*We are on the train.*
La quinta avenida está en la ciudad.	*Fifth Avenue is in the city.*
¿Dónde están las pirámides de los Mayas?	*Where are the Mayan pyramids?*
Las mujeres están en la biblioteca.	*The women are in the library.*

3

Remember

The verb, which carries the action of the phrase, is the essential element of the Spanish sentence or question because of the amount of information it carries.

- **Health**

Yo estoy bien, gracias.	*I am fine, thanks.*
Ella está enferma.	*She is sick.*
Los doctores están enfermos.	*The doctors are sick.*
¿Cómo están Uds.?	*How are you?*
Estamos bien.	*We are well.*

- **Changing mood or condition**

La muchacha está contenta.	*The girl is happy.*
Estoy feliz.	*I am happy.*
Los hombres están cansados.	*The men are tired.*
Estamos alegres.	*We are happy.*
¿Estás enojado?	*Are you angry?*

- **Personal opinion in terms of taste or appearance**
  (English equivalents: *taste/tastes* with food and *look/looks* with appearance)

La comida está buena.	*The meal tastes good.*
El pescado está delicioso.	*The fish tastes delicious.*
La sopa está sabrosa.	*The soup tastes delicious.*
Ella está hermosa hoy.	*She looks pretty today.*
Él está guapo.	*He looks handsome.*

Remember

Often, the pronouns **yo**, **nosotros**, and **tú** are omitted. This is possible because the verb form **estamos** carries the meaning *we are*; **estoy** can only mean *I am*. The same is true of **tú estás**, which means *you are* whether **tú** is omitted or not.

Key Vocabulary

These words will help enhance your ability to communicate. As you learn them, remember to practice them aloud.

Interrogative Words

¿cómo?	*how?*
¿cuál?, ¿cuáles?	*which one?, which ones?*
¿cuándo?	*when?*
¿cuánto?, ¿cuántos?	*how much?, how many?*
¿dónde?	*where?*
¿por qué?	*why?*
¿qué?	*what?*
¿quién?, ¿quiénes?	*who?*

Adverbs of Location

aquí, acá	*here*
allí, allá	*there*

Adverbs of Direction

a la derecha	*to the right*
a la izquierda	*to the left*
derecho, recto	*straight ahead*

Prepositions of Location

al lado de	*next to*
alrededor de	*around*
ante	*before, in front of, in the presence of*
bajo	*under* (more figurative than **debajo de**)
cerca de	*near*
debajo de	*underneath*
delante de	*before, in front of* (physical location)
dentro de	*inside of*
detrás de	*behind*
encima de	*on top of*
enfrente de, frente a	*in front of, opposite, facing, across from*
entre	*between*
fuera de	*outside of*
junto a, pegado a	*close to, right next to*

| lejos de | *far from* |
| tras | *after* (in a set of expressions) |

Adjectives

alegre	*happy, glad*
bonito	*pretty*
bueno	*good*
cansado	*tired*
contento	*happy (contented)*
delicioso	*delicious*
enfermo	*sick*
enojado	*angry*
feliz	*happy*
guapo	*beautiful, handsome*
hermoso	*beautiful, handsome*
lindo	*pretty*
sabroso	*delicious*

NOTE **Guapo** describes people only; **bonito**, **hermoso**, and **lindo** are used to describe both people and things.

Exercise 1.1

Complete the following sentences with the correct form of **estar**. *Indicate whether the sentence expresses health, location, or changing mood.*

EXAMPLES Nosotros __estamos__ en la clase. (__location__)

La profesora __está__ aquí. (__location__)

1. El teléfono y el libro _____ en la mesa. (_____)

2. La mujer _____ bien; el hombre _____ enfermo.

   (_____ , _____)

3. ¿Cómo _____ Uds.? (_____)

4. ¿Dónde _____ ellos? (_____)

5. ¿Dónde _____ el baño, por favor? (_____)

6. El niño _____ enojado y la niña _____ triste.

   (_____ , _____)

7. Los muchachos _____ alegres. (_____)

8. Yo _____ contento. (_____)

9. ¿Quién _____ aquí? (_____)

10. ¿Por qué _____ el perro en la piscina? (_____)

 # Exercise 1.2

Translate the following sentences into Spanish.

1. *The river is near my house.*

   _____

2. *Australia is far from Canada.*

   _____

3. *The white flower is on top of the table.*

   _____

4. *The children are right next to their parents.*

   _____

5. *The school is between the church and the bank.*

   _____

6. *Julia's house is behind the post office.*

   _____

7. *Paula is here with her brothers.*

   _____

8. *Your shoes are underneath my chair.*

   _____

9. *Our problem is under control.*

   _____

10. *Helen's relatives are in Spain. Their suitcases are in the United States.*

    _____

Ser (to be)

Ser is also equivalent to English *to be*. In English, there is only a single verb that means *to be*. We say, for example:

> *The dog is here.*
> *The dog is brown.*

The verb is the same in both cases. But in Spanish, there is a difference, and you have to choose which verb to use.

Following is the conjugation of **ser** in the present tense.

yo **soy**	*I am*	nosotros **somos**	*we are*
tú **eres**	*you are*	vosotros **sois**	*you are*
él **es**	*he is*	ellos **son**	*they are*
ella **es**	*she is*	ellas **son**	*they are*
Ud. **es**	*you are*	Uds. **son**	*you are*

Ser is used to express seven basic concepts: description, profession, point of origin, identification, material, possession or ownership, and where an event takes place.

- **Description**

La casa es roja.	*The house is red.*
El libro es interesante.	*The book is interesting.*
Estas corbatas son feas.	*These ties are ugly.*
Somos fuertes.	*We are strong.*
Estos zapatos son más caros que esas medias.	*These shoes are more expensive than those socks.*

- **Profession**

Yo soy abogado.	*I am a lawyer.*
Él es arquitecto.	*He is an architect.*
Ellas son maestras excelentes.	*They are excellent teachers.*
Somos doctores.	*We are doctors.*
¿Eres tú ingeniero?	*Are you an engineer?*

Spanish does not translate *a/an* when stating an unmodified profession.

UNMODIFIED	Juan es bailarín.	*Juan is a dancer.*
MODIFIED	Juan es un buen bailarín.	*Juan is a good dancer.*

- **Point of origin** (where someone or something is from)

¿De dónde es Ud.?	*Where are you from?*
¿De dónde son Uds.?	*Where are you from?*
Yo soy de Nueva York.	*I am from New York.*
¿De dónde es ella?	*Where is she from?*
Somos de Italia.	*We are from Italy.*
Ellos son de los Estados Unidos.	*They are from the United States.*
El vino es de Portugal.	*The wine is from Portugal.*
La cerveza es de México.	*The beer is from Mexico.*
El café es de Brazil.	*The coffee is from Brazil.*

Remember

In common English usage, we often end a sentence with a preposition, for example, *Where are you from?* This never occurs in Spanish; the preposition can never end a sentence. The preposition, in this case **de**, is placed in front of the interrogative word, which in this case is **dónde**.

- **Identification** (relationship, nationality, or religion)

Somos amigos.	*We are friends.*
José y Eduardo son hermanos.	*Joe and Ed are brothers.*
Pablo es español.	*Paul is Spanish.*
Ella es católica.	*She is Catholic.*

- **Material** (what something is made of)

La mesa es de madera.	*The table is of wood.*
La bolsa es de plástico.	*The bag is of plastic.*
Los zapatos son de cuero.	*The shoes are of leather.*
Las ventanas son de vidrio.	*The windows are of glass.*
La casa es de piedra.	*The house is of stone.*

- **Possession or ownership**

La muñeca es de la niña.	*It's the child's doll. / The doll is the child's. (The doll is of the child.)*
Los amigos son de María.	*They are María's friends. / The friends are María's. (The friends are of María.)*

La idea es de Pedro.	*It's Pedro's idea. /*
	The idea is Pedro's.
	(The idea is of Pedro.)
El barco es del hombre rico.	*The boat belongs to the rich man.*
	(The boat is of the rich man.)
Los perros son del muchacho.	*The dogs belong to the boy.*
	(The dogs are of the boy.)
Los gatos son del niño.	*The cats belong to the child.*
	(The cats are of the child.)
El carro es de los amigos.	*The car belongs to the friends.*
	(The car is of the friends.)

De + **el** (*of* + *the*) = **del**. There are only two contractions in the Spanish language; **del** is one of them. When **de** is followed by the masculine article **el**, meaning *the*, the words contract to **del**, meaning *of the*.

A Word About Possessives

You can see that these translations are not exact. There is no apostrophe in Spanish, so when you think of *Peter's car,* for example, the Spanish structure is *el carro de Pedro.* Make sure you understand this concept, and use whichever English translation is clearest to you.

- **Where an event takes place**

La fiesta es en la casa de José.	*The party is at Joe's house.*
El concierto es en el club.	*The concert is at the club.*
La protesta es en la capital.	*The protest is in the capital.*
La huelga es en la universidad.	*The strike is at the university.*

An equivalent English translation for *is* in the examples above is *take/takes place*:

The party takes place at Joe's house.
The concert takes place at the club.
The protest takes place in the capital.

Ser is also used to tell time and in impersonal expressions.

- **Telling time**

  Spanish uses the third-person singular or plural of **ser** for telling time. **La** refers to **la hora**.

Es la una.	*It is one o'clock.*
Son las dos.	*It is two o'clock.*
Son las tres.	*It is three o'clock.*
Son las cuatro.	*It is four o'clock.*
Son las cinco.	*It is five o'clock.*
Son las seis.	*It is six o'clock.*
Son las siete.	*It is seven o'clock.*
Son las ocho.	*It is eight o'clock.*
Son las nueve.	*It is nine o'clock.*
Son las diez.	*It is ten o'clock.*
Son las once.	*It is eleven o'clock.*
Son las doce.	*It is twelve o'clock.*

- **In impersonal expressions**

Es bueno.	*It is good.*
Es difícil.	*It is difficult.*
Es fácil.	*It is easy.*
Es imposible.	*It is impossible.*
Es importante.	*It is important.*
Es malo.	*It is bad.*
Es mejor.	*It is better.*
Es necesario.	*It is necessary.*
Es posible.	*It is possible.*
Es preciso.	*It is necessary.*
Es probable.	*It is probable.*
Es una lástima.	*It's a shame. / It's a pity.*
Es urgente.	*It is urgent.*

Exercise 1.3

Complete the following sentences with the correct form of **ser***. Indicate whether the sentence expresses description, profession, point of origin, identification, material, possession, or an impersonal expression.*

EXAMPLE   _Es_ la una. (telling time)

1. El hombre _____ director. Él _____ de Chile.

    (_____ , _____)

2. Ellos _____ doctores. Ella _____ profesora.

    (_____ , _____)

3. ¿De dónde _____ los turistas? (_____)

4. Los hermanos de Pablo _____ simpáticos. (_____)

5. El hotel viejo _____ excelente. (_____)

6. Nosotros _____ amigos de Raúl. (_____)

7. Los guantes _____ de cuero. (_____)

8. La mujer y el hombre _____ de Ecuador. (_____)

9. Yo _____ de Puerto Rico. ¿De dónde _____ Ud.?

    (_____ , _____)

10. El apartamento _____ de los estudiantes jóvenes.

    (_____)

11. ¿ _____ tú una estudiante maravillosa? (_____)

12. Los pantalones _____ verdes y rojos. (_____)

13. El café _____ de Colombia. (_____)

14. ¿Quién _____ el presidente de los Estados Unidos?

    (_____)

15. _____ preciso comer bien. (_____)

Exercise 1.4

Complete the following sentences with the correct form of **ser**.

1. Helena _____ de Colombia.

2. El hermano de ella _____ católico.

3. Ellos _____ profesores excelentes.

4. Los carros _____ grises.

5. Nosotros _____ estudiantes.

Complete the following sentences with the correct form of **estar**.

6. San Francisco _____ en California.

7. ¿Cómo está Ud.? Yo _____ bien.

8. El profesor _____ enfermo.

9. Nosotros _____ en la clase.

10. ¿_____ tú triste?

11. Los perros _____ en el carro.

Exercise 1.5

Complete the following sentences with the correct form of either **ser** *or* **estar**.

1. Yo _____ español.

2. Ellos _____ aquí.

3. José y Juan _____ enfermos.

4. Tú _____ abogado.

5. La lección no _____ fácil.

6. Los estudiantes _____ en la ciudad.

7. ¿Cómo _____ Uds.? Nosotros _____ bien, gracias.

8. Hoy _____ miércoles. ¿Dónde _____ los doctores?

9. El profesor _____ contento.

10. Los espejos en el baño _____ grandes.

11. La mesa, las sillas blancas y la lámpara _____ en la casa,

    pero la casa _____ pequeña.

12. La amiga de Sara _____ enferma y Sara _____
    triste.

13. ¿De dónde _____ el vino blanco?

14. Los muchachos y las muchachas _____ en el tren.

    Ellos _____ contentos porque _____ amigos.

15. ¿Quién _____ en el parque?

16. ¿Dónde _____ la sobrina de Fernando?

17. ¿Qué hora _____?

18. _____ las cuatro y media.

19. La presentación _____ a las siete de la noche.

20. ¿De qué color _____ la falda?

Exercise 1.6

Translate the following sentences into Spanish.

1. *The dentists are in their offices.*

   _____

2. *Everyone is sick. Even the doctors are sick.*

   _____

3. *The soup is hot. The meal is delicious.*

   _____

4. *It is necessary to study.*

   _____

5. *Is it possible to learn everything?*

   _____

Common Expressions with *estar*

está bien	*okay, fine*
estar a salvo	*to be safe*
estar bien	*to be fine*
estar con	*to be with*
estar de acuerdo con	*to be in agreement with*
estar de buen genio	*to be in a good mood*
estar de buen humor	*to be in a good mood*
estar de mal genio	*to be in a bad mood*
estar de mal humor	*to be in a bad mood*
estar de pie	*to be standing up*
estar de rodillas	*to be on one's knees*
estar de vacaciones	*to be on vacation*
estar de vuelta	*to be returning*
estar en peligro	*to be in danger*
estar entre la vida y la muerte	*to be between life and death*
estar listo	*to be ready*
estar mal	*to be bad* (adverb)
estar para	*to be about to*
estar por	*to be in favor of*
estar seguro	*to be sure*
estar sin	*to be without*

In general, **estar** is used with the adjectives **frío**, **caliente**, **sucio**, and **limpio**.

El agua está fría.	*The water is cold.*
La sopa está caliente.	*The soup is hot.*
Mi apartamento está sucio.	*My apartment is dirty.*
La casa de María está limpia.	*María's house is clean.*

Common Expressions with *ser*

ser bueno	*to be good*
ser malo	*to be bad*
ser listo	*to be clever*
ser todo oídos	*to be all ears*

Ser and estar and Description

You have learned that **ser** is used for basic description, as in the following examples:

> *The dog is white.*
> *The floor is gray.*
> *We are intelligent.*

However, there are specific situations with description in which **estar** is used. Following are examples of typical uses of **ser** for description, contrasted with related specific uses of **estar**.

- **Food**

    When talking about food in general, use **ser**.

El pescado es bueno para la salud.	*Fish is good for health.*
La carne es mala para la presión.	*Meat is bad for the blood pressure.*

    When giving an opinion about food, use **estar**.

Esta comida está mala.	*This meal is bad.*
El pescado está bueno.	*The fish is good.*
La sopa está sabrosa.	*The soup is delicious.*
Las papas están deliciosas.	*The potatoes are delicious.*

- **Appearance**

    When stating an inherent characteristic, use **ser**.

Ella es hermosa.	*She is beautiful.*
Él es gordo.	*He is fat.*
La actriz es vieja.	*The actress is old.*
Mis amigas son delgadas.	*My friends are slender.*

    When giving an opinion about appearance, use **estar**.

Ella está hermosa.	*She looks beautiful.*
Él está gordo.	*He looks fat to me.*
	(He has gotten fat.)
La actriz está vieja.	*The actress looks old.*

- **Classification**

  When an adjective applies to something that exists without exception, use **ser**.

Los seres humanos son mortales.	*Human beings are mortal.*
La sangre es roja.	*Blood is red.*
El agua es necesaria para la vida.	*Water is necessary for life.*
El oxígeno es indispensable para los seres vivos.	*Oxygen is indispensable for living beings.*
La nieve es blanca.	*Snow is white.*
El cielo es azul.	*The sky is blue.*

  When the description is outside the known or cultural norm, use **estar**.

La nieve está roja por la sangre.	*The snow is red because of the blood.*
El cielo está anaranjado y amarillo por la puesta del sol.	*The sky is orange and yellow because of the sunset.*
La puerta está azul marino por el sol fuerte.	*The door looks navy blue because of the strong sun.*
Los labios del niño están azules porque está congelado.	*The child's lips are blue because he is freezing.*

Exercise 1.7

Complete the following sentences with the correct form of **ser** *or* **estar**, *according to the meaning of the sentence.*

1. El niño _____ de mal genio hoy. Su mamá no sabe que hacer.

2. _____ o no _____; es la cuestión.

3. La reunión _____ en el segundo piso.

4. Las flores que los estudiantes me regalan _____ en el salón.

5. ¿Dónde _____ yo?

6. ¿Cómo sabes quien _____ (tú)?

7. ¿Qué hora _____? _____ las dos.

8. ¿Cuál _____ la fecha de hoy?

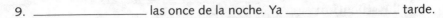

9. _____ las once de la noche. Ya _____ tarde.

10. _____ demasiado temprano para levantarse.

11. Hoy _____ lunes, el cinco de mayo.

12. El estudiante trabaja mucho para _____ doctor.

13. La muchacha llora sin _____ triste.

14. El agua _____ fría.

15. Esta comida de tu madre _____ sabrosa.

16. Con los problemas que él tiene, no me explico como este hombre

    _____ tan contento.

17. Tu rival _____ más listo que tú en esta ocasión.

18. La comida que sirven aquí _____ caliente.

19. Luis y su familia _____ muy alegres de haberse ganado la lotería.

20. Este cuarto _____ la habitación más bonita de la casa.

21. ¿Quién _____ en peligro en una ciudad grande?

22. No hay cupo en el tren y yo tengo que _____ de pie.

23. La mujer _____ muy enferma; _____ entre la vida
    y la muerte.

24. La profesora tiene una opinión pero sus estudiantes no _____
    de acuerdo con ella.

25. Siempre escucho las noticias. Yo _____ todo oídos.

26. El agua _____ necesaria para la vida.

27. La clase _____ para terminar y todo el mundo

    _____ para salir.

28. El cielo _____ gris.

29. Nosotros _____ sin un paraguas.

30. Esta lección _____ difícil.

Reading Comprehension

Machu Picchu
Ancient Mountain

Machu Picchu es uno de los sitios más impresionantes del mundo. La ciudad antigua de los incas, construida en 1450 de piedras enormes y jardines maravillosos, está en Perú a 120 kilómetros de Cuzco, un pueblo colonial.

Es el año 1979. Estoy en Cuzco con un grupo turístico. Al principio, somos un buen grupo. Pero con en el calor insoportable del verano, el grupo cambia y somos todos contra uno y uno contra todos. En este sitio tan espiritual, en la cumbre de las montañas de los incas, bajo una vista majestuosa de las montañas, donde uno está cerca de los dioses de los incas y lejos de la civilización conocida, somos enemigos mortales.

El bus de regreso está lleno de pasajeros. Son las cuatro de la tarde y estamos de vuelta. Estoy sola ahora y según el refrán "es mejor estar sola que mal acompañada".

Verbos

cambiar	*to change*
estar	*to be*
ser	*to be*

Preposiciones

contra	*against*
según	*according to*

Adjetivos

conocido	*known*
construido	*constructed*
insoportable	*unbearable*
lleno	*full*

Expresiones

al principio	*at the beginning*
en la cumbre	*on the top* (of a mountain)

Preguntas

After you have read the selection, answer the following questions in Spanish.

1. ¿Es el/la protagonista mujer u hombre? ¿Cómo sabe Ud.?

   _____

2. ¿Cómo es Machu Picchu?

   _____

3. ¿Es una buena experiencia para el grupo?

   _____

4. ¿Cuál estación es? ¿Cómo es el clima?

   _____

2

Ser and *Estar* in the Preterit and Imperfect Tenses

Preterit Tense

The preterit expresses action completed in the past. The English translation is usually the simple past. The preterit is used to express the following:

- An action completed in the past (action with a definite end)
- A series of actions completed in the past
- A condition that is no longer in effect

 **Key Vocabulary**

This list of words is often used when referring to past actions.

Adverbios y Adjetivos

anoche	*last night*
ayer	*yesterday*
anteayer	*the day before yesterday*
hace	*ago* (when it is used before a period of time in the past)
hace dos días	*two days ago*
pasado	*past, last*
la semana pasada	*last week*
el mes pasado	*last month*
el año pasado	*last year*

Keep in mind that the action or actions expressed by the preterit have been completed. It doesn't make any difference how long the action went on before; the action has a definite end.

Estar in the Preterit

The conjugation of **estar** in the preterit follows. Remember the three primary uses of **estar**: location, health, and changing mood or condition.

estar *to be*	
yo **estuve**	nosotros **estuvimos**
tú **estuviste**	vosotros **estuvisteis**
él **estuvo**	ellos **estuvieron**
ella **estuvo**	ellas **estuvieron**
Ud. **estuvo**	Uds. **estuvieron**

- **Location**

  Estuvimos en la escuela a las once esta mañana.

  ¿Dónde estuviste anoche?

  Mis estudiantes estuvieron en clase ayer a las tres.

  We were at school at eleven o'clock this morning.

  Where were you last night?

  My students were in class yesterday at three o'clock.

- **Health**

  Mi amigo estuvo con gripe el mes pasado, pero está bien hoy.

  Isabel y su hermana estuvieron enfermas el martes, pero están mucho mejor hoy.

  ¿Cómo estuviste tú esta mañana?

  My friend had the flu last month, but he is fine today.

  Isabel and her sister were sick on Tuesday, but they are much better today.

  How were you this morning?

- **Changing mood or condition**

  ¿Estuviste de mal humor ayer?

  Las mujeres estuvieron alegres hasta las dos.

  Estuvimos tristes por una hora.

  Were you in a bad mood yesterday?

  The women were happy until two o'clock.

  We were sad for an hour.

Ser in the Preterit

ser *to be*

yo **fui**	nosotros **fuimos**
tú **fuiste**	vosotros **fuisteis**
él **fue**	ellos **fueron**
ella **fue**	ellas **fueron**
Ud. **fue**	Uds. **fueron**

The preterit of **ser** is used most often for profession and identification.

- **Profession**

  Antonio fue médico de nuestro   *Tony was the doctor of our town.*
      pueblo.

  Fui cantante hace mucho tiempo.   *I was a singer a long time ago.*

  ¿Fue Ud. la maestra de la clase?   *Were you the teacher of the class?*

- **Identification**

  Fue un buen hombre.   *He was a good man.*

  Fuimos amigos.   *We were friends.*

  Las negociaciones fueron a favor   *The negotiations were in favor*
      de la paz.   *of peace.*

Exercise 2.1

Complete the following sentences with the correct preterit form of **ser** *or* **estar**, *according to the context of the sentence.*

1. Ella es profesora hoy, pero antes _____ azafata.

2. Yo _____ gerente por dos años.

3. Nosotros _____ muy contentos ayer porque nos ganamos la lotería.

4. ¿Por qué _____ Manuel en la cárcel sin decirnos nada?

5. Ellos _____ en el supermercado hoy para comprar alimentos.

6. La semana pasada, Raúl _____ en México. Regresó a casa ayer.

7. Los muchachos _____ enfermos anteayer, pero están bien hoy.

8. _____ una buena idea.

9. ¿Dónde _____ la familia de Federico esta tarde?

10. ¿Quiénes _____ en la librería a las nueve y media esta mañana?

11. Yo _____ por irme de vacaciones, pero me faltó valor.

12. Nosotros _____ de pie la mayor parte del concierto.

Ser and estar with Description in the Preterit

On an advanced level, there are situations in which the speaker can decide whether to use **ser** or **estar** in the preterit tense with adjectives. A Spanish speaker can say, for example:

El concierto **fue** fantástico.   *The concert **was** fantastic.*

With this sentence, the speaker transmits a "categorical" judgment, a completed absolute fact.

However, a Spanish speaker may choose to say:

El concierto **estuvo** fantástico.   *The concert **was** fantastic.*

This sentence is more descriptive and represents a "circumstantial" judgment.

A Word About Descriptive Judgments

When examples such as these are presented to native speakers, all generally opine that both are correct, and the majority do not find any perceptible difference between the two. Those who do find some difference are not always able to articulate exactly what this difference is.

La cantante fue maravillosa.   *The singer was marvelous.*
     (statement of fact)

La cantante estuvo maravillosa.   *The singer was marvelous.*
     (opinion indicating that the concertgoer enjoyed the performance)

Me gustó la clase. Fue buena.   *I liked the class. It was good.*
     (statement of fact; a categorical statement about the class)

Me gustó la clase. Estuvo buena.   *I liked the class. It was good.*
     (circumstantial judgment)

Imperfect Tense

The imperfect tense expresses action in the past that is not seen as completed. The imperfect is used to express the following:

- An action that "sets the stage" for another past action
- An action that expresses a narration, background, or situation in the past
- Repeated, habitual, and customary actions in the past
- Continuous actions or actions in progress in the past
- Description in the past
- Point of origin in the past
- Telling time in the past
- Telling one's age (with **tener**) in the past

Estar in the Imperfect

estar *to be*

yo **estaba**	nosotros **estábamos**
tú **estabas**	vosotros **estabais**
él **estaba**	ellos **estaban**
ella **estaba**	ellas **estaban**
Ud. **estaba**	Uds. **estaban**

- **Location**

Los enamorados estaban a la sombra de un árbol.	*The lovers were in the shade of a tree.*
El bolígrafo estaba debajo de la mesa.	*The pen was under the table.*
¿Dónde estaban Uds. anoche?	*Where were you last night?*
Estábamos en el teatro.	*We were in the theater.*

- **Health**

El hombre estaba cansado, pero siguió con su trabajo.	*The man was tired, but he continued with his work.*
Las pacientes estaban en el hospital porque estaban enfermas.	*The patients were in the hospital because they were sick.*

- **Changing mood or condition**

¿Por qué estaba triste la mujer?	*Why was the woman sad?*
Los niños estaban alegres por no tener clases.	*The children were happy because of not having class.*

- **Personal opinion about food or appearance**

La comida estaba buena.	*The meal was good.*
El pescado estaba delicioso.	*The fish tasted delicious.*
Las mujeres estaban bonitas.	*The women looked pretty.*

Ser in the Imperfect

ser *to be*

yo **era**	nosotros **éramos**
tú **eras**	vosotros **erais**
él **era**	ellos **eran**
ella **era**	ellas **eran**
Ud. **era**	Uds. **eran**

You learned that **ser** can be used in the preterit for profession and identification. The other uses of **ser** are best served by the imperfect.

- **Description in the past**

La casa era blanca.	*The house was white.*
Nuestro vecino era viejo, pero tenía el pelo negro.	*Our neighbor was old, but he had black hair.*
Era un caluroso día del mes de julio cuando nos vimos.	*It was a hot day in the month of July when we saw each other.*
Era agosto, lo recuerdo bien.	*It was August, I remember it well.*

- **Point of origin in the past**

El hombre era de Perú.	*The man was from Peru.*
Sus amigos eran de Chile.	*His friends were from Chile.*
Las flores rojas eran de Bolivia.	*The red flowers were from Bolivia.*

- **Telling time in the past**

Eran las cinco y Federico iba a la tienda por última vez.	*It was five o'clock, and Fred was going to the store for the last time.*
¿Qué hora era? Eran las dos de la tarde.	*What time was it? It was two in the afternoon.*
Eran las nueve de la noche y los niños dormían.	*It was nine at night and the children were sleeping.*
Eran las tres menos diez de la tarde cuando el profesor llegó.	*It was ten to three in the afternoon when the professor arrived.*

- **Identification in the past**

Era un buen hombre.	*He was a good man.*
Mi tío siempre era más alto que yo.	*My uncle was always taller than I.*
Éramos siempre buenos amigos.	*We were always good friends.*

Preterit or Imperfect Determined by the Speaker

You can use both the preterit and imperfect tenses in expressing relationships and in impersonal expressions.

- **Relationships**

Fuimos buenos amigos.	*We were good friends.*
Éramos buenos amigos.	*We were good friends.*

In this example, the English translations are the same, but when you use the preterit in Spanish, it means that the action is completed; the friendship is over.

- **Impersonal expressions**

Fue bueno.	*It was good.*
Era bueno.	*It was good.*

The use of the preterit or imperfect in these situations is a choice made by the speaker; the speaker decides whether the action is completed.

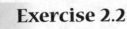

Exercise 2.2

Review **ser** *and* **estar** *in the imperfect, then rewrite the following sentences, changing the verb from the present tense to the imperfect.*

EXAMPLE   Mi padre es de Polonia.   *Mi padre era de Polonia.*

1. Yo soy de Venezuela. _____

2. Ellos son de España. _____

3. ¿Qué hora es? _____

4. Nosotros estamos bien. _____

5. Mi jardín es el más hermoso de la ciudad.

   _____

6. Los tres amigos están aquí. _____

7. No estoy cansada. _____

8. Somos cantantes. _____

9. ¿Dónde estás? _____

10. Yo estoy en la casa con mi hermana.

    _____

Exercise 2.3

Complete the following sentences with the correct form of **ser** *or* **estar** *in the preterit or imperfect, according to the meaning of the sentence.*

EXAMPLE   Lorenzo _fue_ escritor. Ahora es bombero.

1. Yo _____ camarero. Ahora soy maestro.

2. Nosotros _____ en el banco precisamente a las nueve esta mañana.

3. Ayer, _____ un día de mucha lluvia. Hace buen tiempo hoy.

4. El paciente _____ en la oficina del doctor a las siete de la mañana para su operación.

5. Carlos _____ gerente por dos años.

6. _____ la última vez que yo _____ a la playa.

7. ¿Quién _____ el presidente en el año mil novecientos noventa y dos?

8. La situación no _____ tan grave.

9. _____ las dos cuando sonó el despertador.

10. El hombre _____ de Perú.

11. ¿Qué día _____ cuando ella se graduó?

12. Me gustó la obra de teatro. _____ buena.

13. Nosotros _____ enfermos ayer, pero nos sentimos bien hoy.

14. _____ difícil recordar todo.

15. _____ una buena idea, pero no vamos a usarla.

Regular Verbs in the Preterit

Most verbs are regular in the preterit tense.

Regular *-ar* Verbs

To conjugate a regular **-ar** verb in the preterit, drop the ending and add **-é**, **-aste**, **-ó**, **-amos**, **-asteis**, **-aron** to the stem.

ayudar *to help*	
yo ayudé	nosotros ayudamos
tú ayudaste	vosotros ayudasteis
Ud. ayudó	Uds. ayudaron

cantar *to sing*	
yo canté	nosotros cantamos
tú cantaste	vosotros cantasteis
él cantó	ellos cantaron

pensar *to think*	
yo pensé	nosotros pensamos
tú pensaste	vosotros pensasteis
ella pensó	ellas pensaron

recordar *to remember*	
yo recordé	nosotros recordamos
tú recordaste	vosotros recordasteis
ella recordó	ellas recordaron

A Word About Pronunciation

Notice that the first- and third-person singular forms carry written accents. It is very important to practice the pronunciation, stressing the accented syllable. Pronounce the verbs in this way: **yo cant<u>é</u>**, **tú can<u>tas</u>te**, **Ud. can<u>tó</u>**, **nosotros can<u>ta</u>mos**, **vosotros can<u>tas</u>teis**, **ellos can<u>ta</u>ron**. Review the basic pronunciation rules: All words that end in **n**, **s**, or a vowel have the stress on the second-to-last (penultimate) syllable.

The preterit first-person plural **nosotros** form is identical to the present indicative form. Context clarifies whether the verb is in the present or preterit tense.

Regular *-er* and *-ir* Verbs

To conjugate regular **-er** and **-ir** verbs in the preterit, drop the ending and add **-í**, **-iste**, **-ió**, **-imos**, **-isteis**, **-ieron** to the stem. The endings are the same for both **-er** and **-ir** verbs.

-Er Verbs

comer *to eat*	
yo comí	nosotros comimos
tú comiste	vosotros comisteis
él comió	ellos comieron

entender *to understand*	
yo entendí	nosotros entendimos
tú entendiste	vosotros entendisteis
ella entendió	ellas entendieron

ver *to see*	
yo vi	nosotros vimos
tú viste	vosotros visteis
Ud. vio	Uds. vieron

-Ir Verbs

compartir *to share*	
yo compartí	nosotros compartimos
tú compartiste	vosotros compartisteis
él compartió	ellos compartieron

descubrir *to discover*	
yo descubrí	nosotros descubrimos
tú descubriste	vosotros descubristeis
Ud. descubrió	Uds. descubrieron

salir *to leave, to go out*

yo salí	nosotros salimos
tú saliste	vosotros salisteis
ella salió	ellas salieron

 Notice that the verb **ver** is regular. It does not carry an accent mark on the third-person singular form **vio**, because the form has only one syllable. The **nosotros** form of **-ir** verbs in the preterit is identical to the present indicative form. Its meaning becomes clear in context.

-Ir Verbs with Stem Changes in the Third Person

The following verbs have a stem change in the preterit. This stem change occurs only in the third-person singular and plural forms of the preterit.

mentir *to lie*

yo mentí	nosotros mentimos
tú mentiste	vosotros mentisteis
Ud. mintió	Uds. mintieron

pedir *to request, to ask for*

yo pedí	nosotros pedimos
tú pediste	vosotros pedisteis
él pidió	ellos pidieron

dormir *to sleep*

yo dormí	nosotros dormimos
tú dormiste	vosotros dormisteis
ella durmió	ellas durmieron

Irregular Verbs in the Preterit

Verbs that are irregular in the preterit have an irregular stem and a special set of endings. Note that the endings do not carry accent marks. To conjugate an irregular verb in the preterit, add the endings **-e**, **-iste**, **-o**, **-imos**, **-isteis**, **-ieron** to the irregular stems.

andar *to walk, to stroll*

yo anduve	nosotros anduvimos
tú anduviste	vosotros anduvisteis
él anduvo	ellos anduvieron

caber *to fit* (one thing inside another)

yo cupe	nosotros cupimos
tú cupiste	vosotros cupisteis
ella cupo	ellas cupieron

estar *to be*

yo estuve	nosotros estuvimos
tú estuviste	vosotros estuvisteis
Ud. estuvo	Uds. estuvieron

hacer *to do, to make*

yo hice	nosotros hicimos
tú hiciste	vosotros hicisteis
él hizo	ellos hicieron

poder *to be able, can*

yo pude	nosotros pudimos
tú pudiste	vosotros pudisteis
Ud. pudo	Uds. pudieron

poner *to put*

yo puse	nosotros pusimos
tú pusiste	vosotros pusisteis
él puso	ellos pusieron

querer *to want*

yo quise	nosotros quisimos
tú quisiste	vosotros quisisteis
ella quiso	ellas quisieron

saber *to know, to know how*

yo supe	nosotros supimos
tú supiste	vosotros supisteis
Ud. supo	Uds. supieron

tener *to have*

yo tuve	nosotros tuvimos
tú tuviste	vosotros tuvisteis
él tuvo	ellos tuvieron

venir *to come*

yo vine	nosotros vinimos
tú viniste	vosotros vinisteis
él vino	ellos vinieron

When the irregular preterit stem ends in **-j**, the third-person endings become **-o** and **-eron**.

decir *to say, to tell*

yo dije	nosotros dijimos
tú dijiste	vosotros dijisteis
ella dijo	ellas dijeron

producir *to produce*

yo produje	nosotros produjimos
tú produjiste	vosotros produjisteis
Ud. produjo	Uds. produjeron

traer *to bring*

yo traje	nosotros trajimos
tú trajiste	vosotros trajisteis
él trajo	ellos trajeron

Dar, **ir**, and **ser** have different sets of endings.

dar *to give*

yo di	nosotros dimos
tú diste	vosotros disteis
ella dio	ellas dieron

ir *to go*

yo fui	nosotros fuimos
tú fuiste	vosotros fuisteis
Ud. fue	Uds. fueron

ser *to be*

yo fui	nosotros fuimos
tú fuiste	vosotros fuisteis
él fue	ellos fueron

A Word About *haber*

The third-person singular form of **haber** in the preterit is **hubo**, meaning *there was, there were, was there?, were there?*

It is important to memorize the preterit forms of all the irregular verbs, so that you will be able to use any verb you wish in the preterit.

Regular Verbs in the Imperfect

Regular *-ar* Verbs

To conjugate a regular **-ar** verb in the imperfect, drop the ending and add **-aba**, **-abas**, **-aba**, **-ábamos**, **-abais**, **-aban** to the stem. The first- and third-person singular forms (**yo**, **él**, **ella**, **Ud.**) are identical.

acompañar *to accompany*

yo acompañaba	nosotros acompañábamos
tú acompañabas	vosotros acompañabais
él acompañaba	ellos acompañaban

dar *to give*

yo daba	nosotros dábamos
tú dabas	vosotros dabais
ella daba	ellas daban

trabajar *to work*

yo trabajaba	nosotros trabajábamos
tú trabajabas	vosotros trabajabais
Ud. trabajaba	Uds. trabajaban

A Word About the Imperfect

There are no irregular **-ar** verbs in the imperfect. Practice the pronunciation of the verb conjugations above. There are one-syllable, two-syllable, three-syllable, and four-syllable verbs. Be sure to pronounce the imperfect in this way: **yo trabajaba, tú trabajabas, él trabajaba, nosotros trabajábamos, vosotros trabajabais, ellos trabajaban.**

Regular *-er* and *-ir* Verbs

To conjugate regular **-er** and **-ir** verbs in the imperfect, drop the ending and add **-ía, -ías, -ía, -íamos, -íais, -ían** to the stem. The endings are the same for both **-er** and **-ir** verbs. The first- and third-person singular forms are identical.

-Er Verbs

hacer *to do, to make*	
yo hacía	nosotros hacíamos
tú hacías	vosotros hacíais
ella hacía	ellas hacían

poder *to be able, can*	
yo podía	nosotros podíamos
tú podías	vosotros podíais
Ud. podía	Uds. podían

querer *to want*	
yo quería	nosotros queríamos
tú querías	vosotros queríais
él quería	ellos querían

saber *to know, to know how*	
yo sabía	nosotros sabíamos
tú sabías	vosotros sabíais
ella sabía	ellas sabían

tener *to have*	
yo tenía	nosotros teníamos
tú tenías	vosotros teníais
Ud. tenía	Uds. tenían

A Word About *haber*

The third-person singular form of **haber** in the imperfect is **había**, meaning *there was, there were, was there?, were there?*

-Ir Verbs

decir *to say, to tell*	
yo decía	nosotros decíamos
tú decías	vosotros decíais
él decía	ellos decían

sentirse *to feel* (an emotion)	
me sentía	nos sentíamos
te sentías	os sentíais
Ud. se sentía	Uds. se sentían

venir *to come*

yo venía	nosotros veníamos
tú venías	vosotros veníais
él venía	ellos venían

Irregular Verbs in the Imperfect

There are only three irregular verbs in the imperfect.

ir *to go*

yo iba	nosotros íbamos
tú ibas	vosotros ibais
él iba	ellos iban

ser *to be*

yo era	nosotros éramos
tú eras	vosotros erais
ella era	ellas eran

ver *to see*

yo veía	nosotros veíamos
tú veías	vosotros veíais
Ud. veía	Uds. veían

The translation of **ir** in the imperfect is *was going, were going.*

Yo iba a hablar.	*I was going to speak.*
Nosotros íbamos a comprar un carro.	*We were going to buy a car.*

Comparison of Preterit and Imperfect

Remember that the preterit is a completed action. The imperfect is often an action that was repeated in the past.

Ella llegó ayer.	*She arrived yesterday.*
Ella llegaba a la cinco todos los días.	*She arrived at five o'clock every day.*
La semana pasada, leí un buen libro.	*Last week, I read a good book.*
Antes, yo leía mucho.	*Before, I used to read a lot.*
Beatriz vino a verme.	*Beatriz came to see me.*
Él me dijo que Beatriz venía a verme.	*He told me that Beatriz was coming to see me.*

Me levanté a las seis esta mañana.	*I got up at six o'clock this morning.*
Me levantaba tarde.	*I used to get up late.*
Fui a la tienda.	*I went to the store.*
Yo iba a la tienda cuando vi a José.	*I was going to the store when I saw Joe.*
Fuimos a la playa hoy.	*We went to the beach today.*
Íbamos a la playa todos los veranos.	*We used to go the beach every summer.*
¿Qué me dijiste hace dos minutos?	*What did you tell me two minutes ago?*
¿Qué me decías cuando el perro ladró?	*What were you saying to me when the dog barked?*
Marta comió temprano esta mañana.	*Martha ate early this morning.*
Marta siempre comía temprano.	*Martha always ate early.*
Mi papá pagó la cuenta ayer.	*My father paid the bill yesterday.*
Mi papá siempre pagaba la cuenta.	*My father always paid the bill.*
Eduardo hizo su tarea.	*Edward did his homework.*
Eduardo siempre hacía su tarea los lunes.	*Edward always did his homework on Mondays.*
¿Qué compró Ud. ayer?	*What did you buy yesterday?*
¿Qué compraba Ud. cuando lo llamé?	*What were you buying when I called you?*
Caminamos al parque hoy.	*We walked to the park today.*
Caminábamos al parque todos los días.	*We used to walk to the park every day.*
Recibimos un cheque esta tarde.	*We received a check this morning.*
Recibíamos cheques cada semana.	*We used to receive checks every week.*
Ella tuvo una operación anoche.	*She had an operation last night.*
Él no tenía tiempo para verla.	*He didn't have time to see her.*
Anoche, ella durmió hasta las ocho.	*Last night, she slept until eight o'clock.*
Ella siempre dormía hasta tarde.	*She always slept late.*
Conocimos a Silvia en Colombia.	*We met Sylvia in Colombia.*
No la conocíamos bien.	*We didn't know her well.*

Exercise 2.4

Preterit or imperfect? *Complete the following sentences with the correct form of the verb in parentheses.*

1. ¿Por qué no _____ tú la comida ayer? (comprar)

2. Anoche, yo _____ el vino a la fiesta. (traer)

3. _____ mediodía y el niño _____ hambre.
   (ser/tener)

4. _____ a llover y yo _____ la ventana.
   (empezar/cerrar)

5. La muchacha _____ la calle cuando su mamá

   la _____. (cruzar/llamar)

6. ¿Dónde _____ Uds. esta mañana precisamente a las nueve?
   (estar)

7. Nosotros _____ en el parque cuando _____
   el animal exótico. (andar/ver)

8. El taxista nos _____ veinte dólares. ¿Cuánto te

   _____ a ti? (cobrar/cobrar)

9. Nosotros les _____ cartas a nuestros parientes desde Bolivia,

   pero ellos no las _____. (escribir/recibir)

10. Yo _____ por la calle equivocada cuando _____

    que no _____ donde _____.

    (caminar/darse cuenta de/saber/estar)

11. Me agrada su amigo. ¿Dónde lo _____ Ud.? (conocer)

12. Pedro y sus amigos _____ todas las noches antes de acostarse.
    (divertirse)

13. Melisa _____ al cine cada domingo durante su juventud. (ir)

14. Los viajeros de Inglaterra _____ a mi casa la semana pasada

    y _____ conmigo hasta hoy. (llegar/quedarse)

📖 Reading Comprehension

Marianela
por Benito Pérez Galdós

Pérez Galdós nació en las Islas Canarias y es mejor conocido por sus vistas de la sociedad española. Se murió en 1920 en Madrid.

Aquel día Pablo y Marianela salieron al campo. Con ellos iba Choto, su perro fiel. El día estaba hermoso. El aire era suave y fresco, y el sol calentaba sin quemar.

"¿Adónde vamos hoy?" preguntó Pablo, que era ciego de nacimiento.

"Adonde quiera Ud., señor," contestó Marianela, que era su guía.

Marianela parecía crecer y adquirir nuevas fuerzas, cuando estaba al lado de su amo y amigo. Junto a él, se sentía llena de alegría. Al apartarse de él, sentía una profunda tristeza.

Pablo participaba de los mismos sentimientos hacia Marianela. En cierta ocasión le había dicho Pablo a la joven: Antes yo creía que era de día cuando hablaba la gente; y que era de noche, cuando la gente callaba y cantaban los gallos. Ahora, no hago las mismas comparaciones. Es de día cuando estamos juntos tú y yo; es de noche, cuando nos separamos.

Después de caminar un rato, llegaron a un lugar donde había muchas flores. Ambos se detuvieron. Pablo se sentó, y Marianela se puso a recoger flores para su amo. Los dos eran muy felices.

Verbos

adquirir	*to acquire*
apartarse	*to separate*
calentar	*to warm*
callar	*to quiet*
crecer	*to grow*
detenerse	*to detain*
había dicho	*had said* (past perfect tense)
ponerse (a)	*to begin to*
quemar	*to burn*
recoger	*to pick up*

Nombres

el amo	*the boss*
los gallos	*the roosters*

Preposición

hacia   *toward*

Adjetivos

ciego   *blind*
fiel   *faithful*
juntos   *together*

Expresiones

al + *infinitive*   *upon (doing something)*
al apartarse   *upon separating*

Preguntas

After you have read the selection, answer the following questions in Spanish.

1. ¿Quiénes son los personajes en el cuento? ¿Quién los acompaña?

   _____

2. ¿Cómo se sienten juntos?

   _____

3. ¿Cómo se sienten separados?

   _____

3

The Present Progressive Tense

In Spanish, the present progressive tense expresses action that is occurring at the moment, action that is in progress. It is equivalent to the English present progressive (*The woman is singing*, for example). This tense is used to express the following:

- An action that is in progress

- An action that is occurring in the moment

- Emphasis for an action that is happening right now

A Word About the Present Indicative Tense

The present indicative tense in Spanish expresses both the English simple present (*I sing, I do sing*) and the English present progressive (*I am singing*).

Ella **canta** una canción triste.   She ***sings*** a sad song.
She ***does sing*** a sad song.
She ***is singing*** a sad song.

When you don't need to describe what is happening right now, use the simple present tense.

Toco el violín.	*I play the violin.*
Ella nada en el verano.	*She swims in the summer.*
Mis primos viven en México.	*My cousins live in Mexico.*
Siempre nos divertimos los viernes.	*We always have a good time on Fridays.*
¿Por qué te ríes todo el tiempo?	*Why do you laugh all the time?*

The present progressive is a compound tense in Spanish, as it is in English. It is formed by conjugating **estar** in the present tense and adding the present participle of the main verb. The present participle, hereafter referred to as the gerund, is the *-ing* form of a verb in English. The tense is also called the present continuous.

Gerund Formation

The gerund is formed by adding **-ando** or **-iendo** to the stem of the infinitive. In English, the gerund ends in *-ing*. Practice the following verb forms aloud.

-Ar Verbs

To form the gerund of all **-ar** verbs, drop the ending and add **-ando** to the stem.

abrazar	abraz**ando**	*embracing*
adivinar	adivin**ando**	*guessing*
alquilar	alquil**ando**	*renting*
arreglar	arregl**ando**	*arranging, repairing, fixing*
arriesgar	arriesg**ando**	*risking*
bajar	baj**ando**	*descending, going down*
comenzar	comenz**ando**	*beginning*
entregar	entreg**ando**	*delivering, handing in*
esperar	esper**ando**	*waiting*
fregar	freg**ando**	*scrubbing, washing dishes*
jugar	jug**ando**	*playing*
mostrar	mostr**ando**	*showing*
pensar	pens**ando**	*thinking*
probar	prob**ando**	*testing, proving*
recordar	record**ando**	*remembering*
sacar	sac**ando**	*taking out, getting*
soñar	soñ**ando**	*dreaming*
temblar	tembl**ando**	*trembling*
volar	vol**ando**	*flying*

-Er Verbs

To form the gerund of most **-er** verbs, drop the ending and add **-iendo** to the stem.

beber	beb**iendo**	*drinking*
comer	com**iendo**	*eating*
correr	corr**iendo**	*running*
coser	cos**iendo**	*sewing*
devolver	devolv**iendo**	*returning* (an object)
hacer	hac**iendo**	*doing, making*
mover	mov**iendo**	*moving* (an object)
perder	perd**iendo**	*losing*
poner	pon**iendo**	*putting*
volver	volv**iendo**	*returning*

-Ir Verbs

To form the gerund of regular **-ir** verbs, drop the ending and add **-iendo** to the stem.

abrir	abr**iendo**	*opening*
compartir	compart**iendo**	*sharing*
decidir	decid**iendo**	*deciding*
escribir	escrib**iendo**	*writing*
insistir	insist**iendo**	*insisting*
recibir	recib**iendo**	*receiving*
subir	sub**iendo**	*ascending, going up*
sufrir	sufr**iendo**	*suffering*

Orthographic Changes in -er and -ir Verbs

-Er and **-ir** verbs whose stem ends in a vowel form the gerund using **-yendo** instead of **-iendo** in order to avoid having three vowels in a row. These are not irregular forms; it is an orthographic change.

-Er Verbs

atraer	atra**yendo**	*attracting*
caer	ca**yendo**	*falling*
creer	cre**yendo**	*believing*

leer	le**yendo**	*reading*
poseer	pose**yendo**	*possessing*
traer	tra**yendo**	*bringing*

-Ir Verbs

construir	constru**yendo**	*constructing, building*
contribuir	contribu**yendo**	*contributing*
destruir	destru**yendo**	*destroying*
huir	hu**yendo**	*fleeing*
oír	o**yendo**	*hearing*

The Gerund of Irregular *-ir* Verbs

Nearly all gerunds are formed regularly. The only verbs that show an irregularity in the gerund are the **-ir** stem-changing verbs in the present indicative tense. Learn these irregular gerunds now, and you'll be able to form all the gerunds easily.

- Forming the gerund of irregular **-ir** verbs with **o > ue** and **o > u** changes in the stem

Infinitive	Present Tense **o > ue**	Gerund **o > u**	English
dormir	d**ue**rmo	d**u**rmiendo	*sleeping*
morir	m**ue**ro	m**u**riendo	*dying*

- Forming the gerund of irregular **-ir** verbs with **e > ie** and **e > i** changes in the stem

Infinitive	Present Tense **e > ie**	Gerund **e > i**	English
advertir	adv**ie**rto	adv**i**rtiendo	*warning*
hervir	h**ie**rvo	h**i**rviendo	*boiling*
mentir	m**ie**nto	m**i**ntiendo	*lying*
preferir	pref**ie**ro	pref**i**riendo	*preferring*
referir	ref**ie**ro	ref**i**riendo	*referring*
sentir	s**ie**nto	s**i**ntiendo	*regretting*
sugerir	sug**ie**ro	sug**i**riendo	*suggesting*

Infinitive	Present Tense e > i	Gerund e > i	English
bendecir	bendigo	bendiciendo	*blessing*
competir	compito	compitiendo	*competing*
conseguir	consigo	consiguiendo	*obtaining*
corregir	corrijo	corrigiendo	*correcting*
decir	digo	diciendo	*saying, telling*
elegir	elijo	eligiendo	*electing*
freír	frío	friendo	*frying*
gemir	gimo	gimiendo	*groaning*
medir	mido	midiendo	*measuring*
pedir	pido	pidiendo	*requesting*
repetir	repito	repitiendo	*repeating*
seguir	sigo	siguiendo	*following*
servir	sirvo	sirviendo	*serving*
sonreír	sonrío	sonriendo	*smiling*

Exercise 3.1

Write the gerund of the following infinitives.

1. hablar _____
2. besar _____
3. andar _____
4. viajar _____
5. limpiar _____
6. cenar _____
7. sacar _____
8. beber _____
9. comer _____
10. aprender _____
11. agradecer _____
12. escoger _____
13. ver _____

14. abrir _____
15. asistir _____
16. insistir _____
17. permitir _____
18. prohibir _____
19. creer _____
20. leer _____
21. traer _____
22. huir _____
23. oír _____
24. servir _____
25. pedir _____
26. corregir _____

27. repetir	_____	30. morir	_____
28. seguir	_____	31. decir	_____
29. dormir	_____	32. hacer	_____

Formation of the Present Progressive Tense

To form the present progressive tense, conjugate **estar** in the present tense and follow it with the gerund of the main verb.

yo estoy hablando	*I am speaking*
tú estás escuchando	*you are listening*
él está comiendo	*he is eating*
nosotros estamos bebiendo	*we are drinking*
vosotros estáis cocinando	*you are cooking*
ellos están durmiendo	*they are sleeping*

Use of the Present Progressive Tense

The action expressed by the present progressive tense must be action in progress.

Following are examples formed with **estar**.

¿Cuál libro estás leyendo?	*Which book are you reading?*
El niño está jugando en su cuarto.	*The child is playing in his room.*
Está lloviendo.	*It's raining.*
Está nevando.	*It's snowing.*
Está lloviznando.	*It's drizzling.*
¿Qué están Uds. haciendo?	*What are you doing?*
¿Qué están haciendo Uds.?	*What are you doing?*

NOTE The subject pronoun **Uds.** appears in two different positions in the example sentences above. In the first example, it comes between the helping verb **estar** and the gerund. In the second example, **Uds.** follows the gerund. Both are correct.

The negative **no** comes directly before the conjugated form of **estar**.

No estamos hablando.	*We are not talking.*
No está lloviendo.	*It is not raining.*
No estoy mintiendo.	*I am not lying.*

A Word About English

In English, the present progressive tense can be used to describe what is happening right now as well as what will happen in the future.

I am singing right now.
I am singing next Friday.

In Spanish, the present progressive can never be used to describe a future action. For a future action, use **ir** + **a** + *infinitive*.

Estoy cantando en este momento.	*I am singing right now.* (at this moment)
Voy a cantar el viernes que viene.	*I am going to sing next Friday.*

Exercise 3.2

Complete the following sentences with the correct form of the present progressive tense. Be sure to conjugate **estar** *correctly.*

EXAMPLE   Miguel _está cantando_ y su amiga _está tocando_ el piano.
(cantar/tocar)

1. Nuestro profesor _____ muchos exámenes. (corregir)

2. Por fin, nosotros _____ buenas notas. (sacar)

3. Me hace el favor de no hacer ruido, yo _____.
   (estudiar)

4. Los adolescentes les dicen a sus padres, "no _____
   nada." (hacer)

5. Los cocineros _____ la cena. (preparar)

6. ¿Qué _____ tú? (decir)

7. Está lloviendo pero no _____. (nevar)

8. Ya es tarde y los niños _____. (dormir)

9. Son las nueve de la noche y todavía los periodistas

   _____. (escribir)

10. ¿Quiénes _____ por teléfono? (hablar)

11. Tú _____ los huevos para el desayuno. (freír)

12. Son las seis y media y la familia _____. (comer)

Reminder

After a preposition, use the infinitive form of the verb, even though the translation in English might be the gerund -*ing*.

Antes de **comer**, ella se lava las manos.	*Before eating, she washes her hands.*
Después de **cocinar**, la familia disfruta la comida.	*After cooking, the family enjoys the meal.*
Al **entrar** en la clase, los estudiantes se saludan.	*Upon entering the class, the students greet each other.*
A veces, hablamos sin **pensar**.	*At times, we speak without thinking.*
En vez de **leer**, preferimos jugar.	*Instead of reading, we prefer to play.*
A pesar de **despertarme** temprano, llegué tarde a la entrevista.	*In spite of waking up early, I arrived late to the interview.*

Exercise 3.3

Complete the following sentences with the infinitive, present indicative, or present progressive of the appropriate verb. Select from the list of verbs below. Use each verb only once.

almorzar, conocer, devolver, graduarse, hacer, leer, querer, saber, salir, tener, tocar

1. En el avión, en el vuelo de África, parece que los pasajeros están

   _____ sus libros de turismo.

2. ¿Quién _____ nadar?

3. Olivia sigue _____ el violín aunque a su hermano no le gusta el sonido.

4. Antes de _____ a los padres de su novio, Amalia se maquilla la cara.

5. Después de _____ éxito en la escuela secundaria, el estudiante

   _____ ir a una universidad.

6. Los trabajadores tienen hambre a las doce de la tarde; _____

   juntos a las doce y media; _____ de la fábrica a las cinco

   de la tarde.

7. Julia acaba de _____ sus libros a la biblioteca.

8. El hombre tiene veintidós años. Después de _____

de la universidad, no sabe qué _____.

Placement of Object Pronouns

Direct Object Pronouns, Indirect Object Pronouns, and Reflexive Pronouns

Following is a review chart of pronouns: subject, direct object, indirect object, and reflexive.

Subject Pronoun	Direct Object Pronoun	Indirect Object Pronoun	Reflexive Pronoun
yo	me	me	me
tú	te	te	te
él	lo	le	se
ella	la	le	se
Ud.	lo/la/le	le	se
nosotros	nos	nos	nos
vosotros	os	os	os
ellos	los	les	se
ellas	las	les	se
Uds.	los/las/les	les	se

NOTE In English, the direct object *you* can be expressed as **la** in Spanish if the direct object person is female, or **lo** if the direct object person is male. In many countries, **le** is used as the direct object pronoun instead of **lo** or **la**. Similarly, the direct object pronoun *you* in the plural **Uds.** form can be **las**, **los**, or **les**.

La ayudo.	*I help you.* (female)
Lo ayudo.	*I help you.* (male)
Le ayudo.	*I help you.* (either male or female)

This use of **le** as direct object pronoun is called **leísmo**; **le** is borrowed from the indirect object pronoun.

The indirect object pronouns, direct object pronouns, and reflexive pronouns have two possible positions:

- The object pronouns may be placed directly before the helping verb **estar**.

- The object pronouns may be attached to the gerund.

¿Qué me estás diciendo?	*What are you saying to me?*
¿Qué estás diciéndome?	*What are you saying to me?*

The written accent retains the correct pronunciation of the verb.

The placement of the object pronouns does not affect the meaning of the sentence. They can be placed in either position, and the meaning of the sentence is exactly the same.

Yo estoy trayéndote la comida.	*I am bringing the meal to you.*
Te estoy trayendo la comida.	*I am bringing the meal to you.*
Irene no está esperando el tren.	*Irene is not waiting for the train.*
No lo está esperando.	*She is not waiting for it.*
Ella no está esperándolo.	*She is not waiting for it.*
Estamos buscando los gatos de Olivia.	*We are looking for Olivia's cats.*
Los estamos buscando.	*We are looking for them.*
Estamos buscándolos.	*We are looking for them.*

Order of Double Object Pronouns

An indirect object pronoun precedes a direct object pronoun when they occur together. The reflexive object pronoun precedes the direct object pronoun when they occur together. The double object pronouns cannot be separated from one another.

Following is a review chart of double object pronouns.

me lo, me la	*it to me*
me los, me las	*them to me*
te lo, te la	*it to you*
te los, te las	*them to you*
se lo, se la	*it to him, it to her, it to you, it to them*
se los, se las	*them to him, them to her, them to you, them to them*
nos lo, nos la	*it to us*
nos los, nos las	*them to us*
os lo, os la	*it to you*
os los, os las	*them to you*

A Reminder

Se replaces **le** or **les** as the indirect object pronoun when a direct object pronoun follows.

Por fin, la jefa tiene su sueldo.	*At last, the boss has your pay.*
Ella está mandándoselo.	*She is sending it to you.*
Ella se lo está mandando.	*She is sending it to you.*
El papá les está leyendo un cuento a sus hijos.	*The father is reading a story to his children.*
Él se lo está leyendo.	*He is reading it to them.*
Está leyéndoselo.	*He is reading it to them.*

A reflexive object pronoun precedes the direct object pronoun when they occur together.

Estoy lavándome las manos.	*I am washing my hands.*
Estoy lavándomelas.	*I am washing them.*
Me las estoy lavando.	*I am washing them.*
La mujer está peinándose el cabello rubio.	*The woman is combing her blond hair.*
Se lo está peinando.	*She is combing it.*
Está peinándoselo.	*She is combing it.*

Exercise 3.4

Complete the following sentences with the correct present progressive form of the verb in parentheses. Remember to conjugate **estar** correctly.

1. ¿Por qué _____ la pregunta el maestro? (repetir)

2. Los adolescentes no _____ las direcciones. (seguir)

3. Nosotros _____ el libro. (leer)

4. ¿Quiénes _____ tanto ruido? (hacer)

5. Los amigos de Juan _____ en casa hoy. (almorzar)

6. Yo _____ el agua para preparar la sopa. (hervir)

7. El hombre ama a esta mujer. La _____ con su mirada. (seguir)

8. Somos nosotros a quienes ellos _____. (esperar)

Exercise 3.5

Translate the following sentences into Spanish, using the present progressive tense.

1. Are the women talking to the men?

   _____

2. What are you saying to me?

   _____

3. Can you (Ud.) repeat the question? The students are not paying attention to you.

   _____

4. We know that he is searching for an idea. He needs it to write a story.

   _____

5. What is happening?

   _____

6. The fantastic lawyer is dreaming about a trip to Italy.

   _____

Exercise 3.6

Answer the following questions aloud, using the present progressive tense.

1. ¿Quién está estudiando ahora mismo?
2. ¿Por qué estás comiendo chocolate en el salón?
3. ¿Qué está Ud. haciendo ahora mismo?
4. ¿En qué estás pensando?
5. ¿Qué está leyendo el profesor?
6. ¿Quién está huyendo de la policía?

Uses of the Gerund with Verbs Other Than *estar*

- The gerund with **seguir** expresses *to keep/continue (doing something)*.

Los músicos siguen tocando la música y seguimos escuchándola.	*The musicians keep playing the music, and we keep listening to it.*
No hay música, pero la pareja sigue bailando.	*There is no music, but the couple keeps on dancing.*

- The gerund with **ir** expresses *gradually, little by little*.

La estudiante va aprendiendo la lección.	*The student is gradually learning the lesson.*
El paciente va mejorándose.	*The patient is getting better little by little.*
Voy conociendo Madrid.	*I'm getting to know Madrid little by little.*

- The gerund with **llevar** expresses *have been doing*.

Llevo un año estudiando el español.	*I have been studying Spanish for a year.* (literally, *I carry a year studying Spanish.*)
Mi amigo lleva dos años viviendo aquí.	*My friend has been living here for two years.*

After you become accustomed to using the present progressive, you will find that the gerund can sometimes be used without a helping verb.

Puedo pasar el día mirando a la gente.	*I can pass the day looking at the people.*
Los ladrones salieron corriendo.	*The thieves left running.*

Either the gerund or the infinitive can be used after **ver**, **mirar**, **escuchar**, and **oír**. The meaning is the same.

Veo a los niños **jugando**.	*I see the children playing. / I see the children play.*
Veo a los niños **jugar**.	*I see the children playing. / I see the children play.*
Escuchamos al hombre cantar.	*We listen to the man sing. / We listen to the man singing.*
Lo escuchamos cantando.	*We listen to him sing. / We listen to him singing.*
Él vio a María pasar por su casa.	*He saw María passing by his house.*
La vio pasando.	*He saw her pass by.*
Susana oyó los loros hablar.	*Susan heard the parrots speak.*
Ella los oyó hablando.	*She heard them speaking.*

Verbs not generally used in the gerund form are **ser**, **estar**, **poder**, **querer**, **saber**, **tener**, **ir**, and **venir**. These verbs use the present indicative instead of the present progressive.

¿**Puede** Ud. acompañarla?	*Can you accompany her?*
Los nietos de Victoria **quieren** visitar a su abuela.	*Victoria's grandchildren want to visit their grandmother.*
Arturo **tiene** una fiesta cada año para su hijo.	*Arthur has a party every year for his son.*
Susana **va** a la manifestación.	*Susan is going to the demonstration.*
Mucho ruido **viene** de arriba.	*A lot of noise is coming from above.*

NOTES **Poder** is the only **-er** verb with an irregularity in the stem of the gerund: **pudiendo**.
    The gerund of **ir** is **yendo**.

Exercise 3.7

Complete the following sentences with the correct form of either the present indicative or the present progressive of the verb in parentheses.

1. El esposo de Elizabeth no _____ celebrar el día del amor y de la amistad. (querer)

2. ¿Por qué no _____ toda la familia a mi fiesta? (venir)

3. Sócrates _____ que no _____ nada que valga la pena saber. (saber/saber)

4. Favor de no interrumpirme ahora mismo, yo _____. (pensar)

5. Nosotros _____ hablar bien si practicamos. (poder)

6. ¿Por qué lo sigues _____? (llamar)

7. La muchacha triste nunca _____. (sonreír)

8. Los deportistas _____ al tenis todos los veranos. (jugar)

9. Los detectives están contentos ahora porque el criminal _____ su crimen. (confesar)

10. A Paulina y a su amiga no les gusta _____ temprano. (despertarse)

11. Las niñas _____ a su primera fiesta mañana. (ir)

12. La estudiante lleva una hora _____ este ejercicio. (hacer)

Exercise 3.8

Translate the following sentences into English.

1. Vamos a la casa de María porque ella está preparando arroz con pollo.

   _____

2. El mesero nos está sirviendo nuestra comida.

   _____

3. Las niñeras están cuidando a muchos niños en el parque.

   _____

4. Son las ocho de la noche y ya es tarde, pero el hombre sigue leyendo su libro favorito. Sigue leyéndolo hasta las once.

    _____

    _____

5. La muchacha está nadando en la piscina porque sus padres piensan que es peligroso nadar en el océano.

    _____

    _____

6. Los niños están poniendo los platos en el horno. Los están poniendo en el horno para molestar a sus padres.

    _____

    _____

7. ¿Por qué le están Uds. mintiendo?

    _____

8. ¿Quién está riéndose?

    _____

9. El elefante lleva cinco años viviendo en el zoológico.

    _____

10. Seguimos aprendiendo el español.

    _____

Exercise 3.9

Translate the following sentences into Spanish.

1. *Why are the people crying?*

    _____

2. *It is raining.*

    _____

3. *Are you watching television now?*

    _____

4. *Why are the girls laughing?*

_____

5. *It is our turn. We are using the computers now.*

_____

6. *Teresa is waiting for the train, but she is losing patience.*

_____

7. *What are you thinking about?*

_____

8. *We are trying to fall asleep.*

_____

Reading Comprehension

La parada del bus

La mujer se llama Lorena. No es ni joven, ni vieja, ni delgada, ni gorda. Tiene la cara pálida, con ojos marrones y pelo oscuro. No se maquilla mucho pero se nota que le gusta llevar un poco de colorete. Se ve que es conservadora por su vestimenta: su falda que cubre las piernas y la blusa con mangas largas aunque es verano.

Ella llega siempre a la parada del bus, esperando a su esposo. Se puede pasar por la banca y verla allí sentada, hora tras hora, escribiendo en su cuaderno y dibujando el rostro de su esposo amado.

Una mañana de mucho calor, un hombre se sienta cerca de ella y conversa un poco.

Él se llama Roberto; parece ser un buen hombre. Hablan de sus dibujos y como pasa ella el día. Él se entera que ella está separada de su esposo desde hace cinco años, pero siendo católicos los dos, son todavía casados. Roberto, soltero, pasa los días trabajando en computadoras, y sus noches jugando al ajedrez en un club con otros fanáticos.

Después de veinte minutos, otro bus viene, y el hombre, un poco triste ahora de dejarla, sube al bus y se va. Ella lo sigue con los ojos con una mirada llena de soledad. La gente sube al bus; otros se bajan y se van para la casa. Lorena se queda tranquilamente, extrañando a su esposo, esperando que venga en el próximo bus.

Verbos

enterarse	*to become aware*
estar sentado	*to be seated*
irse	*to go* (compared with **ir**, **irse** expresses more immediacy)
maquillarse	*to put makeup on*
se nota	*one notices*
se ve	*one sees*

Nombres

el ajedrez	*chess*
el colorete	*the lipstick*
el fanático	*the fan*

Expresiones

aunque	*although*
hora tras hora	*hour after hour*

Preguntas

1. ¿Qué estación es?

    _____

2. ¿Cómo es el clima?

    _____

3. ¿Qué hace Lorena cada día?

    _____

4. ¿Está casada la mujer?

    _____

5. ¿Está casado Roberto?

    _____

6. ¿Está Roberto interesado en Lorena? ¿Está ella interesada en él?

    _____

7. ¿Piensa Ud. que Roberto va a volver?

    _____

8. ¿Piensa Ud. que Lorena va a seguir esperando?

    _____

4

The Past Progressive Tenses

There are two progressive tenses in the past: the imperfect progressive and the preterit progressive. Both express a past action or actions that were occurring, actions that were in progress. They are equivalent to the English past progressive: *The people were running*, for example. These tenses are used to intensify the following:

- An action that was in progress in the past
- An event that was happening in the past

If you do not want to intensify an action that was in progress in the past, use the simple imperfect tense:

El hombre trabajaba mucho.	*The man was working a lot.*
La mujer cocinaba su cena.	*The woman was cooking her supper.*
Los niños se reían.	*The children were laughing.*
Toda la familia se divertía.	*The whole family was having a good time.*

The Imperfect Progressive Tense

Formation of the Imperfect Progressive Tense

The imperfect progressive is a compound tense in Spanish, as it is in English. It is formed by conjugating **estar** in the imperfect and adding the gerund of the main verb. The tense is also called the imperfect continuous.

58

yo estaba jugando	*I was playing*
tú estabas bebiendo	*you were drinking*
él estaba pintando	*he was painting*
nosotros estábamos corriendo	*we were running*
vosotros estabais sonriendo	*you were smiling*
ellos estaban cenando	*they were dining*

Uses of the Imperfect Progressive Tense

The action expressed by the imperfect progressive tense must be an action that was in progress in the past.

Following are examples formed with **estar**.

El estudiante estaba durmiendo cuando el maestro empezó la clase.	*The student was sleeping when the teacher began the class.*
Yo estaba atravesando la calle cuando vi venir el carro.	*I was crossing the street when I saw the car coming.*
El portero nos estaba ayudando con la maleta.	*The doorman was helping us with the suitcase.*
El gerente estaba mostrándoles la habitación.	*The manager was showing them the room.*
Estábamos bailando cuando se apagaron las luces.	*We were dancing when the lights went out.*

The verbs **seguir**, **ir**, and **venir** can also be conjugated in the imperfect and used with the gerund to form the imperfect progressive tense.

La muchacha iba aprendiendo la lección.	*The girl was learning the lesson little by little.*
Ellas venían hacia nosotros bailando y hablando.	*They were coming toward us dancing and talking.*
Los perros seguían ladrando en la calle.	*The dogs continued barking in the street.*

Verbs not generally used in the gerund form in the past progressive are **ser**, **estar**, **poder**, **querer**, **saber**, **tener**, **ir**, and **venir**. These verbs use the simple imperfect instead of the imperfect progressive.

Hubo un tiempo cuando **podíamos** viajar mucho.	There was a time when we were able to travel a lot.
Ella **quería** ir a España a estudiar.	She wanted to go to Spain to study.
Sócrates dijo que no **sabía** lo que no **sabía**.	Socrates said that he did not know what he did not know.
Yo **iba** a la tienda cuando vi a mi amigo.	I was going to the store when I saw my friend.
Mis primos me dijeron que **venían** a verme, pero no llegaron.	My cousins told me that they were coming to see me, but they didn't arrive.

Exercise 4.1

Translate the following sentences into Spanish, using the imperfect progressive tense.

1. *I was cleaning the house.*

   _____

2. *Rosa continued eating.*

   _____

3. *Pablo was selling medicine to his friends.*

   _____

4. *We were learning to dance.*

   _____

5. *Why was she lying to me?*

   _____

6. *What were you (Ud.) doing?*

   _____

7. *Who was sleeping on the train?*

   _____

8. *Everyone was leaving for the exits.*

   _____

9. *The boys and girls were throwing the ball.*

_____

10. *The politicians were beginning their campaign.*

_____

The Preterit Progressive Tense

Formation of the Preterit Progressive Tense

The preterit progressive also emphasizes action that was taking place in the past. It is formed with the preterit of the verb **estar** followed by the gerund of the main verb.

yo estuve contestando	*I was answering*
tú estuviste gritando	*you were yelling*
ella estuvo bailando	*she was dancing*
nosotros estuvimos charlando	*we were chatting*
vosotros estuvisteis leyendo	*you were reading*
ellas estuvieron explorando	*they were exploring*

Uses of the Preterit Progressive Tense

Unlike the imperfect progressive, the preterit progressive tense expresses an action completed in the past. The name of the tense might seem like a contradiction in terms, but the action, although in a progressive form, is definitely over.

Ayer, en clase de ciencias, el estudiante estuvo escuchando atentamente al profesor hasta que terminó la clase.	*Yesterday, in science class, the student was listening attentively to the professor until the class ended.* (The phrase **hasta que terminó la clase** can also be translated as *until he ended the class.*)
Estuvimos riéndonos a carcajadas hasta que salimos del teatro.	*We were laughing our heads off until we left the theater.*
Anoche, Sofía, una gran pianista, estuvo practicando hasta que su novio la llamó.	*Last night, Sofía, a great pianist, was practicing until her boyfriend called her.*

The gerund is also used with **seguir**, **venir**, and **ir** to form the preterit progressive tense.

La abuela **fue poniéndose** vieja.	*The grandmother was getting older little by little.*
A Guillermo le gusta leer; después de apagar la televisión, **siguió leyendo**.	*William likes to read; after turning off the television, he continued reading.*
Pedro **vino corriendo** a la escuela y llegó a tiempo.	*Peter came running to school and arrived on time.*

Exercise 4.2

Translate the following sentences into English.

1. Nos divertíamos hasta que la obra empezó.

   _____

2. ¿Querían Uds. darles de comer a los pájaros en el parque?

   _____

3. Sabíamos que íbamos a tener éxito.

   _____

4. Las mujeres estuvieron celebrando su jubilación hasta las once de la noche.

   _____

5. Fui conociendo México.

   _____

6. Nuestro profesor estuvo enseñando por una hora ayer.

   _____

7. Estábamos trabajando cuando nuestros amigos llegaron.

   _____

8. ¿De qué estabas hablando?

   _____

9. Ella no me estuvo escuchando.

   _____

10. El camarero no nos estaba sirviendo la comida.

_____

11. Los maestros estuvieron repitiendo las instrucciones hasta que entendimos.

_____

12. ¿Por qué los estabas buscando por tanto tiempo cuando sabías que tus amigos estaban escondiéndose?

_____

_____

13. Estuvimos bailando anoche hasta medianoche.

_____

14. Nadie estaba andando por aquí.

_____

 **Exercise 4.3**

Review (Preterit tense) *Complete the following sentences with the correct preterit form of the verb in parentheses.*

EXAMPLE   Mi amigo no me _*esperó*_ . (esperar)

1. Mis amigos me _____ por una hora. (esperar)

2. Ella no le _____ nada. (decir)

3. ¿Por qué no les _____ Uds. flores? (traer)

4. Las hojas _____ de los árboles. (caerse)

5. Yo nunca les _____ dinero. (dar)

6. Octavio no _____ dormir anoche. (poder)

7. Nosotros no _____ al cine el sábado. (ir)

8. Me _____ mucho la comida. (gustar)

9. Yo sé que tú me _____ en el restaurante. (ver)

10. Ella es amable. ¿Dónde la _____ Ud.? (conocer)

Exercise 4.4

Review (Imperfect tense) *Complete the following sentences with the correct imperfect form of the verb in parentheses.*

EXAMPLE   ¿Dónde _estabas_ cuando la maestra entró? (estar)

1. ¿Qué hora _____ cuando la película empezó? (ser)

2. ¿Cuántos años _____ los gemelos cuando se graduaron? (tener)

3. La doctora no _____ ver a más pacientes. (querer)

4. Yo siempre _____ para los exámenes. (estudiar)

5. En su juventud, Patricio _____ al tenis. (jugar)

6. Antes de la época de la computadora, la gente _____ cartas. (escribir)

7. Ella nunca _____ contenta. Siempre _____. (estar/quejarse)

8. El hombre viejo _____ los dientes en un vaso de agua todas las noches antes de dormirse. (poner)

 Exercise 4.5

Review (Indirect object pronouns) *Complete the following sentences with the correct indirect object pronoun, according to the cue in parentheses.*

1. Yo _____ traigo flores. (*to you*)

2. Susana _____ presta dinero. (*to them*)

3. ¿Por qué _____ hablas en voz alta? (*to her*)

4. ¿Qué _____ estás diciendo? (*to me*)

5. Nosotros no _____ estamos escribiendo ahora. (*to you*).

6. ¿Por qué _____ cobra Ud. tanto? (*to us*)

Exercise 4.6

Review (Direct object pronouns) *Translate the following sentences into English.*

1. Julia busca a su hermana. Ella está buscándola.

2. Cuidamos a los bebés. Los cuidamos.

3. Los dos hermanos ayudan a su familia. La familia aprecia su ayuda.

4. El jardinero mira los pájaros. Los mira volar.

5. Los estudiantes saludan a su maestra. La saludan todos los días.

6. ¿Por qué me llamas hoy? ¿Por qué me estás llamando a casa?

7. Manuel visita a la mujer en Perú. Él quiere casarse con ella en la primavera.

8. Todos los turistas esperan el tren. No les molesta esperarlo porque hace fresco.

Exercise 4.7

Review (Double object pronouns) *Translate the following sentences into English.*

1. Te lo juro.

2. Me pongo los guantes. Me los pongo.

3. La mujer indígena no nos vende agua; ella nos la da.

4. Me gustan los mariscos en este restaurante. El camarero me los sirve con gusto.

_____

_____

5. Ana les trae el postre a sus amigas. Ella se lo trae.

_____

Exercise 4.8

Review (Indirect object pronouns, direct object pronouns, the present tense, the present progressive tense) _Translate the following sentences into Spanish._

1. _Do you tell the truth to your friends? We tell it to you._

_____

2. _I always write letters to him. I am writing them to him now._

_____

3. _Irene gives gifts to her son every Christmas. This year she is going to give them to him on his birthday._

_____

_____

4. _We show the new shoestore to my friend. She looks at the high heels, but she doesn't buy them for us._

_____

_____

5. _Sometimes people don't understand what we say. Sometimes we have to explain it to them._

_____

_____

6. _Enrique reads a story to his children every night at eight o'clock. He is reading it to them now._

_____

_____

Exercise 4.9

Review (Double object pronouns, *se* and the indirect object, the preterit tense) *Translate the following sentences into English.*

1. Miguel no pudo entrar en su casa porque se le perdieron las llaves.

   _____

2. Se me cayó la cuchara y me puse brava.

   _____

3. ¡Cuidado! Se les van a caer los vasos. Ya se nos rompieron dos.

   _____

4. No se me ocurrió trabajar ayer.

   _____

5. No pudiste preparar la sopa de ajo anoche. Se te acabó el ajo.

   _____

6. Se me olvidó hacer mi tarea.

   _____

Reading Comprehension

El hospital

La pobre mamá iba caminando para no mostrarle a su hijo que estaba preocupada. Ella sabía que no era ni catarro, ni gripe, ni pulmonía. Ella sabía que era algo grave. De repente, empezó a correr hacia un taxi para llevárselos a un hospital.

Hacía dos días que su hijo estaba quejándose de un dolor de estómago, un dolor que no lo dejaba dormir. ¿Qué tiene el hijo? Viviendo sola, Silvia no tenía nadie con quien hablar a la medianoche. El taxista los dejó en la entrada del hospital. Ella le pagó y le dio una buena propina. Estuvieron esperando solamente cinco minutos cuando los médicos llegaron. Examinaron al niño que estaba llorando. La mamá, llorando también, trató de ser valiente ante su hijo, pero no pudo. Después de un rato, que le pareció una eternidad, los médicos le ofrecieron dos opciones: operar o no. La mamá, sin duda, optó por la operación y firmó el documento de consentimiento. El niño siguió sollozando.

"Pero mamá," le dijo el niño, "no quiero que me operen."

"Yo lo sé, hijo mío, pero es necesario y vas a estar muy bien y sin dolor después. Los doctores me dijeron que es apendicitis."

Con esta última conversación, los médicos lo pusieron en la camilla de operación y ellos desaparecieron en el largo corredor del hospital. La madre se retiró a la sala de espera, sintiéndose muy desolada en su soledad.

Ella estaba allá, pensando en su hijo, cuando vinieron los doctores con las noticias.

"Todo salió bien," le dijeron, "su hijo está recuperándose en su cuarto y pronto va a estar riéndose y jugando otra vez." La mamá aliviada les agradeció profundamente.

Y dentro de poco, ella y su hijo salieron charlando, ella con la mano preciosa de su hijo en la suya. Abrazándose, entraron en la casa.

Verbos

agradecer	*to thank*
desparecerse	*to disappear*
recuperarse	*to recuperate*
retirarse	*to retire*
sollozar	*to sob*

Expresiones con Verbos

dejar + *infinitive*	*to let (do something)*
llevárselo	*to carry someone or something away*
tratar de + *infinitive*	*to try to (do something)*

Nombres

la camilla	*the stretcher*
el catarro	*the cold*
la gripe	*the flu*
la pulmonía	*pneumonia*

Adjetivos

aliviado	*relieved*
desolado	*desolate*

Pronombres

la suya	*hers* (refers to *her hand*)
hijo mío	*son of mine* (gives more emphasis than **mi hijo** (*my son*))

Expresión

de repente   *suddenly*

Preguntas

1. ¿Por qué fueron al hospital a la medianoche?

   _____

2. ¿Está Ud. de acuerdo con la primera decisión de la madre?

   _____

3. ¿Qué tiene el hijo?

   _____

4. ¿Cuidaron bien los médicos al hijo y a la madre?

   _____

5. ¿Cómo se sienten la madre y su hijo al final del cuento?

   _____

5

The Present Subjunctive

The present subjunctive is a mood in the present tense, widely used in Spanish. The present subjunctive cannot exist alone. Another element in the sentence always causes it to be used. The subjunctive is often needed after the following elements:

- Certain impersonal expressions
- Certain verbs
- Certain conjunctions
- Certain dependent adjectives
- Certain expressions

Formation of the Present Subjunctive

Most verbs form the present subjunctive from the first-person singular **yo** form of the present indicative. Drop the **-o** to get the stem for the present subjunctive.

Verbs that are irregular in the present indicative are irregular in the present subjunctive in the same way.

There are only six verbs that do not form the present subjunctive from the **yo** form of the present indicative.

-*Ar* Verbs

In order to conjugate both regular and irregular **-ar** verbs in the present subjunctive, start with the **yo** form of the present indicative. Drop the **-o** and add -**e**, -**es**, -**e**, -**emos**, -**éis**, -**en** to the stem.

Infinitive	**yo** Form	Present Subjunctive	
bailar	bailo	yo baile	nosotros bailemos
		tú bailes	vosotros bailéis
		ella baile	ellas bailen
cantar	canto	yo cante	nosotros cantemos
		tú cantes	vosotros cantéis
		él cante	ellos canten
cerrar	cierro	yo cierre	nosotros cerremos
		tú cierres	vosotros cerréis
		Ud. cierre	Uds. cierren
pensar	pienso	yo piense	nosotros pensemos
		tú pienses	vosotros penséis
		ella piense	ellas piensen
recordar	recuerdo	yo recuerde	nosotros recordemos
		tú recuerdes	vosotros recordéis
		él recuerde	ellos recuerden

Note that the first-person and third-person singular forms are identical in the present subjunctive.

The first two examples, **bailar** and **cantar**, are regular in the present indicative. The last three, **cerrar**, **pensar**, and **recordar**, show stem changes. Note that the stem changes in the present indicative are also present in the present subjunctive, except in the **nosotros** and **vosotros** forms, which are unaffected by these stem changes.

A Word About the Present Subjunctive

The formation of the subjunctive comes from the conjugation of the first-person singular of the present indicative. Any irregularity that the verb has in the present indicative **yo** form also occurs in the present subjunctive. To learn the subjunctive well, practice the **yo** form of the verbs, because that will be the stem of the present subjunctive.

-*Er* and -*ir* Verbs

In order to conjugate both regular and irregular **-er** and **-ir** verbs in the present subjunctive, drop the **-o** from the first-person singular of the present indicative and add **-a**, **-as**, **-a**, **-amos**, **-áis**, **-an** to the stem.

-*Er* Verbs

Infinitive	**yo** Form	Present Subjunctive	
comer	como	yo coma	nosotros comamos
		tú comas	vosotros comáis
		él coma	ellos coman
querer	quiero	yo quiera	nosotros queramos
		tú quieras	vosotros queráis
		ella quiera	ellas quieran
poder	puedo	yo pueda	nosotros podamos
		tú puedas	vosotros podáis
		Ud. pueda	Uds. puedan
ver	veo	yo vea	nosotros veamos
		tú veas	vosotros veáis
		él vea	ellos vean

-*Ir* Verbs

Infinitive	**yo** Form	Present Subjunctive	
vivir	vivo	yo viva	nosotros vivamos
		tú vivas	vosotros viváis
		él viva	ellos vivan
mentir	miento	yo mienta	nosotros mintamos
		tú mientas	vosotros mintáis
		ella mienta	ellas mientan
pedir	pido	yo pida	nosotros pidamos
		tú pidas	vosotros pidáis
		Ud. pida	Uds. pidan
dormir	duermo	yo duerma	nosotros durmamos
		tú duermas	vosotros durmáis
		él duerma	ellos duerman

NOTE In the irregular **-ir** verbs, there is an additional irregularity in the **nosotros** and **vosotros** forms. Verbs with the stem change **e > ie** or **e > i** have an **-i-** in the **nosotros** and **vosotros** forms. Verbs with the stem change **o > ue** have a -u- in the **nosotros** and **vosotros** forms.

Irregular *-er* and *-ir* Verbs with *-g-* or *-zc-* in the *yo* Form

In the present subjunctive, certain **-er** and **-ir** verbs carry the irregularity of the first-person singular of the present indicative tense throughout the present subjunctive conjugation. There are no **-ar** verbs that have this irregularity.

Infinitive	**yo** Form	Present Subjunctive	
conocer	conozco	yo conozca	nosotros conozcamos
		tú conozcas	vosotros conozcáis
		él conozca	ellos conozcan
decir	digo	yo diga	nosotros digamos
		tú digas	vosotros digáis
		ella diga	ellas digan
hacer	hago	yo haga	nosotros hagamos
		tú hagas	vosotros hagáis
		Ud. haga	Uds. hagan
poner	pongo	yo ponga	nosotros pongamos
		tú pongas	vosotros pongáis
		él ponga	ellos pongan
salir	salgo	yo salga	nosotros salgamos
		tú salgas	vosotros salgáis
		ella salga	ellas salgan
tener	tengo	yo tenga	nosotros tengamos
		tú tengas	vosotros tengáis
		Ud. tenga	Uds. tengan
traer	traigo	yo traiga	nosotros traigamos
		tú traigas	vosotros traigáis
		él traiga	ellos traigan
venir	vengo	yo venga	nosotros vengamos
		tú vengas	vosotros vengáis
		ella venga	ellas vengan

Other regular **-ar** verbs:

alcanzar	*to reach, to overtake*
anular	*to annul*
arrancar	*to pull, to root out*
cargar	*to load*
colocar	*to place*
ignorar	*to be ignorant of*
lograr	*to succeed in*
madrugar	*to get up early*
masticar	*to chew*
pagar	*to pay for*
publicar	*to publish*
rezar	*to pray*
subrayar	*to underline*
tragar	*to swallow*

Other **-er** verbs like **conocer**:

agradecer	*to thank*
amanecer	*to wake up, to brighten*
aparecer	*to appear*
crecer	*to grow*
desaparecer	*to disappear*
establecer	*to establish*
merecer	*to deserve*
nacer	*to be born*
obedecer	*to obey*
ofrecer	*to offer*
padecer	*to suffer*
parecer	*to seem*
pertenecer	*to belong*
reconocer	*to recognize*
yacer	*to lie down*

Other **-ir** verbs with **-zc-** in the **yo** form:

conducir	*to drive*
introducir	*to insert*
lucir	*to light up*
producir	*to produce*

reducir	*to reduce*
traducir	*to translate*

The Spanish equivalent of the English verb meaning *to introduce* is **presentar**.

Te presento a mi familia.	*I introduce you to my family.*

Irregular Verbs

There are only six verbs whose present subjunctive is not formed from the first-person singular of the present indicative. They are irregular in that they are not formed from the **yo** form.

Infinitive	**yo** Form	Present Subjunctive	
dar	doy	yo dé	nosotros demos
		tú des	vosotros deis
		él dé	ellos den
estar	estoy	yo esté	nosotros estemos
		tú estés	vosotros estéis
		ella esté	ellas estén
ir	voy	yo vaya	nosotros vayamos
		tú vayas	vosotros vayáis
		Ud. vaya	Uds. vayan
saber	sé	yo sepa	nosotros sepamos
		tú sepas	vosotros sepáis
		él sepa	ellos sepan
ser	soy	yo sea	nosotros seamos
		tú seas	vosotros seáis
		ella sea	ellas sean
haber	he	yo haya	nosotros hayamos
		tú hayas	vosotros hayáis
		Ud. haya	Uds. hayan

NOTES The present subjunctive form **dé** (from **dar**) has a written accent to distinguish it from **de** (*of*).

The word **hay** comes from the infinitive **haber**; you will not need this form for any other use at this time.

Verbs with Orthographic Changes

Verbs with orthographic changes are not irregular. The spelling changes simply maintain the sound of the **yo** form. Some of the most common spelling changes are the following:

- Verbs that end in **-car** change **c** to **qu**.
- Verbs that end in **-gar** change **g** to **gu**.
- Verbs that end in **-zar** change **z** to **c**.

Infinitive	**yo** Form	Present Subjunctive	
buscar	busco	yo busque	nosotros busquemos
		tú busques	vosotros busquéis
		Ud. busque	Uds. busquen
explicar	explico	yo explique	nosotros expliquemos
		tú expliques	vosotros expliquéis
		Ud. explique	Uds. expliquen
tocar	toco	yo toque	nosotros toquemos
		tú toques	vosotros toquéis
		Ud. toque	Uds. toquen
apagar	apago	yo apague	nosotros apaguemos
		tú apagues	vosotros apaguéis
		él apague	ellos apaguen
llegar	llego	yo llegue	nosotros lleguemos
		tú llegues	vosotros lleguéis
		ella llegue	ellas lleguen
comenzar	comienzo	yo comience	nosotros comencemos
		tú comiences	vosotros comencéis
		ella comience	ellas comiencen
empezar	empiezo	yo empiece	nosotros empecemos
		tú empieces	vosotros empecéis
		él empiece	ellos empiecen

NOTE The change **z** > **c** occurs before the vowel **e** without affecting the sound. The consonants **c** (before **i** and **e**), **s**, and **z** all have the same sound.

> **A Word About Pronunciation of the Present Subjunctive**
> Like the present indicative, the stress in the present subjunctive is on the second-to-last syllable. As you practice, make sure you pronounce the verbs in this way: **yo ca̱nte, tú ca̱ntes, él ca̱nte, nosotros cante̱mos, ellos ca̱nten**. If a word carries a written accent, stress the accented syllable: **vosotros canté̱is**.

Uses of the Present Subjunctive

Remember that the subjunctive mood cannot exist alone; it must always be caused by some other element in the sentence. This is a mood that expresses wishes, doubts, and what is possible, rather than what is certain. The present subjunctive in a dependent clause is caused by the present tense in the main clause. Following are the specific uses of the present subjunctive.

After Certain Impersonal Expressions

A sentence or question may consist of a main clause and a dependent or subordinate clause connected by the Spanish conjunction **que**.

Following is a sentence with a main clause and a subordinate clause that are both in the indicative mood.

THE MAIN CLAUSE	Él sabe
THE DEPENDENT CLAUSE	que yo cocino bien.

However, suppose that the main clause has an impersonal expression, such as **Es dudoso**. This causes the subjunctive to be used in the dependent clause.

Es dudoso que yo **cocine** bien.　　*It is doubtful that I cook well.*

Following are some frequently used impersonal expressions:

es bueno (que)	*it is good (that)*
es difícil (que)	*it is difficult (that)*
es dudoso (que)	*it is doubtful (that)*
es fácil (que)	*it is easy (that)*
es imposible (que)	*it is impossible (that)*
es importante (que)	*it is important (that)*
es malo (que)	*it is bad (that)*
es mejor (que)	*it is better (that)*
es necesario (que)	*it is necessary (that)*

es posible (que)	*it is possible (that)*
es preciso (que)	*it is extremely necessary (that)*
es probable (que)	*it is probable (that)*
es una lástima (que)	*it is a pity (that)*
es urgente (que)	*it is urgent (that)*

Es dudoso que **viajemos** a España.	*It is doubtful that we will travel to Spain.*
Es importante que ella **coma** bien.	*It is important that she eat well.*
Es imposible que él **tenga** razón.	*It is impossible that he is right.*
Es necesario que **estudiemos** para el examen.	*It is necessary that we study for the test.*
¿Es posible que ella **venga** mañana?	*Is it possible that she will come tomorrow?*
Es probable que mi amiga me **vea** en el restaurante.	*It is probable that my friend will see me in the restaurant.*
Es una lástima que Pedro no lo **quiera** hacer.	*It is a pity that Peter doesn't want to do it.*

When you begin a sentence with one of the impersonal expressions above, it is mandatory to use the subjunctive in the dependent clause. You do not have to make any decisions, nor do you have a choice about whether or not to use it. These impersonal expressions in the main clause always trigger the subjunctive in the subordinate clause.

Notice that some of the example sentences and questions above are translated with the future in English. This is because the present subjunctive carries with it a feeling of the future and doubt.

If you want to make a general statement with an impersonal expression, there is neither a dependent clause nor a subjunctive. You simply use the structure you have already learned, which follows English word order.

Es bueno nadar cada día.	*It is good to swim every day.*
Es importante comer bien.	*It is important to eat well.*
¿Es necesario trabajar mucho?	*Is it necessary to work a lot?*
Es posible salir temprano.	*It is possible to leave early.*

Exercise 5.1

Complete the following sentences with the correct present subjunctive form of the verb in parentheses.

EXAMPLE   Es urgente que el chofer _<u>conduzca</u>_ con cuidado. (conducir)

1. Es importante que nuestros amigos _____ a la fiesta. (venir)

2. Es posible que él me _____ la verdad. (decir)

3. Es una lástima que Sara no lo _____. (hacer)

4. ¿Es posible que Uds. _____ a mi amigo Raúl? (conocer)

5. Es necesario que nosotros _____ bien. (dormir)

6. Es importante que ella _____ bien las direcciones. (saber)

7. Es necesario que nosotros _____ mucha agua fría en el verano. (tomar)

8. Es dudoso que ellos _____ temprano. (levantarse)

9. ¿Es posible que ella _____ a tiempo? (llegar)

10. Es posible que yo _____ en Francia. (quedarse)

11. Es probable que mucha gente importante _____ en la conferencia. (estar)

12. Es difícil que yo te _____ una buena respuesta. (dar)

13. Es urgente que tú _____ al doctor hoy. (ir)

14. Es dudoso que ellos _____ ricos. (ser)

15. Es importante que los padres les _____ a sus hijos. (leer)

16. La niña acaba de comer. Es imposible que _____ hambre. (tener)

17. Es probable que nosotros le _____ flores al profesor. (traer)

18. Es bueno que Uds. _____ mejor. (sentirse)

After Certain Verbs

Expressing Wishes or Preferences

Verbs in the main clause that express wishes or preferences with regard to other people will cause the subjunctive mood in the dependent clause. The subject in the main clause must be different from the subject in the dependent clause. Following are verbs that express wishes or preferences:

desear	*to desire*
preferir	*to prefer*
querer	*to desire, to want*

Following is a sentence with a main clause and a subordinate clause that are both in the indicative mood.

THE MAIN CLAUSE   Él sabe
THE DEPENDENT CLAUSE   que yo canto.

However, suppose that the main clause has one of the verbs above, such as **Él quiere**. This causes the subjunctive to be used in the dependent clause:

Él quiere que yo **cante**.   *He wants me to sing.*
                                     (*He wants that I sing.*)

The English equivalent does not always show the distinction in mood like Spanish does. But even in the English translation of the example above, it is clear that the person in the main clause, *he*, wants the other person, *me*, to do something.

Deseamos que ella **esté** bien.   *We want her to be well.*
Ella prefiere que su hijo **juegue** *She prefers that her son play*
  al béisbol.   *baseball.*
Quiero que él **baile**.   *I want him to dance.*

If there is only one subject for the two verbs in a sentence, there is neither a dependent clause nor a subjunctive verb.

Deseamos descansar.   *We want to rest.*
Ella prefiere dormir.   *She prefers to sleep.*
Yo quiero cantar.   *I want to sing.*

Expressing Hope, Happiness, Sadness, or Regret

Verbs in the main clause that express hope, happiness, sadness, or regret with regard to other people will cause the subjunctive mood in the dependent clause. Following are verbs that express hope, happiness, sadness, or regret:

alegrarse de   *to be glad*
esperar   *to hope*
estar contento de   *to be happy*
estar triste de   *to be sad*
gustarle a uno   *to be pleasing to someone*
sentir   *to regret*
temer   *to fear*
tener miedo de   *to be afraid of*

Me alegro de que Uds. **estén** bien.	*I am glad that you are well.*
Esperamos que Ud. **tenga** un buen fin de semana.	*We hope that you have a good weekend.*
La maestra está contenta de que **hagamos** la tarea.	*The teacher is happy that we do the homework.*
¿Estás triste de que no **podamos** aceptar tu invitación?	*Are you sad that we cannot accept your invitation?*
Me gusta que mi familia **venga** a verme.	*It pleases me that my family is coming to see me.*
Lo siento que Ud. nunca se **gane** la lotería.	*I am sorry that you never win the lottery.*
Los padres temen que sus hijos no **quieran** estudiar.	*The parents fear that their children don't want to study.*
El líder tiene miedo de que el grupo no **resuelva** el problema.	*The leader fears that the group will not resolve the problem.*

If there is only one subject for the two verbs in a sentence, the sentence follows the basic structure that you have learned.

Me alegro de estar aquí.	*I am glad to be here.*
Él espera salir dentro de una hora.	*He hopes to leave within the hour.*
Me gusta ir al cine.	*I like to go to the movies.*
Ella tiene miedo de volar.	*She is afraid of flying.*

Expressing Orders, Requests, or Advice

Verbs in the main clause that express orders, requests, or advice will cause the subjunctive mood in the dependent clause. Following are verbs that express orders, requests, or advice:

aconsejar	*to advise*
decir	*to tell (someone to do something)*
dejar	*to permit, to let*
insistir en	*to insist*
mandar	*to order*
pedir	*to request, to ask for*
permitir	*to permit*
prohibir	*to prohibit*
sugerir	*to suggest*

Te aconsejo que **tomes** el tren.	*I advise you to take the train.*
Ella insiste en que yo **me quede**.	*She insists that I stay.*
Les pedimos que **vayan** de vacaciones.	*We ask them to go on vacation.*
Le sugiero que Ud. **lea** este artículo.	*I suggest that you read this article.*

Dejar, **mandar**, **permitir**, and **prohibir** can be used in two ways:

Les dejo que **entren**. Les dejo entrar.	} *I let them enter.*
Te permito que **nades** aquí. Te permito nadar aquí.	} *I permit you to swim here.*
Te prohíbo que **fumes** en la casa. Te prohíbo fumar en la casa.	} *I forbid you to smoke in the house.*
El capitán les manda que los soldados **descansen**.	*The captain orders the soldiers to rest.*
Les manda descansar.	*He orders them to rest.*

As you have learned, **decir** is used to relate a fact. This idea is expressed with the indicative.

José nos dice que el tren viene.	*Joe tells us that the train is coming.*
Ella me dice que le gusta viajar.	*She tells me that she likes to travel.*

However, when **decir** is used as an order, the subjunctive is used in the dependent clause.

Yo te digo que **vayas** al doctor.	*I tell you to go to the doctor.*
Ud. me dice que yo **me quede**.	*You tell me to stay.*
Les decimos que **se acuesten** ahora.	*We tell them to go to bed now.*
Él nos dice que **tengamos** cuidado.	*He tells us to be careful.*
¿Puede Ud. decirle que me **llame**?	*Can you tell her to call me?*

When English *to tell* is used to order someone to do something, the English command form is always the conjugation of the verb *to tell* + infinitive.

An English command is expressed as follows: *I tell him **to stay***. *He tells me **to go***. Compare that to simply relating a fact: *He tells me that the bus is here.*

Expressing Doubt or Uncertainty

Verbs that express doubt or uncertainty in the main clause will cause the subjunctive mood in the dependent clause. Following are verbs that express doubt or uncertainty:

dudar	*to doubt*
no creer	*not to believe*
no pensar	*not to think*

Ella duda que yo **sepa** tocar el piano.	*She doubts that I know how to play the piano.*
La gente no cree que **sea** la verdad.	*The people don't believe that it is the truth.*
No pensamos que Daniel nos **invite** a la fiesta.	*We don't think that Daniel will invite us to the party.*

Exercise 5.2

Complete the following sentences with the correct present subjunctive form of the verb in parentheses.

1. ¿Qué quieres que yo te _____? (decir)

2. Él quiere que su amiga _____ la cuenta. (pagar)

3. Espero que Uds. _____ bien. (sentirse)

4. Ellos se alegran de que el bebé _____. (dejar de llorar)

5. Ellos nos piden que _____ mejor la idea. (explicar)

6. A él no le gusta que yo siempre _____ razón. (tener)

7. Rosa insiste en que su jefe le _____ más dinero. (dar)

8. No creo que Alicia _____ la fecha. (saber)

9. Ellas dudan que _____ mucho tráfico hoy. (haber)

10. Les sugiero a sus padres que _____ de vacaciones. (ir)

11. Me alegro de que no _____ nada grave. (ser)

12. Los expertos nos aconsejan que _____ ejercicio. (hacer)

13. Paula espera que su hermana _____ bien. (estar)

14. Yo dudo que ella lo _____ en la reunión. (besar)

Exercise 5.3

Rewrite the following indicative sentences in the subjunctive mood. Choose any appropriate verb that causes the subjunctive in the dependent clause.

EXAMPLE   Mis estudiantes están en clase.

      Me alegro de que estén en clase.

1. A mis padres les gusta viajar.

    _____

2. Mi amigo tiene malos sueños.

    _____

3. Ella no se divierte mucho.

    _____

4. Nosotros somos buenos estudiantes.

    _____

5. No vamos a volver a los Estados Unidos.

    _____

6. Sara me trae flores a mi casa.

    _____

7. ¿Conoce Ud. a mi tío? [Write a response.]

    _____

8. Mi hermano y yo no nos vemos mucho.

    _____

9. ¿Hay clase los lunes?

10. Carla es de Polonia.

    _____

Exercise 5.4

Indicative or subjunctive? *Complete the following sentences with the correct form of the verb in parentheses.*

EXAMPLES   Yo dudo que Cristina __*cante*__ bien. (cantar)

Yo sé que ella __*canta*__ bien. (cantar)

1. Espero que Uds. _____ un buen fin de semana. (tener)

2. Yo sé que Uds. _____ muchos amigos. (tener)

3. Ricardo prefiere que yo lo _____ en febrero. (visitar)

4. Él quiere que nosotros le _____ regalos. (traer)

5. Nos gusta que él nos _____. (amar)

6. Es importante que nosotros _____ nuestros errores. (corregir)

7. ¿Sabe Ud. que ellos _____ aquí? (estar)

8. Yo pienso que Rosario _____ poco. (quejarse)

9. Dudo que Enrique _____. (quedarse)

10. Sabemos que ellos _____. (irse)

11. El hombre espera que ella _____ con él. (bailar)

12. Sara no quiere que su novio la _____ antes de la boda. (ver)

13. Me alegro de que Uds. _____ aquí. (estar)

14. Es importante que nosotros _____ las direcciones antes de empezar nuestro viaje. (saber)

15. Yo pienso que este hombre _____ médico. (ser)

16. A mi hermano no le importa lo que _____ yo. (hacer)

After Certain Conjunctions

A subjunctive form follows directly after one of the following conjunctions if the main clause has a different subject than the dependent clause.

a pesar de que	*in spite of*
antes de que	*before*
después de que	*after*
en caso de que	*in case*

hasta que	*until*
para que	*in order that, so that*
sin que	*without*

Here is a sentence in which there is only one subject:

Ella practica el piano **antes de cantar**.	*She practices the piano before singing.*

In the following sentence, there are two subjects connected by a conjunction with **que**:

Ella practica el piano **antes de que** él **cante**.	*She practices the piano before he sings.*

The English equivalent does not show this distinction in mood the way Spanish does. However, there are clearly two subjects in the example above: *she* and *he*.

In the example sentences below, there are two subjects in each sentence, and the subjunctive follows the conjunction:

Voy a esperar **hasta que** tú **llegues**.	*I am going to wait until you arrive.*
Él enseña **para que** los estudiantes **aprendan**.	*He teaches so that the students learn.*
Lo voy a hacer **sin que** Ud. me **ayude**.	*I'm going to do it without your helping me.*

If there is one subject in the sentence, an infinitive follows the preposition.

Después de trabajar, ella descansa.	*After working, she rests.*
Ella estudia para aprender.	*She studies in order to learn.*
Él habla sin pensar.	*He speaks without thinking.*

Some conjunctions of time always cause the subjunctive, whether there are two subjects or only one in the sentence. Following are a few conjunctions of this type:

a menos que	*unless*
luego que	*as soon as*
tan pronto como	*as soon as*

Vamos a bailar **a menos que**
no **haya** música.

We are going to dance unless
there is no music.

Voy a llegar **tan pronto como**
yo **pueda**.

I am going to arrive as soon as
I can.

After *cuando*

The subjunctive form directly follows **cuando** if the future is implied.

Vamos a viajar **cuando**
tengamos tiempo y dinero.

We are going to travel when
we have time and money.

¿Me puedes llamar **cuando**
llegues a casa?

Can you call me when you
arrive home?

El niño quiere ser bombero
cuando sea grande.

The child wants to be a fireman
when he grows up.

When **cuando** introduces a question, the indicative form is used.

¿Cuándo vas a estar en casa?

When are you going to be home?

¿Cuándo quieren Uds. viajar?

When do you want to travel?

When **cuando** introduces a sentence that involves either a repeated action or a general statement in the present, the indicative mood is used.

Cuando hace frío, los niños
juegan en la nieve.

When it is cold, the children play
in the snow.

Ella se siente alegre cuando baila.

She feels happy when she dances.

Cuando voy a la playa, siempre
me divierto.

When I go to the beach, I always
have a good time.

Exercise 5.5

Complete the following sentences with the conjunction indicated and the correct form of the verb in parentheses.

EXAMPLE   Vamos de vacaciones ___tan pronto como___ (as soon as)

nosotros ___podamos___ (to be able to).

1. Él va a limpiar su apartamento _____ (before) su familia

   lo _____ (to visit).

2. _____ (after) yo _____ (to bathe myself),

   voy a vestirme.

3. No voy _____ (unless) Uds. _____ (to go) también.

4. Él va a invitar a su amiga a la fiesta _____ (as soon as)

   él _____ (to have) confianza.

5. Les doy las instrucciones _____ (so that) ellos

   _____ (to know how) llegar.

6. Uds. pueden jugar al baloncesto _____ (as soon as)

   Uds. _____ (to finish) su tarea.

7. _____ (before) su novio _____ (to come)

   a verla, Rosa va a arreglarse.

8. Te presto el dinero _____ (so that) tú _____
   (to be able to) comprar un carro usado.

9. Vamos a estar aquí _____ (until) ellos _____
   (to arrive).

10. _____ (in case) Uds. no _____ (to have)

    nada que hacer mañana, ¿podemos ir al cine?

11. A Ricardo no le gusta estudiar. Pero va a estudiar _____

    (so that) sus padres _____ (to be) contentos.

12. _____ (in spite of) _____ (to be) frío,

    ellos quieren dar una vuelta.

13. Tú puedes venir a mi casa _____ (without) yo

    te _____ (to invite).

14. Graciela va a descansar _____ (after) sus nietos

    _____ (to go away).

15. _____ (when) Ud. _____ (to be able),

    ¿me puede acompañar al tren?

16. Elena me va a ver _____ (when) nosotros

    _____ (to meet) en México.

17. _____ (when) ellos _____ (to return)

    a los Estados Unidos, van a comprar una casa pequeña.

18. El hombre va a estar contento _____ (when)

    _____ (to learn) a manejar.

In Certain Dependent Adjective Clauses

The subjunctive mood is used in the dependent clause if the object or person described in the main clause is indefinite or nonexistent. In the following examples, the objects and persons described in the main clause are not known.

Busco **un apartamento** que **sea** grande y barato.	*I am looking for an apartment that is big and cheap.*
¿Conoce Ud. a **alguien** que **sepa** hablar alemán?	*Do you know anyone who knows how to speak German?*
¿Hay **alguien** aquí que **baile** bien?	*Is there anyone here who dances well?*
No hay **nadie** que siempre **tenga** razón.	*There is no one who is always right.*

After the Expressions *por más que* and *por mucho que*

Por más que ella **limpie,** su casa está siempre desordenada.	*No matter how much she cleans, her house is always a mess.*
Por mucho que él **coma**, no se engorda.	*No matter how much he eats, he doesn't get fat.*

After *ojalá*

An interjection of Arabic origin, **ojalá** means *would to God that* or *may God grant that* and expresses great desire. It can also be translated as *I hope.*

Ojalá que ella **tenga** suerte.	*Would to God that she has luck.*
Ojalá que él **se quede**.	*May God grant that he stay.*
Ojalá que Uds. **reciban** el cheque.	*I hope you receive the check.*

After *acaso, quizás,* or *tal vez*

Acaso él me **visite** mañana.	*Perhaps he will visit me tomorrow.*
Quizás ellos me **digan** la verdad.	*Perhaps they will tell me the truth.*
Tal vez me **digan** mentiras.	*Perhaps they will tell me lies.*

After *aunque*

The subjunctive mood is used if the action has not yet occurred.

Voy al cine **aunque** no **vayan** mis amigos.	*I am going to the movies, although my friends may not go.*
Aunque Pedro **se quede** esta noche, yo voy a salir.	*Although Peter may stay tonight, I am going to leave.*
Aunque sea difícil, él lo puede hacer.	*Although it may be difficult, he can do it.*

If **aunque** introduces a sentence or question that expresses a known fact, a repeated action, or a general statement in the present, the indicative mood is used.

Aunque **es** verano, la mujer siempre lleva guantes.	*Although it is summer, the woman always wears gloves.*
Aunque el doctor **está** enfermo, va al hospital.	*Although the doctor is sick, he is going to the hospital.*
Aunque le **duele** la voz, la cantante decide cantar en la ópera.	*Although her voice hurts, the singer decides to sing in the opera.*
Elena no quiere ir al parque aunque sus amigos siempre **van**.	*Elena doesn't want to go to the park, although her friends always go.*

After Compounds of *-quiera*

Compounds of **-quiera**—**adondequiera** (*wherever*), **cualquiera** (*whichever*), **dondequiera** (*wherever*), and **quienquiera** (*whoever*)—all indicate uncertainty and therefore cause the subjunctive to follow.

Adondequiera que **vayas**, te deseo lo mejor.	*Wherever you go, I wish you the best.*
Cualquiera que **sea** sincero puede ser un buen amigo.	*Whichever one is sincere can be a good friend.*
Dondequiera que **estén ellos**, los voy a buscar.	*Wherever they are, I am going to look for them.*
Quienquiera que **esté** aquí puede salir con nosotros.	*Whoever is here can leave with us.*

After *como*

The subjunctive mood is used after **como** only if the meaning is *however*.

Ellas van a preparar la comida   *They are going to prepare the meal*
como tú **quieras**.   *however you want.*

Exercise 5.6

Complete the following sentences with the correct present subjunctive form of the verb in parentheses.

1. Tal vez ellos _____ por la comida. (enfermarse)

2. Ojalá que nosotros _____ hoy. (descansar)

3. Aunque él _____ mañana, no quiero lavar el baño. (llegar)

4. Por mucho que ellas _____, no van a hacer nada. (quejarse)

5. Quienquiera que _____ bien puede ser experto. (cocinar)

6. Ojalá que tú _____ bien esta noche. (dormir)

7. Aunque _____ mucho tráfico, queremos viajar. (haber)

8. Mi amiga busca un apartamento que _____ tres cuartos. (tener)

9. Carlos necesita una casa que _____ en el campo. (estar)

10. El hombre quiere hacer el proyecto como Ud. lo _____. (querer)

11. No conozco a nadie que me _____ a la playa. (acompañar)

12. Ella busca un novio que _____ inteligente. (ser)

13. Quizás él _____ la semana que viene. (venir)

14. Por más que Tomás _____, no sabe nada. (hablar)

Other Tenses That Cause the Present Subjunctive

You have learned so far that the present indicative in the main clause can cause the present subjunctive in the subordinate clause. This is the most common use of the subjunctive mood.

Two additional tenses, the present progressive and the future periphrastic (**ir** + **a** + *infinitive*) can cause the subjunctive mood as well.

Present Progressive as Cause for the Present Subjunctive

The present progressive in the main clause can cause the present subjunctive in the dependent clause.

La preocupada mamá está esperando que su hijo regrese a casa.	*The anxious mother is hoping that her son returns home.*
El papá le está diciendo a su hijo que juegue en el parque.	*The father is telling his son to play in the park.*
Los padres les están rogando que tengan cuidado.	*The parents are begging them to be careful.*
Les estamos sugiriendo que los niños hagan más ejercicio.	*We are suggesting to them that the children exercise more.*

NOTE The present tense and the present progressive are both present tenses.

Future (*ir* + *a* + infinitive) as Cause for the Present Subjunctive

The present subjunctive can also be caused by the future tense in the main clause.

Vamos a estar contentos de que Susana tenga éxito.	*We are going to be happy that Susan is successful.*
Raimundo va a pedirle a su jefe que le compre un carro.	*Raymond is going to ask his boss to buy him a car.*
Voy a insistir que mis amigos me acompañen al cine.	*I am going to insist that my friends accompany me to the movies.*
Marisa va a estar alegre cuando consiga un buen apartamento.	*Marisa is going to be happy when she gets a good apartment.*

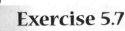

Exercise 5.7

Complete the following sentences with the correct present subjunctive form of the verb in parentheses. The verb in the main clause is in the present indicative. Make sure you know why the present subjunctive is used in each case.

EXAMPLE   El doctor me aconseja que yo __*haga*__ más exámenes médicos. (hacer)

1. Espero que Uds. _____ bien. (estar)

2. Nos alegramos mucho de que el sol no te _____. (picar)

3. Me gusta que mi sobrina _____ un buen trabajo. (obtener)

4. Paulina insiste en que su familia _____ a su compañero. (conocer)

5. Es imposible que Roberto _____ todo. (saber)

6. Dudamos que los inquilinos _____ contra el dueño. (ganar)

7. Ojalá que los huéspedes _____. (venir)

8. ¿Hay alguien aquí que me _____ cien dólares? (prestar)

9. Enseño para que los estudiantes _____. (aprender)

10. Presentamos la obra de teatro después de que los actores _____. (ensayar)

Exercise 5.8

Complete the following sentences with the correct present subjunctive form of the verb in parentheses. The verb in the main clause is in the present progressive.

EXAMPLE   La doctora está esperando que no _sea_ nada grave. (ser)

1. Catarina está aconsejándonos que _____ la puerta. (abrir)

2. Te estoy sugiriendo que _____. (irse)

3. ¿Por qué me sigues diciendo que yo te _____? (perdonar)

4. Los padres del niño le están pidiendo que no _____ en aguas peligrosas. (nadar)

5. Les estamos esperando que el tren _____ a tiempo. (llegar)

Exercise 5.9

*Complete the following sentences with the correct present subjunctive form of the verb in parentheses. The verb in the main clause is in the future periphrastic (**ir** + **a** + infinitive).*

EXAMPLE   El hombre idealista va a esperar que la mujer perfecta _venga_. (venir)

1. ¿Va a ser imposible que los adolescentes _____ a sus padres? (escuchar)

2. Voy a pedir que la gente no _____ más. (fumar)

3. Vamos a esperar que el piloto no _____. (perderse)

4. El paciente no va a tomar su medicina hasta que el doctor

   le _____ que se la _____. (decir/tomar)

5. La obra de teatro no se va a acabar hasta que la mujer gorda

   _____. (cantar)

📖 Reading Comprehension

Estimados lectores,

   Espero que a Uds. les guste la siguiente historia. Está en forma
de diálogo y basada en acontecimientos de la vida real. Intenten adivinar
quien es el personaje principal según las claves que aparecen en esta
escena. Para que gocen de lo lindo y para que aprendan de la historia,
es necesario que Uds. lean con cuidado.
La autora

El juicio

*La escena tiene lugar en la corte griega ante una asamblea de 501
ciudadanos.*

   El protagonista entra y empieza a hablar.

PROTAGONISTA Tengo sesenta años y es la primera vez que me ven
   en la corte. ¿Cuál es la primera acusación contra mí?

ACUSADOR Ud. es culpable de investigar bajo la tierra y en el cielo
   y de enseñarles a los otros las mismas cosas.

PROTAGONISTA No tengo nada que ver con estas acusaciones y no es
   verdad.

ACUSADOR Pero, ¿cuál es el problema, entonces? ¿Por qué hay tantos
   prejuicios contra Ud. si no hace algo diferente de los demás? Nos puede
   decir Ud. lo que es, para que le demos un veredicto justo.

PROTAGONISTA Bueno. Voy a decirles toda la verdad. Me dan esta
   reputación por cierta sabiduría que tengo. Menciono el dios de Delfos
   para que él sea mi testigo. ¿Se acuerdan Uds. de Querefón? Él fue
   al dios de Delfos y le preguntó si hay una persona más sabia que yo.
   El dios contestó que no hay nadie. Pero, ¿qué significa la idea de que
   yo soy el hombre más sagaz de todos? Me tocó investigar la cuestión.
   Yo fui a ver a un hombre que tiene la reputación de ser sagaz.

Lo examiné. No es necesario que les diga su nombre, él es un político, y esto es el resultado.

Cuando yo hablé con él, me di cuenta que él no era sabio. Cuando me fui, pensaba, "Yo soy más sabio que este hombre; ninguno de nosotros no sabe nada que valga la pena saber, pero él piensa que él tiene la sabiduría cuando él no la tiene, y yo, sin saber nada, no pienso que yo sea sagaz. No pienso que sé lo que no sé." Después, fui a ver a los poetas, pensando que ellos iban a ser más sagaces que yo. Pero averigüé que no es por la sabiduría que los poetas crean sus poemas sino por una inspiración divina. Por fin, fui a ver a los artesanos. Ellos sabían lo que yo no sabía y por eso eran más sabios que yo. Pero me pareció que cada uno se creía extremadamente sagaz en cuestiones importantes porque eran hábiles en su propio arte.

Mucho prejuicio contra mi ha resultado de mi investigación. Y yo sigo investigando y examinando a cada persona que pienso es sagaz y si él no es sagaz yo se lo digo. Estoy tan ocupado en mi investigación que no he tenido tiempo ni para servir en posiciones del estado ni de ganar dinero. Como resultado, yo soy pobre. Es verdad lo que les dije. Y yo sé que por esta investigación de la gente hay mucha rabia contra mí. Pero lo que Uds. escuchan es mi defensa contra estas primeras acusaciones.

Verbos

adivinar	*to guess*
averiguar	*to check out, to verify*
darse cuenta (de)	*to realize*
examinar	*to examine*
gozar	*to enjoy*
ha resultado	*has resulted* (present perfect tense)
he tenido	*have had* (present perfect tense)
intentar	*to intend, to try*
servir	*to serve*
tener que ver con	*to have something to do with*
valer	*to value*

Nombres

los acontecimientos	*the events*	la clave	*the key, the code*
la acusación	*the accusation*	la corte	*the court*
la asamblea	*the assembly*	la cuestión	*the issue*
el ciudadano	*the citizen*	la defensa	*the defense*

los demás	*the rest*	el personaje	*the character*
el diálogo	*the dialogue*	el político	*the politician*
el dios de Delfos	*the god of Delphi*	el prejuicio	*the prejudice*
la escena	*the scene*	la sabiduría	*the knowledge*
la investigación	*the investigation*	el/la testigo	*the witness*
el/la juez	*the judge*	el veredicto	*the verdict*
el juicio	*the judgment*		

Adjetivos

culpable	*guilty*	sabio	*wise, clever*
justo	*fair, just*	sagaz	*wise*
principal	*main, principal*	siguiente	*following*

Preguntas

1. ¿En qué sitio empieza la acción?

   _____

2. ¿Contra quién se defiende el protagonista?

   _____

3. ¿Cuántas personas hay en la asamblea griega?

   _____

4. ¿Cuál es la acusación contra él?

   _____

5. ¿Qué hizo el protagonista después de escuchar que él es el más sabio de todos?

   _____

6. ¿Qué hace el protagonista en su vida diaria?

   _____

7. Según el protagonista, ¿qué significa la sabiduría?

   _____

8. ¿Se defiende bien el protagonista?

   _____

9. ¿Es inocente o culpable el protagonista?

   _____

10. ¿Quién es el protagonista?

    _____

11. ¿Quién escribió el diálogo de la defensa?

    _____

6

Commands

The command form, also called the imperative, is used to tell someone to do or not to do something. The command form is considered a mood, and exists only in the immediate present. The Spanish affirmative command is equivalent to English commands, such as *turn here* or *follow the directions*. The Spanish negative command is equivalent to English *don't scream* or *don't drink the water,* for example. Except for the affirmative **tú** command, all the constructions use a form that is the same as the present subjunctive, so your knowledge of the subjunctive is a great help.

Even though there are other ways to request that people do things, the command form is necessary in many situations. For example, let's say you need to give someone directions:

> **Go** straight ahead, and then **turn** to the right.
> **Follow** the red line.
> **Walk** in the direction of the traffic.

Sometimes you need the command form to tell people not to do something, and you don't have very much time to do it in.

> **Don't touch** the light socket!
> **Don't jump** in the water—there are sharks!
> **Don't move**.
> **Don't worry**.

Affirmative *tú* Commands

The affirmative command form in the familiar **tú** is the same as the third-person singular of the present indicative. If the third-person indicative form is irregular, so is the command form.

-*Ar* Verbs

REGULAR IN THE PRESENT	Baila. Canta.	*Dance. Sing.*
	Mira. Escucha.	*Look. Listen.*
IRREGULAR IN THE PRESENT	Empieza. Piensa.	*Begin. Think.*

-*Er* and -*ir* Verbs

REGULAR IN THE PRESENT	Come. Bebe.	*Eat. Drink.*
	Lee. Escribe. Decide.	*Read. Write. Decide.*
IRREGULAR IN THE PRESENT	Duerme. Sonríe.	*Sleep. Smile.*

Irregular *tú* Commands

The following are the only irregular commands in the affirmative **tú** form. It is a good idea to learn these imperatives right away.

Infinitive	**tú** Command	English
decir	di	*say*
hacer	haz	*do*
ir	ve	*go*
poner	pon	*put*
salir	sal	*leave*
ser	sé	*be*
tener	ten	*have*
venir	ven	*come*

Haz tus ejercicios, por favor.	*Do your exercises, please.*
Ven acá.	*Come here.*
Pon tus zapatos en el armario.	*Put your shoes in the closet.*
Ten cuidado.	*Be careful.*

NOTE The command form can be softened by adding **por favor** (*please*).

Exercise 6.1

*Translate the following regular **tú** commands into English.*

1. Toma tu medicina y llama al doctor en la mañana.

   _____

2. Sigue a la derecha, por favor.

   _____

3. Cierra la puerta, por favor, y abre la ventana.

   _____

4. Corre a la tienda y compra la leche.

   _____

5. Prepara la comida esta noche y después, saca la basura, por favor.

   _____

6. Lee *Don Quixote* para la clase y escribe tu opinión acerca del tema principal.

   _____

7. Come más frutas y verduras.

   _____

8. Cuenta conmigo.

   _____

Exercise 6.2

*Write the affirmative **tú** command form for the following verbs.*

1. apagar   *to turn off*   _____
2. compartir   *to share*   _____
3. decidir   *to decide*   _____
4. devolver   *to return* (an object)   _____
5. doblar   *to turn*   _____
6. mirar   *to look at, to watch*   _____
7. oír   *to hear*   _____

    8. regresar   *to return*   _____

    9. terminar   *to end*   _____

   10. tirar   *to throw*   _____

✎ Exercise 6.3

*Complete the following sentences with the **tú** command form of the verb in parentheses. Both regular and irregular commands are included.*

EXAMPLE   ¿Por qué no vienes acá? __*Ven*__ acá.

1. Tú nunca dices la verdad. _____ la verdad. (decir)

2. Tú debes portarte bien. _____ un buen niño. (ser)

3. _____ tu pregunta, por favor. (leer)

4. _____ el correo electrónico. (escribir)

5. Hay mucho peligro en la selva. _____ cuidado. (tener)

6. _____ la ropa en el cajón, por favor. (poner)

7. _____ acá. (venir)

8. Tú te vas a engordar si no haces ejercicios. _____ ejercicios por lo menos tres veces a la semana. (hacer)

9. Necesitamos arroz para preparar la comida. _____ el arroz, por favor. (traer)

10. _____ a tu hermanita. (esperar)

Placement of Object Pronouns with Affirmative *tú* Commands

All object pronouns are attached to the affirmative form of the imperative. When two object pronouns occur together, the indirect object pronoun precedes the direct object pronoun.

Escribe la carta.	*Write the letter.*
Escríbeme la carta.	*Write the letter to me.*
Escríbemela.	*Write it to me.*
Enseña la lección.	*Teach the lesson.*
Enséñanos la lección.	*Teach us the lesson.*
Enséñanosla.	*Teach it to us.*

Presta el dinero.	*Lend the money.*
Préstale el dinero a María.	*Lend the money to María.*
Préstaselo.	*Lend it to her.*
Tráeles las galletas a tus colegas.	*Bring the cookies to your colleagues.*
Tráeselas.	*Bring them to them.*
Dame la sartén.	*Give me the frying pan.*
Dámela.	*Give it to me.*
Dinos la idea.	*Tell us the idea.*
Dínosla.	*Tell it to us.*
Perdóname.	*Pardon me. / Excuse me.*

NOTE The written accent maintains the stress on the correct syllable in the imperative: **es<u>cri</u>be**, **es<u>crí</u>beme**, **es<u>crí</u>bemela**, for example.

In Spanish, the reflexive command form is very important. The reflexive object pronoun is attached the affirmative command form, and the written accent is again used to maintain stress on the correct syllable. Practice these examples aloud.

Infinitive	**tú** Command	English
acordarse	Acuérdate.	*Remember.*
acostarse	Acuéstate.	*Go to bed.*
despertarse	Despiértate.	*Wake up.*
dormirse	Duérmete.	*Go to sleep.*
levantarse	Levántate.	*Get up.*
sentarse	Siéntate.	*Sit down.*

When a reflexive object pronoun and a direct object pronoun occur together, the reflexive object pronoun precedes the direct object pronoun.

Lávate las manos.	*Wash your hands.*
Lávatelas.	*Wash them.*
Quítate los zapatos.	*Take off your shoes.*
Quítatelos.	*Take them off.*
Ponte el abrigo.	*Put on your coat.*
Póntelo.	*Put it on.*

Exercise 6.4

Write the affirmative **tú** *command form for the following verbs. All responses require a written accent to maintain stress on the correct syllable, except* **irse**. *Pronounce each response aloud.*

1. fijarse   *to notice*   _____
2. animarse   *to cheer up*   _____
3. callarse   *to be quiet*   _____
4. arreglarse   *to get ready*   _____
5. moverse   *to move*   _____
6. irse   *to go away*   _____
7. quedarse   *to stay*   _____
8. pararse   *to stand up*   _____
9. cepillarse   *to brush one's teeth*   _____
10. vestirse   *to get dressed*   _____
11. divertirse   *to have a good time*   _____
12. dormirse   *to fall asleep*   _____

Negative *tú* Commands

The negative **tú** command form is the same as the present subjunctive form.

To form the negative **tú** command, begin with the **yo** form of the present indicative tense. Drop the final **-o** to get the stem of the present subjunctive.

*   For **-ar** verbs, add **-es** to the stem.

*   For **-er** and **-ir** verbs, add **-as** to the stem.

-Ar Verbs

No grites.   *Don't yell.*
No fumes en mi casa, por favor.   *Don't smoke in my house, please.*
No juegues con fósforos.   *Don't play with matches.*
No toques el enchufe.   *Don't touch the light socket.*

-Er and -ir Verbs

No mientas.	*Don't lie.*
No corras con tijeras.	*Don't run with scissors.*
No comas comida rápida.	*Don't eat fast food.*
No subas la montaña solo.	*Don't climb the mountain alone.*
No bebas esa agua.	*Don't drink that water.*

Pronounce the commands listed above aloud. Take time to write down both the affirmative and negative commands you need in everyday life, pronounce them, and try to learn them by memory. The negative commands are very important.

Placement of Object Pronouns with Negative *tú* Commands

All object pronouns precede the verb in a negative command. The indirect object pronoun precedes the direct object pronoun if they appear together.

No abras la ventana.	*Don't open the window.*
No la abras.	*Don't open it.*
No cierres la puerta.	*Don't close the door.*
No la cierres.	*Don't close it.*
No lo hagas.	*Don't do it.*
No me lo digas.	*Don't say it to me.*
No me traigas las tortas.	*Don't bring me the cakes.*
No me las traigas.	*Don't bring them to me.*
No nos cuentes el mismo cuento.	*Don't tell us the same story.*
No nos lo cuentes.	*Don't tell it to us.*
No le escribas una carta a Federico.	*Don't write a letter to Fred.*
No se la escribas.	*Don't write it to him.*
No les prestes dinero.	*Don't lend them money.*
No se lo prestes.	*Don't lend it to them.*
No le des nada a Dorotea.	*Don't give anything to Dorothy.*

The reflexive object pronoun also precedes the verb in a negative **tú** command.

No te enfades.	*Don't get angry.*
No te vayas.	*Don't go.*
No te quejes.	*Don't complain.*
No te asustes.	*Don't be afraid.*

If a reflexive verb and a direct object appear in the same phrase, the reflexive object pronoun precedes the direct object pronoun.

No te pongas el abrigo en el verano.	*Don't put on your coat in the summer.*
No te lo pongas.	*Don't put it on.*
No te quites el sombrero en el invierno.	*Don't take off your hat in the winter.*
No te lo quites.	*Don't take it off.*

Review of *tú* Commands

Regular *tú* Commands

	Affirmative	Negative
cantar	canta	no cantes
beber	bebe	no bebas
abrir	abre	no abras

Irregular *tú* Commands

	Affirmative	Negative
decir	di	no digas
hacer	haz	no hagas
ir	ve	no vayas
poner	pon	no pongas
salir	sal	no salgas
ser	sé	no seas
tener	ten	no tengas
venir	ven	no vengas

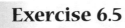

Exercise 6.5

Translate the following commands into English.

1. Hazme un favor. _____

2. Dinos la verdad. _____

3. Vete. _____

4. Ponte las medias. _____

5. Sal ahora. _____

6. Sé un buen perro. _____

7. Ten cuidado. _____

8. Ven acá. _____

Exercise 6.6

*Write the correct affirmative and negative **tú** commands for the following verbs, according to the example given. Pronounce each command aloud.*

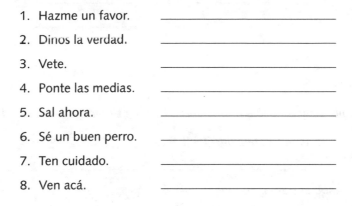

	AFFIRMATIVE	NEGATIVE
EXAMPLE cruzar	*cruza (tú)*	*no cruces*
1. correr	_____	_____
2. caminar	_____	_____
3. beber	_____	_____
4. seguir	_____	_____
5. repetir	_____	_____
6. hablar	_____	_____
7. mirar	_____	_____
8. romper	_____	_____
9. vender	_____	_____
10. abrir	_____	_____
11. subir	_____	_____
12. empezar	_____	_____

13. mentir _____ _____

14. salir _____ _____

15. poner _____ _____

16. tocar _____ _____

Exercise 6.7

*Translate the following sentences into Spanish. Use the **tú** form for commands.*

1. *Don't eat the salad in Guatemala. Don't eat it.*

   _____

2. *Don't run; another train is coming.*

   _____

3. *Don't tell me the secret. Don't tell it to me.*

   _____

4. *Don't do it.*   _____

5. *Don't touch it.*   _____

6. *Don't be afraid.*   _____

7. *Don't lend money to her. Don't lend it to her.*

   _____

8. *Don't come late to the parade.*

   _____

9. *Don't give us bad news.*

   _____

10. *Don't bring candies to the child. Don't bring them to him.*

   _____

11. *Don't go away.*   _____

12. *Don't worry.*   _____

13. *Don't wait for me.*   _____

14. *Don't be jealous.*   _____

Ud. and Uds. Commands

The command forms for **Ud.** and **Uds.** are identical to the present subjunctive.

- To form the **Ud./Uds.** commands for **-ar** verbs, begin with the **yo** form of the present indicative. Drop the **-o** and add **-e** (**Ud.**) or **-en** (**Uds.**) to the stem.

- To form the **Ud./Uds.** commands for **-er** and **-ir** verbs, begin with the **yo** form of the present indicative. Drop the **-o** and add **-a** (**Ud.**) or **-an** (**Uds.**) to the stem.

- There are only five irregular **Ud./Uds.** command forms. All regular **Ud./Uds.** commands are formed from the **yo** form of the present indicative.

Affirmative Ud. Commands

-Ar Verbs

Tome una aspirina si tiene dolor de cabeza.	*Take an aspirin if you have a headache.*
Firme aquí.	*Sign here.*
Entre Ud., por favor.	*Enter, please.*
Cante. Baile. Escuche música.	*Sing. Dance. Listen to music.*
Espere Ud.	*Wait.*

NOTE The command can be softened by adding **Ud.** or **Uds.**

-Er and -ir Verbs

Abra la ventana, por favor.	*Open the window, please.*
Coma. Beba.	*Eat. Drink.*
Venga a mi casa a las siete.	*Come to my house at seven o'clock.*
Tenga cuidado.	*Be careful.*
Haga sus ejercicios.	*Do your exercises.*

Negative Ud. Commands

The verb form for negative **Ud.** commands is the same as the present subjunctive. Affirmative and negative **Ud.** command forms are identical.

No tome una aspirina.	*Don't take an aspirin.*
No entre Ud.	*Don't enter.*
No grite Ud.	*Don't yell.*
No abra la ventana.	*Don't open the window.*
No coma, no beba.	*Don't eat, don't drink.*
No venga a mi casa a las siete; sino a las ocho.	*Don't come to my house at seven, but rather at eight.*

Affirmative *Uds.* Commands

Add an **-n** to the **Ud.** form of the imperative to form the **Uds.** command.

-Ar Verbs

Compren la casa.	*Buy the house.*
Apaguen la luz.	*Turn off the light.*
Caminen Uds.	*Walk.*

-Er and *-ir* Verbs

Repitan la frase, por favor.	*Repeat the sentence, please.*
Lean el periódico.	*Read the newspaper.*

Negative *Uds.* Commands

No hablen.	*Don't talk.*
No fumen en la casa.	*Don't smoke in the house.*
No griten.	*Don't yell.*
No salgan.	*Don't leave.*
No prendan la luz.	*Don't turn on the light.*
No pongan su ropa en el piso.	*Don't put your clothes on the floor.*

Pronounce the commands listed above aloud. Now list the commands that you need in everyday life. Make your own list of commands and practice them.

Placement of Object Pronouns with Affirmative *Ud./Uds.* Commands

The reflexive, indirect, and direct object pronouns are attached to the affirmative command. When an object is added to the command form, a written accent is placed over the stressed syllable to maintain the sound of the verb.

Affirmative *Ud.* Commands

Diga. Dígame. Dígamelo.   *Tell. Tell me. Tell it to me.*
Escúcheme.   *Listen to me.*
Bésela.   *Kiss her.*
Siéntese Ud.   *Sit down, please.*
Sirva el postre, por favor.   *Serve the dessert, please.*
Sírvalo.   *Serve it.*
Créame.   *Believe me.*

Affirmative *Uds.* Commands

Ayúdenla.   *Help her.*
Denles su dinero.   *Give them their money.*
Espérenme, por favor.   *Wait for me, please.*
Siéntense Uds.   *Sit down, please.*
Quédense.   *Stay.*
Enséñennos la idea. Enséñennosla.   *Teach us the idea. Teach it to us.*

NOTE The **-nn-** combination is very rare in Spanish.

Placement of Object Pronouns with Negative *Ud./Uds.* Commands

The reflexive, indirect, and direct object pronouns precede the verb in a negative **Ud./Uds.** command. The verb forms for affirmative and negative commands are the same.

Negative *Ud.* Commands

No me traiga agua.   *Don't bring me water.*
No le diga nada a nadie.   *Don't say anything to anybody.*
No nos espere.   *Don't wait for us.*
No se caiga.   *Don't fall down.*
No se desespere.   *Don't despair.*
No se preocupe.   *Don't worry.*

Negative *Uds.* Commands

No lo toquen.   *Don't touch it.*
No se preocupen.   *Don't worry.*
No se vayan.   *Don't go.*
No se rían.   *Don't laugh.*

Review of *Ud./Uds.* Commands

Regular *Ud./Uds.* Commands

	Affirmative		Negative	
	Ud.	Uds.	Ud.	Uds.
caminar	camine	caminen	no camine	no caminen
comer	coma	coman	no coma	no coman
escribir	escriba	escriban	no escriba	no escriban

Irregular *Ud./Uds.* Commands

There are only five **Ud./Uds.** command forms that are not formed from the **yo** form of the present indicative.

	Affirmative		Negative	
	Ud.	Uds.	Ud.	Uds.
dar	dé	den	no dé	no den
estar	esté	estén	no esté	no estén
saber	sepa	sepan	no sepa	no sepan
ser	sea	sean	no sea	no sean
ir	vaya	vayan	no vaya	no vayan

NOTE Remember that commands such as **diga**, **haga**, and **tenga** are not irregular. They are formed from the **yo** form of the present indicative tense.

Other Ways of Asking People to Do Things

- **Favor de** + *infinitive* (easy to use and very polite)

Favor de abrir la ventana.	*Please open the window.*
Favor de sentarse al frente.	*Please sit in front.*
Favor de esperarnos.	*Please wait for us.*

- **Tener la bondad de** + *infinitive*

¿Tiene Ud. la bondad de acompañarme al hotel?	*Will you be kind enough to accompany me to the hotel?*
¿Tienes la bondad de regalarme el anillo?	*Will you be kind enough to give me the ring?*
¿Tienen Uds. la bondad de prestarnos su carro?	*Will you be kind enough to lend us your car?*

- **Puede Ud.** + *infinitive*

¿Puede Ud. cerrar la ventana?	*Can you close the window?*
¿Puedes ayudarme, por favor?	*Can you help me, please?*

- **Hacer el favor de** + *infinitive* with *indirect object* (similar to **favor de**)

¿Me hace Ud. el favor de traernos el libro?	*Will you do me the favor of bringing us the book?*
¿Nos haces el favor de escribirle?	*Will do you us the favor of writing to her?*
¿Me hace Ud. el favor de bailar conmigo?	*Will you do me the favor of dancing with me?*

- Present indicative with *indirect object pronoun* or *direct object pronoun*

¿Me ayudas, por favor?	*Will you help me, please?*
¿Nos acompaña Ud. al tren?	*Will you accompany us to the train?*
¿Me prestas tu carro?	*Will you lend me your car?*
¿Nos da dinero?	*Will you give us money?*
¿Nos llevan Uds. al hotel?	*Will you take us to the hotel?*

A Word About the Word "Will"

In all of the constructions mentioned above, the English translation using the word "will" does not indicate a future tense, but rather a voluntary mood.

Exercise 6.8

Translate the following sentences into English, then pronounce these commands aloud.

1. No naden en este lago.

   _____

2. No caminen en el lodo.

   _____

3. No se acueste tarde.

＿＿＿＿＿＿＿＿＿＿＿＿＿＿＿＿＿＿＿＿＿＿＿＿

4. No nos lo dé.

＿＿＿＿＿＿＿＿＿＿＿＿＿＿＿＿＿＿＿＿＿＿＿＿

5. No dejen los platos sucios en la mesa.

＿＿＿＿＿＿＿＿＿＿＿＿＿＿＿＿＿＿＿＿＿＿＿＿

6. No trabajen tanto.

＿＿＿＿＿＿＿＿＿＿＿＿＿＿＿＿＿＿＿＿＿＿＿＿

7. No venga a clase el lunes.

＿＿＿＿＿＿＿＿＿＿＿＿＿＿＿＿＿＿＿＿＿＿＿＿

8. No lleguen tarde.

＿＿＿＿＿＿＿＿＿＿＿＿＿＿＿＿＿＿＿＿＿＿＿＿

 ## Exercise 6.9

*Write both the affirmative and negative **Ud.** commands for the following verbs. Practice pronouncing all commands aloud.*

		AFFIRMATIVE	NEGATIVE
EXAMPLE	cantar	*Cante.*	*No cante.*
1.	decir		
2.	hacer		
3.	trabajar		
4.	entrar		
5.	leer		
6.	esperar		
7.	beber		

Exercise 6.10

*Write both the affirmative and negative **Uds.** commands for the following reflexive verbs. Practice pronouncing all commands aloud.*

		AFFIRMATIVE	NEGATIVE
EXAMPLE	irse	*Váyanse.*	*No se vayan.*
1.	quedarse	_____	_____
2.	sentarse	_____	_____
3.	levantarse	_____	_____
4.	acostarse	_____	_____
5.	dormirse	_____	_____

Reading Comprehension

Perdida en Nicaragua

"Vaya recto hasta llegar a la iglesia. Cuando llegue a la iglesia, doble a la derecha.

"Siga recto hasta llegar al ayuntamiento; camine diez minutos más, suba una colina, cruce la calle y ya está en la universidad. Si sale ahora, va a llegar mucho antes de su primera clase a las diez."

El año era 1987. Eran las siete de una mañana caliente y húmeda como siempre era en agosto en Managua. Empecé mi caminata con mucha confianza y alegría, siendo muy independiente. Caminé con las direcciones escritas en un papelito. Después de quince minutos comencé a prestar mucha atención, buscando la iglesia blanca y grande como era la descripción de ella. La temperatura siguió subiendo. No vi a nadie para pedir direcciones. No hallé ninguna iglesia, ni grande, ni pequeña, ni blanca ni de otros colores.

Desesperada, di la vuelta y seguí la misma pista que me trajo hasta este punto y volví a la pensión. Sudada, miré al grupo, todos alegres, comiendo el desayuno y charlando.

"Nunca vi la iglesia," les relaté a los dueños. Mis colegas me miraron sin poder aguantar la risa.

"Ah," me contestaron. "Ud. no es nicaragüense y no conoce bien ni la ciudad ni esta área. Le dirigimos adonde la iglesia estaba antes de la guerra."

Verbos

aguantar la risa	*to hold back laughter*
cruzar	*to cross*
dar una vuelta	*to take a walk*
doblar	*to turn*
hallar	*to find*
relatar	*to relate*

Nombres

el ayuntamiento	*town hall*
la colina	*the hill*
la pista	*the trail*

Adjetivo

sudado	*sweaty*

Direcciones

a la derecha	*to the right*
recto	*straight ahead*

Preguntas

1. ¿A qué hora es la clase de la protagonista?

   _____

2. ¿Cómo se siente ella al empezar el camino?

   _____

3. ¿Estaba ella sola o acompañada?

   _____

4. ¿Cómo volvió a la pensión?

   _____

5. ¿Por qué se rieron sus colegas?

   _____

The *nosotros* Command: "Let us . . ."

"*Let's* do something," or "*Let's not* do something" expresses the **nosotros** command forms. The **nosotros** command forms are the same as the present subjunctive.

Begin with the present indicative **yo** form of the verb, and drop the **-o**. That gives you the stem for the command form.

- For **-ar verbs**, add **-emos** to the stem.

- For **-er** and **-ir** verbs, add **-amos** to the stem.

- The affirmative and negative **nosotros** commands have the same form.

-Ar Verbs

Cantemos. Bailemos.	*Let's sing. Let's dance.*
Esperemos un momento.	*Let's wait a moment.*
Tomemos un café.	*Let's have coffee.*
Empecemos la lección.	*Let's begin the lesson.*

-Er and *-ir* Verbs

Salgamos ahora.	*Let's leave now.*
Abramos el libro.	*Let's open the book.*
Leamos este capítulo en clase.	*Let's read this chapter in class.*

The indirect object pronouns and direct object pronouns are attached to the affirmative command.

Digamos la verdad.	*Let's tell the truth.*
Digámosla.	*Let's tell it.*
Hagamos la tarea.	*Let's do the homework.*
Hagámosla.	*Let's do it.*
Traigámosle las flores al maestro.	*Let's bring flowers to the teacher.*
Besemos a los niños.	*Let's kiss the children.*
Besémoslos.	*Let's kiss them.*
Crucemos la calle.	*Let's cross the street.*
Crucémosla.	*Let's cross it.*

The negative **nosotros** command form is the same as the affirmative **nosotros** command form. The object pronouns (reflexive, indirect, and direct) precede the command.

No fumemos.	*Let's not smoke.*
No le digamos nada al doctor.	*Let's not say anything to the doctor.*
No les compremos nada.	*Let's not buy them anything.*
No nos acostemos tarde.	*Let's not go to bed late.*

Vamos is used instead of **vayamos** for *let's go.* In the negative, **vayamos** is used.

Vamos al cine. No vayamos al museo.	*Let's go to the movies. Let's not go to the museum.*

In the affirmative **nosotros** command form of a reflexive verb, the final **-s** is dropped before the **-nos** is added.

irse	vamos + nos	Vámonos. *Let's go.*
sentarse	sentemos + nos	Sentémonos. *Let's sit down.*
acostarse	acostemos + nos	Acostémonos. *Let's go to bed.*
ducharse	duchemos + nos	Duchémonos. *Let's take a shower.*
levantarse	levantemos + nos	Levantémonos. *Let's get up.*

The final **-s** of the command form is dropped if the indirect object pronoun **se** is added. The **-s** is dropped before the **se** is added. This is done to eliminate the **-ss-** combination.

Ella quiere un perro. Comprémoselo. (compremos + se + lo)	*She wants a dog. Let's buy it for her.*
Gloria necesita nuestra ayuda. Démosela. (demos + se + la)	*Gloria needs our help. Let's give it to her.*

In the stem-changing **-ir** verbs, there is an irregularity in the **nosotros** command form. Verbs with the **e > ie** or **e > i** change in the stem have an **-i-** in the stem of the **nosotros** command. Verbs with the **o > u** change in the stem have a **-u-** in the stem of the **nosotros** command. This is the same stem change seen in the present subjunctive.

e > ie

Adv**i**rtamos a los otros. *Let's warn the others.*

e > i

Rep**i**tamos la pregunta. *Let's repeat the question.*
S**i**rvamos la cena. *Let's serve supper.*
S**i**gamos las señales. *Let's follow the signs.*

o > u

D**u**rmámonos ahora. Ya es tarde. *Let's go to sleep now. It's already late.*

Exercise 6.11

Write the affirmative **nosotros** *command for the following verbs.*

1. decir _____
2. empezar _____
3. seguir _____
4. irse _____
5. despertarse _____
6. jugar _____
7. esperar _____
8. entrar _____
9. tomar _____
10. cruzar _____
11. dormirse _____
12. almorzar _____
13. comer _____
14. descansar _____
15. volver _____

Affirmative *vosotros* Commands

The **vosotros** form is used only in Spain. The affirmative, familiar plural **vosotros** command is formed by dropping the final **-r** of the infinitive and adding **-d**. There are no exceptions.

Mirad. Escuchad. Caminad.	*Look. Listen. Walk.*
Bebed. Comed. Tened cuidado.	*Drink. Eat. Be careful.*
Id. Salid. Venid. Decid.	*Go. Leave. Come. Tell.*

In the affirmative **vosotros** command, both the direct and indirect object pronouns are attached to the verb form.

Leed el libro. Leedlo.	*Read the book. Read it.*
Cerrad la puerta. Cerradla.	*Close the door. Close it.*
Abrid la ventana. Abridla.	*Open the window. Open it.*

In the affirmative **vosotros** command of a reflexive verb, the final **-d** is dropped before the **-os** is added:

despertad + os − -d- = desperta(d)os = despertaos

Desayunaos. Bañaos.	*Have breakfast. Bathe.*
Poneos la chaqueta. Ponéosla.	*Put on your jacket. Put it on.*
Divertíos en vuestras vacaciones.	*Have a good time on your vacation.*

Negative *vosotros* Commands

The negative **vosotros** command is the same as the subjunctive. The reflexive, indirect, and direct object pronouns precede the verb.

No cantéis esa canción.	*Don't sing that song.*
No bailéis aquí.	*Don't dance here.*
No comáis este pescado. No lo comáis.	*Don't eat this fish. Don't eat it.*
No bebáis el agua. No la bebáis.	*Don't drink the water. Don't drink it.*
No le traigáis el paquete a Susana. No se lo tragáis.	*Don't bring the package to Susan. Don't bring it to her.*

No cerréis aquella puerta.	*Don't close that door.*
No la cerréis.	*Don't close it.*
No os sentéis en esta silla rota.	*Don't sit down in this broken chair.*
No os vayáis.	*Don't go.*
No os caigáis.	*Don't fall.*
No os preocupéis.	*Don't worry.*

For the negative **vosotros** command, as for the affirmative **nosotros** command, stem-changing **-ir** verbs show an irregularity in the command form. Verbs with the **e > ie** or **e > i** change in the stem have an **-i-** in the stem of the **vosotros** command. Verbs with the **o > u** change in the stem have a **-u-** in the stem of the **vosotros** command. This is the same as is found in the present subjunctive.

No mintáis.	*Don't lie.*
No os muráis.	*Don't die.*
No me corrijáis.	*Don't correct me.*
No repitáis vuestra idea.	*Don't repeat your idea.*
No sigáis a un mal líder.	*Don't follow a bad leader.*

A Word About the *vosotros* Command

The **vosotros** command is used only in Spain. It is good to know this form, however, especially when you begin to read literature by Spanish writers, or if you are planning a trip to Spain.

Exercise 6.12

Write the Spanish translation for the following commands as quickly as you can, according to the cue in parentheses. You often you have very little time to ask someone to do or not to do something. (Try to say each of the following Spanish commands in five seconds or less.)

1. *Don't touch it.* (tú)   _____

2. *Don't say it to me.* (tú)   _____

3. *Don't do it.* (tú)   _____

4. *Help me.* (Ud.)   _____

5. *Give her the book.* (Ud.)   _____

6. *Give it to her.* (Ud.)   _____

7. *Don't give it to her.* (Ud.)   _____

8. *Kiss me.* (tú)   _____

9. *Sit down, please.* (Uds.)   _____

10. *Let's begin.* (nosotros)   _____

11. *Wait for us.* (Uds.)   _____

12. *Go to the right.* (Uds.)   _____

13. *Be careful.* (tú)   _____

14. *Fill out this form, please.* (Ud.)   _____

15. *Don't drink so much.* (tú)   _____

16. *Take out the garbage.* (tú)   _____

17. *Don't go away.* (Ud.)   _____

18. *Don't worry.* (Uds.)   _____

19. *Let's follow the directions.* (nosotros)   _____

20. *Drive slower, please.* (Ud.)   _____

21. *Please stay.* (Uds.)   _____

22. *Call me.* (tú)   _____

23. *Don't buy anything.* (Ud.)   _____

24. *Don't laugh.* (Uds.)   _____

25. *Let's go.* (nosotros)   _____

Exercise 6.13

Subjunctive, present indicative, or infinitive? *Complete the following sentences with the correct form of the verb in parentheses.*

1. Quiero que Ud. _____. (quedarse)

2. ¿Qué quieres que yo te _____? (decir)

3. Es importante _____ bien. (comer)

4. Esperamos que Jorge y su hermana _____. (mejorase)

5. Paulina sabe que yo la _____. (buscar)

6. Es cierto que a los niños les _____ jugar. (gustar)

7. No me gusta que ella _____ a verme. (venir)

8. Los turistas buscan un hotel que _____ cómodo. (ser)

9. No sabemos quien _____ ser presidente. (querer)

10. Ojalá que toda la familia nos _____. (visitar)

11. Helena nos dice que el tren _____. (llegar)

12. El profesor les dice a los estudiantes que _____ la tarea. (hacer)

13. Vamos a estar alegres cuando _____ un buen apartamento. (comprar)

14. Me alegro _____ aquí. Me alegro de que tú

    _____ aquí también. (estar/estar)

15. Antes de _____ al concierto, las mujeres se visten bien. (ir)

16. ¿Es verdad que a la gente le _____ usar la computadora? (gustar)

17. Espero que a Uds. les _____ esta lección. (gustar)

18. Mi amigo me va a esperar hasta que yo lo _____. (llamar)

19. Buscamos una piscina que _____ limpia. (estar)

20. ¿Conoce Ud. a alguien que _____ tocar el violín? (saber)

21. ¿Sabe ella de donde _____ tú? (ser)

22. Yo le aconsejo a Alicia que ella _____ al dentista. (ir)

23. Es imposible que la mayoría siempre _____ razón. (tener)

24. Dudo que _____ mucho tráfico hoy. (haber)

As you read the following story, underline the command forms.

Reading Comprehension

La Noche de Brujas

"Ven acá m'hija," dijo su padre. "Ven acá para que yo pueda verte de cerca. Qué bonita estás en tu disfraz."

"Vuelve a las nueve como nos prometiste," le pidió su madre. "Y no hables con nadie, sino con tu grupito de chicas."

"Sí, no se preocupen." Y después, le murmura a su papá para que su mamá no la oiga: "Tú sabes, papá, que mamá va a seguirme, escondiéndose, detrás de los árboles."

"Eres muy lista. Yo no sabía que tú sabías. Ten cuidado, niñita, y no cruces la calle sin mirar en ambas direcciones."

"Sí, sí, papá." Les cantó a sus padres el canto de la Noche de Brujas: "Triqui triqui Halloween, quiero dulces para mí," y se fue.

El papá las mira salir; primero su hija, y después su esposa. Sus dos mujeres; una mayor, la otra menor. Él se sienta en su sillón favorito, en la casa cómoda, entre sus libros. Pasan las nueve; pasan las diez y nadie llegó. Empezó a oír todos los sonidos de la casa, el reloj, la radio, el viento contra la ventana, menos el sonido que él quería oír—las voces de su esposa e hija, llenas de cuentos de sus aventuras.

Verbos

esconderse	*to hide*
murmurar	*to mumble, to whisper*
ser listo	*to be clever* (**Estar listo** means *to be ready.*)

Nombre

el disfraz	*the disguise*

Expresiones

m'hija	*my daughter* (combination of **mi** and **hija**; a term of affection)
grupito	*small group* (When you add **-ito** or **-ita** to a word, it makes the object smaller or less.)
niñita	*dear girl* (When you add **-ito** or **-ita** to a word, it can be a term of affection.)
triqui triqui	*trick or treat* (from the sound of English *trick or treat*)

Preguntas

1. ¿Adónde van la madre e hija?

   _____

2. ¿Por qué no va con ellas el papá?

   _____

3. ¿Piensa Ud. que ellas van a regresar?

   _____

4. ¿Es una familia feliz o infeliz?

   _____

II

Nouns, Articles, Adjectives, Pronouns; Present and Past Perfect Tenses

7

Nouns, Articles, Adjectives, and Pronouns

Nouns and Articles

A noun is a person, place, or thing. In Spanish, all nouns are either masculine or feminine. The definite article (**el**, **la**, **los**, **las**), agrees with its noun in gender and number, as does the indefinite article (**uno**, **una**, **unos**, **unas**).

Most of the time, inclusion of the article in Spanish is the same as it is in English.

El carro rojo cuesta treinta mil dólares.	*The red car costs 30,000 dollars.*
La comida estaba deliciosa.	*The meal was delicious.*
Los guantes de cuero son costosos.	*The leather gloves are expensive.*
Las revistas están en la mesa.	*The magazines are on the table.*
Una muchacha fue al concierto.	*A girl went to the concert.*
Un adulto la acompañó.	*An adult accompanied her.*
Unos músicos tocaron bien.	*Some musicians played well.*
Unas personas salieron contentas.	*Some people left happy.*

Similarly, omission of the article in Spanish often corresponds to English usage.

Escuchamos música.	*We listen to music.*
Escuchamos la música clásica.	*We listen to the classical music.*
El hombre enfermo toma medicina.	*The sick man takes medicine.*
Él toma la medicina que el doctor le dio.	*He takes the medicine that the doctor gave to him.*

A Word About the Definite Article
Even without many rules, you will be able to use the articles effectively.

Inclusion and Omission of Articles

Spanish does not translate *a/an* when stating an unmodified profession. If the profession is modified, the indefinite article (**un/una**) becomes necessary.

UNMODIFIED	Juan es pintor.	*Juan is a painter.*
MODIFIED	Juan es un pintor maravilloso.	*Juan is a wonderful painter.*
UNMODIFIED	Paula es doctora.	*Paula is a doctor.*
MODIFIED	Paula es una buena doctora.	*Paula is a good doctor.*
UNMODIFIED	José es maestro.	*Joseph is a teacher.*
MODIFIED	José es un mal maestro.	*Joseph is a bad teacher.*
UNMODIFIED	Eres estudiante.	*You are a student.*
MODIFIED	Eres una estudiante fantástica.	*You are a fantastic student.*

The definite article is used with days of the week. The English word *on* is not translated.

Ella salió el martes.	*She left on Tuesday.*
Ramón va a volver el sábado.	*Ramón is going to return on Saturday.*
Tenemos clase los jueves.	*We have class on Thursdays.*

The only time the article is omitted when expressing the day of the week is following a form of **ser**.

Hoy es miércoles.	*Today is Wednesday.*
¿Qué día es? Hoy es viernes.	*What day is it? Today is Friday.*

The definite article is used with seasons of the year, even though the English equivalent may not include it.

La primavera es bonita.	*Spring is beautiful.*
El verano es ideal.	*Summer is ideal.*
Me encanta viajar en el otoño.	*To travel in the autumn enchants me.*
No nos gusta esquiar en el invierno.	*To ski in the winter is not pleasing to us.*

The definite article is used after forms of **gustar** and verbs that are used like **gustar** (for example, **doler**, **encantar**, **fascinar**, **importar**), whether the English translation includes it or not.

Me gustan los vegetales.	*Vegetables are pleasing to me.*
A Paula le encanta el cine.	*Movies are very pleasing to Paula.*
A Fernando y a sus amigos les importa la verdad.	*The truth is important to Fernando and his friends.*

The Spanish definite article never follows a form of **haber**. Nouns, adjectives, and indefinite articles can follow **haber**, but not the definite article (**el**, **la**, **los**, **las**).

Hay una persona aquí.	*There is one person here.*
Había algunos libros en la mesa, pero ahora no los veo.	*There were some books on the table, but now I don't see them.*
No hay ningún buen hotel por aquí.	*There is not one good hotel around here.*
Hay poca gente en la ciudad.	*There are few people in the city.*
Hubo mucho tráfico ayer.	*There was a lot of traffic yesterday.*
Había dos fiestas el día de las madres.	*There were two parties on Mother's Day.*

When the verb **hablar** is followed by the name of a language, the definite article is omitted.

Ella habla español, pero no habla inglés.	*She speaks Spanish, but she doesn't speak English.*
Los portugueses hablan francés y portugués.	*The Portuguese speak French and Portuguese.*

The definite article is used in front of each noun if there is more than one noun stated, as in a series.

El museo tiene el arte, la escultura y los dibujos.	*The museum has art, sculpture, and drawings.*
El estudiante tiene el lápiz, la pluma y la computadora en su cuarto.	*The student has the pencil, the pen, and the computer in his room.*

The definite article is used with the name of subject matter.

Enrique estudia la ley.	*Henry studies law.*
María escribe la historia de su país.	*María writes the history of her country.*
Platón enseñó la filosofía.	*Plato taught philosophy.*
Oscar y Fernanda escriben sobre el periodismo.	*Oscar and Fernanda write about journalism.*

The definite article is used before a noun in a general statement.

Los cigarrillos son malos.	*Cigarettes are bad.*
El agua es buena.	*Water is good.*

The definite article is used before abstract nouns.

La sinceridad es importante.	*Sincerity is important.*
La honestidad es rara.	*Honesty is rare.*

The definite article is used to refer to all members of a class.

Los delfines son inteligentes.	*Dolphins are intelligent.*
Las computadoras son necesarias.	*Computers are necessary.*
Los bebés duermen mucho.	*Babies sleep a lot.*

The definite article is used in front of a personal title in Spanish, even when it is not used in the English equivalent.

El señor Muñoz está aquí.	*Mr. Muñoz is here.*
La profesora Hernández llegó ayer.	*Professor Hernández arrived yesterday.*
La señorita López cantó anoche.	*Ms. López sang last night.*

The definite article is omitted before a personal title when the person is being addressed directly.

Hola, señorita López.	*Hello, Ms. López.*
¿Cómo está Ud., señor Rodríguez?	*How are you, Mr. Rodriguez?*

NOTE The definite article is not used in front of **don/doña** or **Santo/San/ Santa**. **Santo** is used only before words beginning with **Do-** or **To-** (**Santo Domingo** and **Santo Tomás**, for example). **Santo** becomes **San** when used before words beginning with any other letters.

Don Juan tiene una mala reputación.	*Don Juan has a bad reputation.*
Doña Barbara vive en Santo Domingo.	*Doña Barbara lives in Santo Domingo.*
Santa Clara y Santo Tomás la visitan allá.	*Saint Clara and Saint Thomas visit her there.*
San Pedro quiere ir a San Juan.	*Saint Peter wants to go to San Juan.*
Desean ver San Diego, California.	*They want to see San Diego, California.*

The definite article is used before nouns of measurement, where it carries the meaning *per.*

Pagamos cien dólares la libra.	*We pay 100 dollars per pound.*
Los bananos cuestan cincuenta centavos el kilo.	*The bananas cost 50 cents per kilo.*
Ella vendió el perfume a diez dólares la onza.	*She sold the perfume at $10 per ounce.*

When two nouns are joined by **de** to form a compound noun, the definite article is omitted before the second noun.

Ella tiene un dolor de cabeza.	*She has a headache.*
A ella le gusta la casa de vidrio.	*She likes the glass house.*
María leyó dos libros de historia.	*María read two history books.*
La novia recibió un anillo de diamantes.	*The girlfriend received a diamond ring.*

The article is omitted before ordinal numbers in the names of kings, queens, and other rulers.

Carlos V (quinto)	*Carlos the fifth*
Louis XIV (catorce)	*Louis the fourteenth*

Before an apposition, which is a noun or noun phrase that is used in the same way and describes the same thing as the noun before it, the definite article is omitted.

Cervantes, **escritor**, era de España.	*Cervantes, the writer, was from Spain.*
Hugo Chávez, **presidente** de Venezuela, fue elegido en 2000.	*Hugo Chávez, president of Venezuela, was elected in 2000.*

Baryshnikov, **bailarín**, empezó a bailar en Moscú.	*Baryshnikov, the dancer, began to dance in Moscow.*
Bogotá, **capital** de Colombia, tiene una población de siete millones de habitantes.	*Bogotá, capital of Colombia, has a population of seven million inhabitants.*

Exercise 7.1

Definite article or not? *Complete the following sentences with the correct definite article where it is necessary. Mark an **X** where no article is needed.*

1. Quiero que mi hermano me dé _____ libro de _____ medicina.

2. Yo soy _____ abogado pero no me gusta _____ ley.

3. Francamente, yo fumo pero sé que _____ cigarrillos son malos para

   _____ salud.

4. ¿Qué quiere hacer _____ verano que viene?

5. El gobernador tuvo un accidente y le dolieron mucho _____ costillas.

6. ¿Son buenas _____ computadoras?

7. Hugo Chávez, _____ presidente de Venezuela, le da gasolina

   a _____ gente pobre.

8. A _____ familia le encantan _____ vacaciones.

9. Sinceramente, el mesero no sabe si _____ comida está buena en este restaurante.

Possessive Adjectives

A possessive adjective agrees in gender and number with the noun it modifies.

Short-Form Possessive Adjectives

A short-form possessive adjective precedes the noun it modifies.

mi, **mis** *my*

Mi cumpleaños es bueno.	*My birthday is good.*
Mis regalos son malos.	*My gifts are bad.*

tu, **tus** *your* (**tú** form)

Tu jardín tiene muchas flores.	*Your garden has many flowers.*
Tus hijos siembran las semillas.	*Your children sow the seeds.*

su, **sus** *your* (**Ud./Uds.** forms), *his, her, their*

Su hermano tiene varias casas.	*Your brother has several houses.* (also possible: *His/Her/Their brother*)
Sus amigos lo visitan.	*His friends visit him.* (also possible: *Your/Her/Their friends*)

In Spanish, a single form (**su/sus**) expresses the third-person possessive for *your* (**Ud./Uds.** forms), *his, her,* and *their*. This means that **su/sus** can be ambiguous, so the construction noun + **de** + pronoun is often used to clarify the meaning.

El hermano de Ud. tiene varias casas.	*Your brother has several houses.*
Los amigos de él lo visitan.	*His friends visit him.*

nuestro, **nuestra**, **nuestros**, **nuestras** *our*

Nuestro abuelo es viejo.	*Our grandfather is old.*
Nuestra abuela es mayor.	*Our grandmother is older.*
Nuestros hermanos son jóvenes.	*Our siblings are young.*
Nuestras hijas son menores.	*Our daughters are younger.*

vuestro, **vuestra**, **vuestros**, **vuestras** *your* (**vosotros** form)

Like **vosotros**, this form is used only in Spain. It is explained here so that you will be aware of it, but when you need the word for *your* in Spanish, use **su/sus**.

Vuestro sobrino tiene suficiente dinero.	*Your nephew has enough money.*
Vuestra sobrina vive en Portugal.	*Your niece lives in Portugal.*
Vuestros tíos viven en España.	*Your uncles and aunts live in Spain.*
Vuestras parientes van a viajar a ambos países.	*Your (female) relatives are going to travel to both countries.*

Exercise 7.2

Complete the following sentences with the most appropriate possessive adjective from the list below.

mi, mis, tu, tus, su, sus, nuestro, nuestra, nuestros, nuestras

1. Soy estudiante: _____ libros están en la mesa.

2. Él es un buen profesor; _____ cursos son interesantes.

3. Ellos son abogados; _____ clientes pueden ser culpables o inocentes.

4. Nuestra amiga es maestra; _____ padres enseñan también.

5. Ella es mi suegra; _____ casa está en México.

6. El cuñado de Cecilia es carpintero: _____ nombre es Manuel.

7. Liliana está en Texas; _____ familia vive en Arizona.

8. Vivo con cuatro amigos, un gato y un conejo; _____ casa es grande.

9. Somos principiantes; _____ tarea es difícil.

10. La hija de Beatriz es doctora; _____ hijo es arquitecto.

Long-Form Possessive Adjectives

Spanish also has a set of long-form possessive adjectives that are used to stress one possessor over another:

*This is **my** car, not **your** car.*

They are used less frequently than the short-form possessive adjectives.

- Long-form possessive adjectives are placed after the noun, and they agree in gender and number with the noun they modify. All have four forms that indicate both gender and number.

- Long-form possessive adjectives are used to emphasize the possessor, and they are the equivalent of the English *of mine, of yours, of his, of hers, of theirs, of ours.*

- Long-form possessive adjectives are used in direct address and exclamations: **¡Dios mío!** for example.

mío, **mía**, **míos**, **mías** *my, of mine*

Tu carro es viejo. El carro **mío** es nuevo.	*Your car is old. **My** car is new.*
Tu casa es azul. La casa **mía** es blanca.	*Your house is blue. **My** house is white.*
Queridos amigo **míos**, ¿cómo están Uds.?	*Dear friends **of mine**, how are you?*

tuyo, **tuya**, **tuyos**, **tuyas** *your (**tú** form), of yours*

No me gusta mi apartamento. Prefiero el apartamento **tuyo**.	*I don't like my apartment. I prefer **your** apartment.*
Mis plumas no tienen tinta. ¿Me puedes prestar las plumas **tuyas**?	*My pens have no ink. Can you lend me **your** pens?*

suyo, **suya**, **suyos**, **suyas** *your (**Ud./Uds.** forms), of yours; his, of his; her, of hers; their, of theirs*

Tomás y Helena están aquí. Necesito el carro **suyo**.	*Thomas and Helen are here. I need his car. (also possible: her/their car)*
¿El carro de él o el carro de ella?	*His car or her car?*

Remember that in Spanish there is only one form for the third-person possessive adjective. This means that **suyo/suya/suyos/suyas** can be ambiguous. The construction noun + **de** + pronoun or noun is used to clarify the meaning.

Sara y José escriben cuentos. Los artículos de ella son aburridos, pero los artículos **suyos** son interesantes.	*Sara and Joe write short stories. Her articles are boring, but **his** articles are interesting.*
A Ana le agrada David. Ana es una amiga **suya**. A David le agrada Ana. David es un amigo **suyo**.	*Ana likes David. Ana is a friend **of his**. David likes Ana. David is a friend **of hers**.*
Las ideas **suyas** son estupendas.	*The ideas of **yours/his/her/theirs** are great.*
¿Las ideas de quiénes? Las ideas de Uds.	*The ideas of whom? Your ideas.*

nuestro, **nuestra**, **nuestros**, **nuestras** *our, of ours*

Ud. tiene una familia grande.	*You have a big family.*
La familia **nuestra** es pequeña.	***Our** family is small.*
Los parientes de Enrique viven en Ecuador.	*Henry's relatives live in Ecuador.*
Los parientes **nuestros** viven en Inglaterra.	***Our** relatives live in England.*

vuestro, **vuestra**, **vuestros**, **vuestras** *your (**vosotros** form), of yours*

Mis amigos son de los Estados Unidos.	*My friends are from the United States.*
Los amigos **vuestros** son de España.	***Your** friends are from Spain.*
Mis primas viven en California.	*My cousins live in California.*
Las primas **vuestras** viven en Madrid.	***Your** cousins live in Madrid.*

Long-form possessive adjectives can also occur with the indefinite article—**un**, **uno**, **una**, **unos**, **unas**.

Un estudiante **suyo** recibe buenas notas.	*A student **of yours** receives good marks.*
El maestro explica una idea **nuestra**.	*The teacher explains an idea **of ours**.*
Unos amigos **míos** van de vacaciones.	*Some friends **of mine** are going on vacation.*
Unas amigas **tuyas** prefieren trabajar.	*Some friends **of yours** prefer to work.*

Exercise 7.3

Complete the following sentences with the correct possessive adjective, according to the cue in parentheses.

1. Querido amigo _____, ¿vienes a visitarme? (*of mine*)

2. El libro _____ es más pesado que el libro _____. (*yours/mine*)

3. Tus zapatos son viejos; los zapatos _____ son costosos y nuevos. (*of hers*)

4. A los dos compañeros de cuarto siempre se les pierden las llaves. Afortunadamente, tienen otras llaves _____. (*of theirs*)

5. Unas primas _____ quieren ir a México; la otra no quiere viajar. (*of mine*)

6. La idea de Ofelia es mala; la idea _____ es mejor. (*our*)

7. Favor de venir acá, hijo _____. (*of mine*)

8. Los guantes de Rebeca son de cuero; los guantes _____ son de algodón. (*of theirs*)

Possessive Pronouns

A pronoun takes the place of a noun. A possessive pronoun tells who owns or possesses the noun it is replacing.

Your bicycle is yellow. **Mine** *is red.*

Mine is used instead of *my bicycle*, and it is a possessive pronoun because it replaces the noun, *bicycle*, and tells who owns the noun.

Formation and Uses of Possessive Pronouns

- A possessive pronoun agrees in number and gender with the thing possessed.

- A possessive pronoun is similar to the possessive adjective. In most sentences and questions, it is used with the definite article.

- The definite article is omitted before the possessive pronoun only when the possessive pronoun is followed by a form of **ser**.

el mío, la mía, los míos, las mías *mine*

Tu carro es nuevo; **el mío** es viejo y feo.	*Your car is new;* **mine** *is old and ugly.*
Tu casa es grande; **la mía** tiene cuatro cuartos.	*Your house is big;* **mine** *has four rooms.*
Yo sé que tus amigos están aquí, pero ¿dónde están **los míos**?	*I know that your friends are here, but where are* **mine**?

Notice how important gender is in the use of possessive pronouns in Spanish. It is clear that **el mío** replaces **tu carro**, because it is masculine. Similarly, **la mía** replaces **su casa** because it is feminine.

el tuyo, **la tuya**, **los tuyos**, **las tuyas** *yours* (**tú** form)

No tengo una pluma. ¿Puedo usar **la tuya**?	*I don't have a pen. May I use* ***yours***?
Dejé mis libros en la oficina. ¿Me puedes prestar **los tuyos**?	*I left my books in the office. Can you lend me* ***yours***?

el suyo, **la suya**, **los suyos**, **las suyas** *yours* (**Ud./Uds.** forms), *his, hers, theirs*

Compré mi libro ayer. ¿Compró Ud. **el suyo**?	*I bought my book yesterday. Did you buy* ***yours***?
La casa de Susana es grande. Mi casa es pequeña. No me gusta la mía. Prefiero **la suya**.	*Susan's house is big. My house is small. I don't like mine. I prefer* ***hers***.
Jaime no tiene mis zapatos. Tengo **los suyos**.	*Jim doesn't have my shoes. I have* ***his***.
David no sabe dónde están mis llaves. **Las suyas** están en el carro.	*David doesn't know where my keys are.* ***His*** *are in the car.*

Remember that the third-person possessive pronouns, both singular and plural, are often ambiguous. **Prefiero la suya** can be translated as *I prefer his, I prefer yours,* or *I prefer theirs,* in addition to *I prefer hers.* It can be clarified in the following manner: **Prefiero la casa de él / de ella / de Ud. / de ellos / de ellas / de Uds.**

el nuestro, **la nuestra**, **los nuestros**, **las nuestras** *ours*

La guitarra de Gloria es vieja. **La nuestra** es nueva y costosa.	*Gloria's guitar is old.* ***Ours*** *is new and expensive.*
Elena tiene su propio radio. No quiere **el nuestro**.	*Elena has her own radio. She doesn't want* ***ours***.
¿Dónde pusieron Uds. sus libros? Encontramos **los nuestros** en el estudio.	*Where did you put your books? We found* ***ours*** *in the study.*

el vuestro, **la vuestra**, **los vuestros**, **las vuestras** *yours* (**vosotros** form)

Mi tren llega de Barcelona el lunes. **El vuestro** llega de Madrid.	*My train arrives from Barcelona on Monday.* ***Yours*** *arrives from Madrid.*

Mis revistas están encima del piano.	*My magazines are on top of the piano.*
No puedo ver **las vuestras**.	*I can't see **yours**.*

✎ Exercise 7.4

Complete the following sentences with the correct possessive pronoun, according to the cue in parentheses.

1. El himno nacional de Canadá es más bonito que _____. (*ours*)

2. Nuestros tíos vinieron a vernos ayer. ¿Cuándo vienen _____? (*yours*)

3. Enrique quiere vender su cámara. Me gusta _____, pero voy a

   comprar _____. (*his/yours*)

4. La mujer quería llevar su chaqueta en clase, pero yo tenía calor, y me quité

   _____. (*mine*)

5. Los hijos de Sonia se duermen a las ocho todas las noches; _____

   se duermen a las nueve. (*ours*)

6. Esta alcoba es más pequeña que _____. (*mine*)

7. Este hotel de tres estrellas es menos cómodo que _____. (*ours*)

8. ¿Cuál de los pasteles desea Ud.? El pastel que deseo es más sabroso que

   _____. (*yours*)

Omission of the Article Following *ser* with Possessive Pronouns

When a possessive pronoun follows any form of **ser**, the article (**el**, **la**, **los**, **las**) is omitted.

El gusto es mío.	*The pleasure is mine.*
La casa es mía.	*The house is mine.*
Los zapatos son míos.	*The shoes are mine.*
Estas opiniones son mías.	*These opinions are mine.*
El vestido es tuyo.	*The dress is yours.*
La corbata es tuya.	*The tie is yours.*

Los trajes son tuyos.	*The suits are yours.*
Las faldas son tuyas.	*The skirts are yours.*
El piano es suyo.	*The piano is yours.*
	(also possible: *is his/her/theirs*)
La guitarra es suya.	*The guitar is his.*
	(also possible: *is yours/hers/theirs*)
Los tambores son suyos.	*The drums are hers.*
	(also possible: *are yours/his/theirs*)
Las flautas son suyas.	*The flutes are theirs.*
	(also possible: *are yours/his/hers*)
El violín es nuestro.	*The violin is ours.*
La computadora es nuestra.	*The computer is ours.*
Los coches son nuestros.	*The cars are ours.*
Las bicicletas son nuestras.	*The bicycles are ours.*

Exercise 7.5

Complete the following sentences with the correct possessive pronoun, according to the cue in parentheses. In these sentences, it appears after a form of **ser**.

1. El libro es _____. (*mine*)

2. Estos espejos son _____. (*yours*)

3. Los mapas son _____. (*ours*)

4. Los gatos son _____. (*his*)

5. La planta es _____. (*hers*)

6. La televisión es _____. (*theirs*)

Exercise 7.6

Complete the following sentences with the correct possessive pronoun, according to the cue in parentheses. In these sentences, it appears after a word other than a form of **ser**.

1. Mi libro está aquí. ¿Dónde está _____? (*yours*)

2. El chaleco guatemalteco cuesta veinte pesos. ¿Cuánto cuesta

    _____? (*his*)

3. El maestro tiene su libro. ¿Quién tiene _____? (*mine*)

4. Los carros de Jaime son costosos; son mejores que _____. (*ours*)

5. No tengo una buena maleta para mi viaje. ¿Me puedes prestar

     _____? (*yours*)

6. ¿Hay platos para la fiesta? ¿Nos pueden Uds. traer _____? (*yours*)

Relative Pronouns

Relative pronouns are related to a noun that has been previously stated.

Que

Que, meaning *that, which,* or *who,* is the most commonly used, all-purpose relative pronoun in Spanish. Referring to persons, places, or things, it comes right after the noun to which it refers.

Este hombre, que habla mucho, es mi amigo.	*This man, who talks a lot, is my friend.*
Tengo la información que necesitas.	*I have the information that you need.*

Que is also used after prepositions. As the object of a preposition, **que** refers to a thing or things only, not to a person or persons.

El edificio en que vivo es viejo.	*The building in which I live is old.*
Tengo la pluma con que él escribe.	*I have the pen with which he writes.*
Los libros de que hablo son interesantes.	*The books of which I am speaking are interesting.*

Quien

Quien means *who* and is used instead of **que** when a form of **ser** is used in the main clause.

Es ella **quien** canta bien.	*It is she who sings well.*
Son ellos **quienes** bailan.	*It is they who dance.*
Soy yo **quien** escribe.	*It is I who is writing.*

Quien and **quienes**, meaning *whom,* are used after prepositions to refer to people.

Ella es la mujer con quien Eduardo vive.	*She is the woman with whom Ed lives.*
El cantante a quien conozco llegó hoy.	*The singer whom I know arrived today.*
Los estudiantes a quienes vi ayer no están aquí hoy.	*The students whom I saw yesterday are not here today.*

Cuyo, cuya, cuyos, cuyas

Cuyo, which means *whose,* can serve as a relative pronoun or relative adjective. It most often acts as an adjective, however, because it typically precedes the noun that it modifies and agrees with it in gender and number.

Los niños **cuya familia** vive lejos se sienten solos.	*The children whose family lives far away feel lonely.*
El hombre **cuyo libro** tengo se fue ayer.	*The man whose book I have left yesterday.*
La doctora **cuyos clientes** son exigentes trabaja duro.	*The doctor whose clients are demanding works hard.*
El guitarrista **cuyas canciones** son originales gana mucho dinero.	*The guitarist whose songs are original earns a lot of money.*

Lo que

Lo que means *that which* and is often translated as *what.* It is a neuter relative pronoun and refers to an abstract idea.

Julia siempre entiende lo que le enseñamos.	*Julia always understands what we teach her. (Julia always understands that which we teach her.)*
Lo que quiero decirles es la verdad.	*What I want to say to you is the truth.*
Lo que Ud. hizo me sorprendió.	*What you did surprised me.*
Fernando tiene lo que necesitas.	*Fernando has what you need.*
¿Oyen Uds. lo que yo oigo?	*Do you hear what I hear?*

When **lo que** is used to mean *whatever*, it is followed by the present subjunctive.

El día de tu cumpleaños, puedes   *On your birthday, you can do*
   hacer lo que quieras.   *whatever you want.*

Exercise 7.7

Complete the following sentences with the appropriate relative pronoun. Choose from the list below.

lo que, que, quien, quienes, cuyo

1. Sabemos _____ Luisa sabe.

2. Los hombres, _____ jugaban tenis contra sus esposas, perdían.

3. Este hotel, en _____ pasamos nuestras vacaciones, es maravilloso.

4. Samuel y su hermano, _____ viven en el décimo piso, son carpinteros.

5. Graciela tiene dos nietos con _____ viaja.

6. Ella tiene un bastón con _____ caminar.

7. _____ Raúl hace no le sirve.

8. ¿Eres tú _____ baila bien?

9. Somos nosotros _____ cantan bien.

10. ¿Entendieron Uds. _____ yo les enseñé?

11. ¿Compraste la casa _____ me gustó?

12. No tengo nadie con _____ hablar.

13. A este hombre _____ esposa tiene tres coches no le gusta manejar.

14. Mi mejor amigo, _____ hermanos bailan y cantan, toca bien el violín.

Exercise 7.8

Translate the following sentences into English.

1. Rita vendió la casa que me gustó.

   _____

2. Lo que Ud. dijo era verdad.

   _____

3. No sé si este hombre conocido, que estudia la filosofía, quiere ir a Grecia con sus amigos.

   _____

El que, la que, los que, las que

El que and its related forms are translated as *that, which, who, the one that, the ones that, the one who,* and *the ones who.* They refer to people or things, show gender and number, and can be used instead of **que** for emphasis or clarification. **Que** is used much more in conversation, while the forms of **el que** are used more in written Spanish. This form is not commonly used in speech as a connector. It is good to know these forms, but for conversation, you'll probably use **que**.

Mi hermana, la que es baja, compró tacones.	*My sister, who is short, bought high heels.*
El turista, el que llegó ayer, está cansado.	*The tourist, the one who arrived yesterday, is tired.*
Las mesas, las que son de vidrio, son caras.	*The tables, the ones that are made of glass, are expensive.*
Mis sobrinos, los que estudian la ley, quieren ser abogados.	*My nephews, who study law, want to be lawyers.*

El cual, la cual, los cuales, las cuales

El cual and its related forms also mean *that, which,* or *who.* They are interchangeable with **el que**, **la que**, **los que**, and **las que**. Like the latter forms, these are used more in writing than in speech.

This form replaces **que** when there is some doubt about the reference, or if the relative pronoun is at a distance from the antecedent. These relative pronouns also show gender and number, so they are used to avoid confusion when there is more than one possible noun to which they might refer.

El padre de mi amiga, **el cual** es científico, fue a Alemania a estudiar.

My friend's father, who is a scientist, went to Germany to study.

La madre de Federico, **la cual** canta y baila, es actriz.

Fred's mother, who sings and dances, is an actress.

Los hermanos de Susana, **los cuales** trabajan en España, hablan español.

Susan's brothers, who work in Spain, speak Spanish.

Las hijas de Gabriel, **las cuales** están alegres, viajan mucho.

Gabriel's daughters, the ones who are happy, travel a lot.

El cual and its related forms are most frequently used after prepositions other than **a**, **de**, **con** and **en**. They are especially common with compound prepositions.

La razón por la cual Isabel viaja es un misterio.

The reason why Isabel travels is a mystery.

Había una guerra durante la cual muchas personas murieron.

There was a war during which many people died.

Éste es el edificio enfrente del cual vi el accidente.

This is the building in front of which I saw the accident.

Éstas son las calles debajo de las cuales hay varias líneas de metro.

These are the streets under which there are several subway lines.

Aquí está la fuente detrás de la cual Lorenzo y Laura se enamoraron.

Here is the fountain behind which Lorenzo and Laura fell in love.

NOTE **La razón por la cual** is translated *the reason why* in English. Literally, the translation is *the reason through which*.

 ## Exercise 7.9

Complete the following sentences with the most appropriate relative pronoun.

1. Es ella _____ lo ama.

2. Yo sabía _____ los estudiantes estaban alegres.

3. Muchas personas murieron durante la guerra _____
   no era necesaria.

4. La razón por _____ Paulina y Raúl se enamoraron es obvia.

5. Las vacas y los búfalos comen hierba, _____ dan leche.

6. Susana necesita un bastón con _____ andar.

7. Ella necesita una persona con _____ estar.

8. Es un buen barrio en _____ vivir.

9. ¿Cuál es el tema de _____ tú hablas?

10. ¿A _____ buscan Uds.?

11. ¿Es ésta la puerta por _____ entramos?

Demonstrative Adjectives and Pronouns

The demonstrative adjectives and demonstrative pronouns look similar.

Demonstrative Adjectives

Masculine	Feminine	
este	esta	*this*
estos	estas	*these*
ese	esa	*that*
esos	esas	*those*
aquel	aquella	*that (over there)*
aquellos	aquellas	*those (over there)*

Demonstrative Pronouns

Demonstrative pronouns carry a written accent.

The demonstrative pronoun replaces the noun. Whereas **este libro** means *this book*, **éste** (referring to **el libro**) means *this one* and replaces **el libro** (*the book*). The pronunciation is the same for both forms.

	Masculine	Feminine	
NEAR THE SPEAKER	éste	ésta	*this one*
	éstos	éstas	*these (ones)*
NEAR THE LISTENER	ése	ésa	*that one*
	ésos	ésas	*those (ones)*
FAR FROM BOTH	aquél	aquélla	*that one (over there)*
SPEAKER AND LISTENER	aquéllos	aquéllas	*those (over there)*

Los zapatos suyos son más elegantes que **éstos** que están en la ventana.	*Your shoes are more elegant than **these** that are in the window.*
Estos perros feroces ladran mucho, pero **aquéllos** son mansos.	*These wild dogs bark a lot, but **those (over there)** are tame.*
Nos gusta este carro, pero vamos a comprar **ése**.	*We like this car, but we are going to buy **that one**.*
Esta vista de la ciudad es hermosa, pero prefiero **ésa**.	*This view of the city is beautiful, but I prefer **that one**.*

The demonstrative pronoun is also used to express former and latter.

Dos personas, Julia y Ana, se quieren mucho.	*Two people, Julia and Ana, love each other a lot.*
Ésa es alta y delgada; **ésta** es baja y cariñosa.	***The former** is tall and thin; **the latter** is short and affectionate.*

There are three neuter demonstrative pronouns that do not carry written accents. They refer to an object that is not known, a statement, or a general idea.

esto	*this*
eso	*that*
aquello	*that* (farther away in place or time)

¿Qué es **esto**?	*What is **this**?*
¡**Eso** es imposible!	***That** is impossible!*
Aquello me molesta.	***That** annoys me.*

📖 Reading Comprehension

Mi viaje

Estoy preparándome para mis vacaciones en México y se me perdió
el pasaporte. ¿Es necesario que yo tenga un pasaporte? Pienso que sí.
¿A quién le pregunto? Debo llamar a mi amigo Juan que viaja mucho.
Ojalá que sepa. El año pasado viajó a Oaxaca, una ciudad en México
la cual está a seis horas por bus desde la capital. Le gustó mucho o me
dijo que le gustó.

    Estoy pensando en ir a los Galápagos también donde las tortugas viven
más de cien años y los animales y los pájaros actúan como dueños de la
isla porque no les tienen miedo a los turistas, los cuales pasean por las islas
todo el día, día tras día. Si Juan no está en casa, lo voy a llamar a su celular,
el que lleva consigo todo el tiempo. ¿Cuál es su número de teléfono?
Se me olvidó.

Verbos

actuar	*to act*
olvidarse	*to forget* (by accident)
pasear	*to take a walk, to stroll*
perderse	*to lose* (by accident)

Preposición

consigo	*with himself*

Preguntas

1. ¿Adónde quiere viajar el protagonista?

   _____

2. ¿Quién es Juan?

   _____

3. ¿Puede Ud. describir los Galápagos?

   _____

4. ¿Cómo son los animales de la isla?

   _____

The Neuter *lo* + Adjective Used as a Noun

The neuter article **lo** followed by the masculine form of an adjective acts as a noun.

Lo difícil es pensar por sí mismo.	*The difficult thing is to think for oneself.*
Lo más importante es preguntar.	*The most important thing is to ask.*
Lo mejor de todo es poder vivir bien.	*The best (thing) of all is to be able to live well.*
Se ve lo bueno y lo malo por todas partes.	*One sees the good and the bad everywhere.*

The neuter article **lo** followed by **de** means *the matter of, the issue of.*

Lo de la mujer le interesa a José.	*The matter of the woman interests Joe.*
Lo de la tecnología le fascina al científico.	*The issue of technology interests the scientist.*

Expressions with *lo*

lo antes posible	*as soon as possible*
lo más posible	*the most possible*
lo más pronto posible	*the fastest possible*
lo menos posible	*the least possible*

 ## Exercise 7.10

Complete the following sentences with the correct form of the article: **el**, **la**, **los**, **las**, *or* **lo**. *In some cases, the article is part of the contraction* **al**. *Remember that the article may also be omitted. If no article is needed, mark an* **X**.

Hoy es (1.) _____ domingo, (2.) _____ 27 de junio. Eduardo fue

(3.) _____ cine ayer. Le gustó (4.) _____ película *María Llena de Gracia.*

(5.) _____ público le gustó mucho también. Me dijo que (6.) _____ bueno

de la película era (7.) _____ de (8.) _____ vida actual en Bogotá,

(9.) _____ capital de Colombia. A Eduardo todo (10.) _____ del cine le interesa. Él va todos (11.) _____ sábados por (12.) _____ noche. Cuando

tiene tiempo, estudia (13.) _____ historia del cine. A veces, (14.) _____

películas que ve son malas, pero no le importa. (15.) _____ importante es que

Eduardo goza mucho de (16.) _____ experiencia. A mí no me gusta ir

(17.) _____ cine. Prefiero (18.) _____ teatro donde (19.) _____ actores

actúan ante nosotros. Cuando yo fui joven, quería ser (20.) _____ actriz,

pero a la edad de cuarenta, decidí hacerme (21.) _____ directora.

Exercise 7.11

Complete the following sentences with **el cual**, **la cual**, **los cuales**, **las cuales**, **cuyo**, **cuya**, **cuyos**, **cuyas**, **quien**, *or* **quienes**. *Use each relative pronoun only one time.*

1. La radio de mi hermano, _____ me gustó, era un regalo de mi amigo.

2. Olivia es la persona de _____ hablábamos.

3. La ciudad construyó un nuevo rascacielos desde _____ hay vistas maravillosas.

4. Los estudiantes _____ maestro es excelente ganaron todos los premios académicos.

5. Conozco a esa mujer _____ madre es de Colombia.

6. Roberto y Jorge vinieron a vernos, _____ son de México.

7. Los muchachos con _____ el jefe hablaba son los mejores estudiantes de la clase.

8. Este hombre, _____ opiniones son interesantes, se llama Teodoro.

9. Tengo buenas gafas por _____ puedo ver bien.

10. A Leonardo le molesta su vecino _____ perros ladran toda la noche.

Adjectives Used as Nouns

Spanish adjectives can be used as nouns when the noun they modify is omitted.

Me gusta la camisa azul.	*The blue shirt is pleasing to me.*
También me gusta la camisa roja.	*The red shirt is also pleasing to me.*
A Paula le gusta la camisa roja.	*The red shirt is pleasing to Paula.*
Le gusta **la roja**.	***The red one** is pleasing to her.*
Íbamos a comprar un carro viejo, pero cambiamos la decisión y escogimos el carro nuevo.	*We were going to buy an old car, but we changed our mind and we chose the new car.*
Escogimos **el nuevo**.	*We chose **the new one**.*
No nos gustó **el viejo**.	***The old one** wasn't pleasing to us.*
¿Por qué compró Ana la casa azul, si le gusta la casa amarilla?	*Why did Ana buy the blue house, if the yellow house is pleasing to her?*
¿Por qué no compró **la amarilla**?	*Why didn't she buy **the yellow one**?*

 ## Exercise 7.12

Complete the following sentences with the correct adjective used as a noun, according to the cue in parentheses.

EXAMPLE   El hombre viejo no camina bien. La mujer vieja usa un bastón.

_____Los dos viejos_____ dan un paseo cada mañana. (*the two old people*)

1. ¿Por qué no te gusta este nuevo restaurante chino?

   ¿Prefieres _____? (*the old one*)

2. Los dos carros son económicos: uno es verde; el otro es blanco.

   Voy a comprar _____. (*the white one*)

3. Al hombre le gustan dos apartamentos: un apartamento grande

   y costoso y otro apartamento mediano y barato. Decide comprar

   _____. (*the big one*)

Pronouns Used as Nouns

Pronouns are words that refer to a noun or take the place of a noun.

El de, la de, los de, las de

The articles **el**, **la**, **los**, **las** followed by **de** can replace a noun when that noun is omitted.

El libro de Olivia y **el** (libro) **de** su hermano son interesantes.	*Olivia's book and **that of** her brother are interesting.*
Tu blusa y la (blusa) de María son hermosas.	*Your blouse and **that of** María are beautiful.*
Los perros feroces viven en el campo.	*The wild dogs live in the countryside.*
Los de mi hermano son animales domesticados.	***My brother's** are pets.* (*My brother's = Those of my brother = My brother's dogs*)
Estas camisas son caras.	*These shirts are expensive.*
Las de Alicia son baratas.	***Alice's** are cheap.* (*Alice's = Those of Alice = Alice's shirts*)

El que, la que, los que, las que

The articles **el**, **la**, **los**, **las** followed by **que** can replace a noun when that noun is omitted.

Los dos hombres son amigos.	*The two men are friends.*
El que se llama Alonso juega al baloncesto.	***He who** is called Alonso plays basketball.*
Hay dos mujeres que aman a David.	*There are two women who love David.*
La que está a su lado es su esposa.	***The one who** is at his side is his wife.*
Hay documentos en mi escritorio.	*There are documents on my writing table.*
Los que están en el banco son de mi sobrina.	***Those that** are in the bank are my niece's.*

📖 Pronunciation Practice

Practice the following selection aloud.

Los maderos de San Juan
Un poema por José Asunción Silva

José Asunción Silva nació en 1865 y se murió en 1896 en Bogotá, Colombia. Él comparte con Rubén Darío y otros la estética literaria conocida bajo el nombre de modernismo.

> Y aserrín
> aserrán
> los maderos
> de San Juan
> piden queso,
> piden pan;
> los de Roque
> Alfandoque;
> los de Rique,
> Alfeñique;
> los de Trique,
> Triquitrán.
> ¡Trique, trique, trique, tran!
> ¡Trique, trique, trique, tran!

Nombres

aserrán	*nonsense word*
aserrín	*sawdust*
los maderos	*logs*

📖 Reading Comprehension

Lo fatal

Un poema por Rubén Darío

Rubén Darío nació en 1867 en Metapa, Nicaragua, y se murió en su país en 1916. Es considerado como la figura más representativa del modernismo.

Dichoso el árbol que es apenas sensitivo,
y más la piedra dura porque ésa ya no siente,
pues no hay dolor más grande que el dolor de ser vivo,
ni mayor pesadumbre que la vida consciente.

Ser, y no saber nada, y ser sin rumbo cierto,
y el temor de haber sido y un futuro terror...
Y el espanto seguro de estar mañana muerto,
y sufrir por la vida y por la sombra y por

lo que no conocemos y apenas sospechamos,
y la carne que tienta con sus frescos racimos,
y la tumba que aguarda con sus fúnebres ramos,

¡y no saber adónde vamos,
ni de dónde venimos!...

Verbos

aguardar	*to keep*
haber sido	*to have been* (present perfect tense)
sospechar	*to suspect*
tentar	*to tempt*

Nombres

el espanto	*the fright*
la pesadumbre	*the sorrow*
los racimos	*the clusters/bunches*
los ramos	*the bouquets*
el rumbo	*the path*

Expresiones

apenas	*hardly*
sin rumbo	*without direction*

Preguntas

1. Según el poema, ¿por qué son dichosos el árbol y la piedra?

   _____

2. ¿De qué sufre el poeta?

   _____

3. ¿Cuál es el tema del poema?

   _____

4. ¿Cuál es la opinión de Ud. acerca de las ideas del poema?

   _____

8

The Present Perfect Tense

The present perfect tense expresses past action closely related to the present.

The present perfect is a compound tense formed with the present tense of the helping verb **haber** and the past participle of the main verb. The English equivalent of **haber** + past participle is *to have done something*. In the present tense, it corresponds to the present perfect in English: *I have eaten there many times*, for example.

The present perfect tense expresses the following:

- An action that we are waiting for, but that hasn't yet happened
- An action that began in the past and continues to the present
- An action that has happened at various times in the past and may happen again

Formation of the Past Participle

-Ar Verbs

To form the past participle of all **-ar** verbs, drop the ending and add **-ado** to the stem.

alquilar	alquil**ado**	*rented*
apretar	apret**ado**	*squeezed, tightened*
aumentar	aument**ado**	*increased, augmented*
borrar	borr**ado**	*erased*

154

decepcionar	decepcion**ado**	*disappointed*
empujar	empuj**ado**	*pushed*
estacionar	estacion**ado**	*parked*
estar	est**ado**	*been*
llegar	lleg**ado**	*arrived*
marcar	marc**ado**	*dialed, marked*
tomar	tom**ado**	*taken*
usar	us**ado**	*used*
viajar	viaj**ado**	*traveled*

-*Er* and -*ir* Verbs

To form the past participle of most **-er** and **-ir** verbs, drop the ending and add **-ido** to the stem.

-*Er* Verbs

beber	beb**ido**	*drunk*
comer	com**ido**	*eaten*
entender	entend**ido**	*understood*
perder	perd**ido**	*lost*
ser	s**ido**	*been*
torcer	torc**ido**	*twisted*

-*Ir* Verbs

advertir	advert**ido**	*warned*
añadir	añad**ido**	*added*
convertir	convert**ido**	*converted*
dormir	dorm**ido**	*slept*
hervir	herv**ido**	*boiled*
ir	**ido**	*gone*
oprimir	oprim**ido**	*pressed*
recibir	recib**ido**	*received*

Pronunciation Reminder

In all regular past participles, the Spanish **d** is pronounced like the soft **th** sound in English *other*. Practice the pronunciation of past participles with a **th** sound.

-Er and **-ir** verbs whose stem ends in a vowel have a written accent above the **-i-** in the past participle to maintain the **-ido** sound.

atraer	atra**ído**	*attracted*
caer	ca**ído**	*fallen*
creer	cre**ído**	*believed*
leer	le**ído**	*read*
oír	o**ído**	*heard*
traer	tra**ído**	*brought*

Verbs that end in **-uir** do not carry a written accent in the past participle.

construir	constru**ido**	*constructed*
destruir	destru**ido**	*destroyed*
huir	hu**ido**	*fled*

Irregular Past Participles

Following are the 12 basic irregular past participles in Spanish. Pronounce each of them as you learn them.

abrir	abierto	*opened*
cubrir	cubierto	*covered*
decir	dicho	*told, said*
escribir	escrito	*written*
freír	frito	*fried*
hacer	hecho	*done*
morir	muerto	*died*
poner	puesto	*put*
pudrir	podrido	*rotted*
romper	roto	*broken*
ver	visto	*seen*
volver	vuelto	*returned*

When a prefix is added to any of the irregular verbs above, the past participle shows the same irregularity.

describir	descrito	*described*
descubrir	descubierto	*discovered*
devolver	devuelto	*returned* (an object)
disolver	disuelto	*dissolved*

envolver	envuelto	*wrapped*
oponer	opuesto	*opposed*
resolver	resuelto	*resolved*

Exercise 8.1

Write the past participle of the following verbs. Pronounce each past participle aloud, and make sure you know the meaning of the verb.

1. jugar _____
2. buscar _____
3. conocer _____
4. entrar _____
5. devolver _____
6. ser _____
7. estar _____
8. dar _____
9. ver _____
10. escribir _____

11. romper _____
12. tener _____
13. querer _____
14. hacer _____
15. decir _____
16. ir _____
17. abrir _____
18. cerrar _____
19. morir _____
20. amar _____

Formation of the Present Perfect Tense

To form the present perfect tense in Spanish, conjugate the helping verb **haber** (the English auxiliary verb *to have*) in the present tense and follow it with the past participle of the main verb.

yo he comido	*I have eaten*
tú has hablado	*you have spoken*
él ha vuelto	*he has returned*
nosotros hemos sonreído	*we have smiled*
vosotros habéis ido	*you have gone*
ellos han dicho	*they have said*

NOTE The verb **haber** is used as an auxiliary or helping verb to form the perfect tenses. The verb **tener** means *to have* in the sense of possession: **yo tengo dos libros**. **Tener** is never used as an auxiliary verb.

The helping verb **haber** cannot be separated from the past participle. In a question, place the subject after the verb form.

¿Dónde **han estado** Uds.?	*Where have you been?*
¿**Han salido** las mujeres?	*Have the women left?*

Exercise 8.2

Complete the following phrases with the correct past participle of the verb in parentheses. Practice pronouncing each phrase aloud.

1. yo he _____ (ser)

2. tú has _____ (tener)

3. ella ha _____ (poder)

4. nosotros hemos _____ (estar)

5. vosotros habéis _____ (querer)

6. ellas han _____ (saber)

7. yo he _____ (decir)

8. tú has _____ (dar)

9. Ud. ha _____ (volver)

10. nosotros hemos _____ (poner)

11. vosotros habéis _____ (hacer)

12. Uds. han _____ (llegar)

Complete the following phrases with the correct form of the present perfect tense of the verb in parentheses.

13. yo _____ (dormir)

14. tú _____ (romper)

15. ella _____ (abrir)

16. nosotros _____ (estar)

17. vosotros _____ (escribir)

18. ellas _____ (ver)

Uses of the Present Perfect Tense

The present perfect tense expresses an action closely related to the present. Its English equivalent corresponds to the present perfect tense in English. The present perfect tense expresses the following:

- An action that we are waiting for, but that hasn't yet happened

- An action that began in the past and continues to the present

- An action that has happened at various times in the past and may happen again

¿Por qué han apagado Uds. las luces?	*Why have you turned off the lights?*
¿Has comido ya?	*Have you already eaten?*
Los viajeros no han vuelto de México todavía.	*The travelers haven't returned from Mexico yet.*
¿Jamás ha estado en Europa?	*Have you ever been in Europe?*
He andado por este pueblo antes.	*I have walked through this town before.*

NOTE The words **jamás** (meaning *ever* in an affirmative sentence or question), **ya** (meaning *already*), and **todavía** (meaning *still* or *yet*) frequently occur in sentences using the present perfect tense.

Action Waited for or Hoped for

Todavía no he llamado.	*I haven't called yet.* (I might still call.)
Mis invitados no han llegado.	*My guests haven't arrived.*

Compare the following sentences. The first sentence of each pair is in the preterit and the second is in the present perfect.

No llamaron.	*They didn't call.* (The action is complete.)
No han llamado.	*They haven't called.* (There is a possibility that they will call.)
No llegaron.	*They didn't arrive.*
No han llegado.	*They haven't arrived.*

Action That Began in the Past and Continues to the Present

He dormido aquí por cinco horas.	*I have slept here for five hours.*
Hemos vivido en Londres por dos meses.	*We have lived in London for two months.*

Action That Happened in the Past and May Happen Again

Often the actions expressed can be counted.

Eva ha estado en Nueva York tres veces.	*Eva has been in New York three times.*
¿Cuantas veces han comido Uds. en este restaurante?	*How many times have you eaten in this restaurant?*
Hemos comido allí cinco veces.	*We have eaten there five times.*
¿Cuántas veces han visitado México?	*How many times have they visited Mexico?*
Camillo ha visitado México siete veces; Antonio ha ido dos veces.	*Camillo has visited Mexico seven times; Antonio has gone two times.*
Yo he viajado a la ciudad de México cuatro veces. Me he quedado en el mismo hotel dos veces.	*I have traveled to Mexico City four times. I have stayed in the same hotel twice.*

Placement of Object Pronouns with the Present Perfect Tense

The reflexive, indirect, and direct object pronouns are placed directly before the helping verb. This is the only possible position for object pronouns used with the present perfect tense. The object pronouns are never attached to the past participle.

Ellos no **me** han llamado.	*They haven't called me.*
¿Por qué no **le** has hablado a Oscar?	*Why haven't you spoken to Oscar?*
Paula **se lo** ha dicho.	*Paula has said it to you.*
Yo **te** he devuelto el dinero.	*I have returned the money to you.*
Yo **la** he visto antes.	*I have seen her before.*

¿**Te** has duchado hoy?   *Have you showered today?*
El doctor **se** ha lavado las manos   *The doctor has washed his hands*
    tres veces.   *three times.*
No **nos** hemos levantado todavía.   *We haven't gotten up yet.*

 ## Exercise 8.3

Complete the following sentences with the correct form of the present perfect tense of the verb in parentheses.

1. Laura nos _____ la carta. (traer)

2. Nosotros todavía no la _____. (recibir)

3. Los hoteleros no me _____. (llamar)

4. Sus hermanos nunca le _____ dinero. (prestar)

5. ¿Por qué jamás me _____ tú? (amar)

6. Por fin, mis amigos _____. (volver)

7. El bisabuelo que tenía cien años _____. (morirse)

8. ¿Adónde _____ ellos? (irse)

9. Uds. _____ bien el trabajo. (hacer)

10. Tus colegas siempre _____ bien de ti. (hablar)

11. Irene y su hermano jamás _____. (viajar)

12. Yo la _____ recientemente. (ver)

13. Yo no _____ dormir. (poder)

14. Ellas ya _____. (acostarse)

15. Nosotros _____ a otra casa. (mudarse)

Use of the Infinitive *haber* and the Past Participle

The infinitive form of the helping verb **haber** is used after a preposition.

Me alegro de **haber llegado**   *I am glad to have arrived on time.*
    a tiempo.
Ella se alegra de **haber hecho**   *She is glad to have done her*
    su tarea.   *homework.*

Después de **haber encontrado** sus llaves, el taxista empezó su trabajo.	*After having found his keys, the cabdriver began his work.*
Después de **haber ido** al dentista, Monica se sintió mejor.	*After having gone to the dentist, Monica felt better.*

Because object pronouns can never be attached to the past participle, when they are needed in an infinitive + past participle construction, they must be attached to the infinitive, in this case, **haber**.

Me alegro de **haberte** conocido.	*I'm glad to have met you.*
Los padres de Laura están muy felices después de **habernos** visto.	*Laura's parents are very happy after having seen us.*
Pedro está contento de haber cerrado la puerta.	*Peter is happy to have closed the door.*
Está contento de **haberla** cerrado.	*He is happy to have closed it.*

Exercise 8.4

*Complete the following sentences with the correct form of **haber**.*

1. Después de _____ leído el párrafo, los estudiantes están contentos.

2. Nosotros _____ corrido a casa.

3. Sus padres les _____ dado una bienvenida.

4. Después de _____ comido galletas y leche, los niños están listos para acostarse.

5. Nosotros ya _____ leído el libro.

6. El muchacho _____ entendido la lección.

7. Sus profesores les _____ enseñado bien.

8. Después de _____ aprobado el examen, ellos se sienten satisfechos.

9. ¿_____ hecho bien los niños?

10. Los alumnos _____ empezado a aprender mucho.

Exercise 8.5

Rewrite the following sentences in the present perfect tense. You may include additional words or expressions in the sentence if you wish.

EXAMPLE   Julia no toma mucha cerveza.

Julia no ha tomado mucha cerveza (todavía).

1. Cruzo la calle a la escuela.

_____

2. Jamás entro en la clase.

_____

3. Mis compañeros entran también.

_____

4. Le decimos "hola" al profesor.

_____

5. Nos sentamos.

_____

6. Escribo con lápiz.

_____

7. Mis amigos usan una computadora.

_____

8. Contestamos las preguntas.

_____

9. Almorzamos juntos.

_____

10. Nos despedimos del profesor.

_____

11. Vamos en bus a casa.

_____

12. Les saludamos a nuestros padres al llegar a casa.

_____

Exercise 8.6

Translate the following sentences into Spanish.

1. *How have you been?*

   _____

2. *Where have all the flowers gone?*

   _____

3. *Who has just called?*

   _____

4. *What have you done?*

   _____

5. *We have sent the document.*

   _____

6. *Have they had breakfast today?*

   _____

7. *I have turned on the oven and have put in the chicken. I have to cook it for an hour.*

   _____

   _____

8. *It is no longer hot, because the students have opened all the windows in the classroom.*

   _____

   _____

9. *The exterminators have killed all the cockroaches.*

   _____

10. *Laura and her daughter have just arrived in Italy.*

   _____

A Word About *acabar de*

Remember: When you want to say *to have just done something,* use the expression **acabar de** in the present tense, not the verb **haber** with the present perfect tense.

Yo **acabo de** llegar.	*I have just arrived.*
Tú **acabas de** cantar.	*You have just sung.*
Él **acaba de** salir.	*He has just left.*
Nosotros **acabamos de** decidir.	*We have just decided.*
Vosotros **acabáis de** pagar.	*You have just paid.*
Ellos **acaban de** volver.	*They have just returned.*

Reading Comprehension

El apartamento

¿Desde cuándo viven los inquilinos en este edificio en la calle cuarenta y seis con la novena avenida? ¿Quién sabe? La gente no se mete en la vida de nadie. Pero yo sí sé porque me gusta observar la ida y vuelta de la muchedumbre. Es verdad que hay muchos inquilinos que ya se han ido o les han alquilado su apartamento a otros. Los apartamentos son pequeños, pero agradables, y bastante baratos en comparación a otros lugares en la ciudad. Por mi parte, sigo firmando el contrato de arrendamiento año de por medio con muchísimas ganas de quedarme. Los porteros son agradables y el superintendente, que vive solo en el primer piso, nos trata bien.

Una pareja del octavo piso ha tenido un bebé hace ocho meses y están viviendo felices. En el décimo piso, dos personas, una mujer que está vieja ya, aunque tiene solamente cuarenta y cinco años, y su compañero (nunca se han casado) se pelean, gritan, y comen mucha comida rápida de restaurantes. (Veo a los mensajeros con pizza o con comida china todo el tiempo). Una mujer muy simpática del tercer piso se ha muerto, y otra mujer del cuarto piso, pelirroja, cuyo perro se ha desaparecido, vive desesperada y triste. En el piso once, un hombre amargado sin amigos sube y baja en el ascensor todos los días. Cuando voy vagando por el edificio, escucho a veces sonidos de amor por la noche en el sexto y el séptimo. En el quinto piso vive un hombre a quien le gusta patinar. Hace muchos años, él tenía una novia bonita e inteligente. Se separaron de repente, y este hombre, tan fuerte y guapo en días pasados, nunca ha tenido otra compañera. Un día voy a escribir un libro, pero por ahora, estoy satisfecha, mirando a la gente, escuchándola ir y venir en la vida cotidiana.

Verbos

estar viejo	*to feel old*
meterse	*to become involved*
patinar	*to skate*
pelear	*to fight*
vagar	*to wander*

Nombres

el contrato de arrendamiento	*the lease*
el inquilino	*the tenant*
la muchedumbre	*the crowd*
el portero	*the doorman*
el superintendente	*the superintendent*

Adjetivos

bonita e inteligente	*pretty and intelligent* (The word **e** is used instead of **y** before words that begin with an emphasized **i-** or **hi-**.)
cotidiano	*daily*
pelirrojo	*red headed*

Expresión

año de por medio	*every other year*

Preguntas

1. ¿Se conoce la gente en este edificio?

   _____

2. ¿Cuántos pisos hay?

   _____

3. ¿Cuántas personas están felices en el edificio?

   _____

4. ¿Cómo sabe tanto de la gente la protagonista?

   _____

9

The Past Perfect Tense

The past perfect tense refers to action that occurred in the past prior to another past action. It is a compound tense. The past perfect tense in Spanish corresponds to the same tense in English: *I had eaten,* for example.

Formation of the Past Perfect Tense

To form the past perfect tense in Spanish, conjugate the helping verb **haber** in the imperfect, and follow it with the past participle of the main verb.

yo había vuelto	*I had returned*
tú habías empezado	*you had begun*
ella había hecho	*she had done*
nosotros habíamos sabido	*we had known*
vosotros habíais dicho	*you had said*
ellas habían comido	*they had eaten*

Uses of the Past Perfect Tense

The past perfect tense occurs in sentences and questions that are directly linked to the past. It expresses an action that precedes another action: A sentence may begin with the imperfect or preterit and continue with the past perfect.

Ud. sabía	que habíamos salido.
You knew (imperfect)	*that we had left.* (past perfect)

167

Yo creí   que él se había muerto.
I believed (preterit)   *that he had died.* (past perfect)

Ellos vieron a la mujer   que no había dicho nada.
They saw the woman (preterit) *who hadn't said anything.* (past perfect)

The reflexive, indirect, and direct object pronouns precede the helping verb
haber.

Ella sabía que él no **me** había   *She knew that he hadn't written*
   escrito.   *to me.*
Me di cuenta de que ellos no   *I realized that they hadn't done it.*
   lo habían hecho.

The infinitive form of the helping verb **haber** is used after a preposition.

Después de **haber llegado**   *After having arrived in Peru,*
   a Perú, los aventureros   *the adventurers looked for*
   buscaron un hotel en Cuzco.   *a hotel in Cuzco.*
Después de **haber comido**,   *After having eaten, I went to*
   fui a la plataforma del tren.   *the train platform.*
El actor aprendió el diálogo   *The actor learned the dialogue*
   sin **haber ensayado** mucho.   *without having rehearsed much.*

 **Exercise 9.1**

Translate the following sentences into Spanish.

1. *The children thought that their parents had left.*

   _____

2. *I had already set the table when my family arrived.*

   _____

3. *Roberto went to a country that he had never visited before.*

   _____

4. *My colleagues told me that they had finished their work.*

   _____

Exercise 9.2

Translate the following sentences into English.

1. El profesor sabía que yo había estudiado.

   _____

2. La niña pensaba que su perro había vuelto.

   _____

3. Ellos dijeron que habían devuelto los libros a la biblioteca.

   _____

4. Creíamos que nuestros amigos nos habían escrito.

   _____

5. Estuvimos seguras que los jóvenes habían tenido éxito.

   _____

6. Pensábamos que los ladrones habían estado en el banco.

   _____

7. El policía creía que nosotros los habíamos visto.

   _____

8. Les dijimos a los detectives que no habíamos sido buenos testigos.

   _____

Exercise 9.3

Complete the following sentences with the correct form of the verb in parentheses.

1. Todo el mundo había _____ para el verano. (ir)

2. ¿Habían _____ Uds. mucho tiempo antes de

   _____ al doctor? (esperar/ver)

3. Yo había _____ antes de _____.
   (descansar/cenar)

4. Antes de _____, Anita había _____ sus deudas.
   (jubilarse/pagar)

5. ¿Por qué no le habías _____ al camarero una buena propina

   antes de _____ del restaurante? (dar/salir)

6. Nadie le había _____ a la senadora que ella había

   _____ la elección. (decir/perder)

Reading Comprehension

El sueño

Después de haber leído su libro y de haber apagado la tele, Octavio
se acostó. Las noches anteriores él no había podido dormir bien por sus
sueños, digamos, pesadillas, pero esta noche él tenía la determinación
de soñar con buenas cosas. Trató de pensar en algo bueno. ¿Qué será?,
pensaba. El martes, había pensado en el amor y eso le cogió mal, el
miércoles, había pensado en el dinero, pero tampoco le salió bien el sueño.
El jueves pensó en tomar algunas vacaciones en Hawái y muchos tiburones
llenaban sus sueños. Se despertó exhausto, luchando contra los peces.
Hoy siendo viernes, se quedó despierto toda la noche, la única solución
en la cual Octavio podía pensar.

Verbos

cogerle bien/mal a alguien	*to go well/badly for someone*
digamos	*let's say* (the **nosotros** command form of **decir**)
luchar	*to struggle*
salirle bien/mal a alguien	*to go well/badly for someone*
soñar con	*to dream about*
tratar de	*to try to*

Nombres

la pesadilla	*the nightmare*
el pez, los peces	*the fish* (sing. and pl.)
el tiburón	*the shark*

Adjetivos

despierto	*wide-awake*
exhausto	*exhausted*

Expresión

¿qué será?   *What could it be?* (literally, *What will it be?*)

Preguntas

1. ¿En qué trata de pensar Octavio?

_____

2. ¿Cómo son sus sueños?

_____

3. ¿Cuál es su solución?

_____

📖 Reading Comprehension

Recordando Nicaragua

En el año 1987 Nicaragua estaba sufriendo los fines de su guerra civil. Los sandinistas luchaban contra el ejército de Somoza, los contras luchaban contra los sandinistas. Daniel Ortega era presidente y líder de los sandinistas, el nombre y el movimiento inspirados por Augusto César Sandino, héroe nacional de Nicaragua que había muerto muchos años atrás.

Era mucho que entender—quien estaba luchando contra quien y por qué.

Fui a Managua, capital de Nicaragua, con un grupo de intérpretes y científicos. Llegamos en agosto a una casa agradable entre gente amable. Desde el principio, nos sentíamos cómodos en nuestra pensión; los dueños nicaragüenses nos trataban bien, nos servían las comidas, y nos mostraban su poesía. (Nos parecía que toda la gente era poeta.)

Después de haber estado en Managua dos días, empezamos nuestro trabajo en la universidad, enseñándoles a los estudiantes avanzados las matemáticas, la ciencia, la medicina, y la astrofísica.

Por la noche volvíamos a la casa y pasábamos muchas noches agradables con amigos; hablábamos de la guerra, de las drogas, de la felicidad. Lo increíble era que a pesar de todo, los nicaragüenses habían mantenido un amor profundo por la vida. Mientras tanto, la guerra continuaba.

Preguntas

1. ¿Por qué estaba sufriendo Nicaragua?

   _____

2. ¿Cómo eran los nicaragüenses?

   _____

3. ¿Quién escribía poesía?

   _____

4. ¿De qué hablaban en las noches?

   _____

The Past Participle as an Adjective

Now that you have learned the past participle, your vocabulary will expand even more, because the past participle is also used as an adjective. As an adjective, the past participle follows the noun it describes, and it agrees with its noun in gender and number.

el restaurante preferido	*the preferred restaurant*
el teléfono perdido	*the lost telephone*
los huevos podridos	*the rotten eggs*
el enemigo conocido	*the known enemy*
la ventana cerrada	*the closed window*
las puertas abiertas	*the open(ed) doors*

Exercise 9.4

Complete the following phrases with the past participle of the verb in parentheses used as an adjective. Remember that the adjective agrees in gender and number with its noun. Practice pronouncing the phrases aloud.

1. la comida _____ (quemar)

2. la mesa _____ (romper)

3. el pájaro _____ (morir)

4. la tarea bien _____ (hacer)

5. las ideas bien _____ (expresar)

6. el niño _____ (dormir)

7. el amigo _____ (querer)

8. los carros _____ (vender)

9. las blusas _____ (comprar)

10. el año _____ (pasar)

11. los problemas _____ (resolver)

12. el apartamento _____ (alquilar)

13. el tesoro _____ (esconder)

14. las cartas _____ (entregar)

15. la telenovela _____ (grabar)

The Past Participle as an Adjective with *estar*

The past participle as an adjective is usually used with **estar**.

Estoy cansada.	*I am tired.*
¿Estás vestido?	*Are you dressed?*
El baño está ocupado.	*The bathroom is occupied.*
La mesa está puesta.	*The table is set.*
El televisor está prendido.	*The television set is on.*
Estamos enojados.	*We are angry.*
Estamos sentados.	*We are seated.*
Uds. están equivocados.	*You are mistaken.*
Los trabajadores están preocupados.	*The workers are worried.*

When the past participle is used as an adjective with **estar**, it indicates that the idea expressed is the result of an action.

Susana va a escribir un libro. > Ella está escribiendo un libro.
> El libro **está escrito**.

Susana va a escribir un libro.	*Susan is going to write a book.*
Ella está escribiendo un libro.	*She is writing a book.*
El libro **está escrito**.	*The book is written.*

Los músicos van a grabar la canción. > Están grabando la canción.
> La canción **está grabada**.

Los músicos van a grabar la canción.	*The musicians are going to record the song.*
Están grabando la canción.	*They are recording the song.*
La canción **está grabada**.	*The song is recorded.*

La niña va a esconder su muñeca. > Ella está escondiendo su muñeca.
> La muñeca **está escondida**.

La niña va a esconder su muñeca.	*The girl is going to hide her doll.*
Ella está escondiendo su muñeca.	*She is hiding her doll.*
La muñeca **está escondida**.	*The doll is hidden.*

El hombre va a morir. > Él está muriendo. > El hombre **está muerto**.

El hombre va a morir.	*The man is going to die.*
Él está muriendo.	*He is dying.*
El hombre **está muerto**.	*The man is dead.*

NOTE Whether you are aware of this concept or not, you can still use **estar** + past participle with confidence when you are describing someone or something.

Exercise 9.5

*Complete the following sentences with the correct form of **estar** + past participle as an adjective.*

1. El dueño va a cerrar la tienda. Está cerrando la tienda. La tienda

   _____.

2. En la mañana, este hombre va a abrir la tienda. Está abriéndola. La tienda

   _____.

3. Shakira va a escribir una canción. Está escribiéndola. La canción

   _____.

4. Vamos a construir una casa. Estamos construyéndola. La casa

   _____.

5. Los estudiantes van a hacer su tarea. Están haciéndola. La tarea

   _____.

6. Las abejas van a morir. Están muriendo. Las abejas

   _____.

7. Los padres van a freír unos huevos. Están friéndolos. Los huevos

   _____.

8. Vamos a resolver nuestros problemas. Estamos resolviéndolos. Los problemas

   _____.

 Exercise 9.6

Write the past participles that appear in the following rhymes. Repeat these rhymes aloud to practice your pronunciation.

1. La mujer está triste
   Triste está la mujer
   La tienda está cerrada
   Y no sabe qué hacer.

   _____

2. El doctor está herido
   Herido está el doctor
   Los médicos preocupados
   Lo cuidan con amor.

   _____

3. El cielo está nublado
   Parece que va a llover
   La gente no quiere mojarse
   Y empieza a correr.

   _____

4. El baúl está arreglado
   Arreglado está el baúl
   La pareja va al Caribe
   A nadar en el agua azul.

   _____

5. La pareja está separada
Dividido está el hogar
Los amantes no se acuerdan
Cuando se dejaron de amar.

The Past Participle with *ser* and the Passive Voice

The past participle is also used with **ser**. When used with **ser**, the past participle expresses the action itself, in this case, the passive voice, rather than the result of an action. The passive voice consists of **ser** + past participle and is often followed by **por**. The past participle agrees in gender and number with the subject of the sentence.

- In the preterit

El libro *Don Quixote* **fue escrito por** Cervantes.	*The book* Don Quixote *was written by Cervantes.*
La puerta **fue abierta por** el portero.	*The door was opened by the doorman.*
Las casas **fueron robadas por** los ladrones.	*The houses were robbed by the thieves.*
Las iglesias en Guatemala **fueron construidas por** los españoles.	*The churches in Guatemala were constructed by the Spaniards.*
La comida **fue servida por** el camarero.	*The meal was served by the waiter.*

- In the present perfect and past perfect

La carta **ha sido entregada por** el cartero.	*The letter has been delivered by the mailman.*
Los impuestos **han sido preparados por** los contadores.	*The taxes have been prepared by the accountants.*
Los testigos **habían sido advertidos por** el juez.	*The witnesses had been warned by the judge.*
El apartamento **había sido alquilado por** dos amigos.	*The apartment had been rented by two friends.*

In speech, it is generally much better to use the active voice. The passive voice is used infrequently in Spanish. For example, the passive voice is used in this sentence:

El almuerzo **fue preparado por**   *The lunch was prepared by the*
    el cocinero.   *cook.*

However, it is better to use the active voice you already know.

El cocinero preparó el almuerzo.   *The cook prepared the lunch.*

Exercise 9.7

Rewrite the following passive sentences as sentences in the active voice.

EXAMPLE   La carta fue escrita por Carla.

        Carla escribió la carta.

1. Los vasos fueron hallados por los antropólogos.

   _____

2. El país ha sido gobernado por un dictador.

   _____

3. La clase fue enseñada por el maestro.

   _____

4. El criminal fue reconocido por la víctima.

   _____

5. Los regalos fueron ofrecidos por los padres.

   _____

6. Las camisas habían sido planchadas por Catalina.

   _____

7. Las luces fueron apagadas por los inquilinos.

   _____

8. Se dice que las Américas fueron descubiertas por Colón en 1492.

   _____

📖 Reading Comprehension

El conde Lucanor
por Don Juan Manuel

Don Juan Manuel nació en Escalona, Toledo, y se murió en 1348 en Peñafiel, Valladolid. Él pertenece a la tradición literaria-didáctica de la Edad Media.

Había en la corte de Castilla un hombre de gran inteligencia y virtud llamado don Sancho, el cual era muy estimado por el rey. Una de las expresiones favoritas de don Sancho era la siguiente: "Todo lo que nos pasa es siempre para lo mejor."

Algunos nobles le tenían envidia y lo acusaron de que preparaba una revolución. El rey les creyó y envió un mensajero para que don Sancho viniera inmediatamente a la corte. Al mismo tiempo, el rey daba órdenes para matarlo en camino.

Don Sancho se apresuró a obedecer, pero al bajar de prisa las escaleras de su casa, se cayó y se rompió una pierna. En medio del dolor, repetía: "Todo lo que nos pasa es siempre para lo mejor."

A causa del accidente, no pudo ir a la corte del rey. Mientras tanto, éste descubrió la falsedad de las acusaciones contra don Sancho y castigó a los culpables. Don Sancho se dirigió, por fin, a la corte, donde fue recibido con grandes honores.

Verbos

apresurarse	*to hurry*	enviar	*to send*
caerse	*to fall down*	romperse	*to break*
dirigirse	*to make one's way, to direct oneself*	viniera	*came* (past subjunctive form of **venir**)

Preguntas

1. ¿En qué año nació el autor del cuento?

_____

2. ¿Por qué lo acusaron a don Sancho de ser revolucionario?

_____

3. ¿Por qué no lo mataron los mensajeros del rey?

_____

4. ¿Cuál es la moraleja del cuento?

_____

III

Future and Conditional Tenses; Past Subjunctive; Idioms

10

The Future Tense

The future tense is used to express actions that take place in the future. It refers to both the immediate and the remote future. This is a simple tense, in that it has no helping verb in Spanish. In English, the auxiliaries *will* or *shall* are used: *Irene will drink the water*, for example.

Formation of the Future Tense

Most verbs in the future tense are regular. To form the future tense, use the infinitive as the stem and add the following endings to the infinitive: **-é**, **-ás**, **-á**, **-emos**, **-éis**, **-án**. The endings are the same for all **-ar**, **-er**, and **-ir** verbs. Notice that only the **nosotros** form does not carry a written accent. The following list includes new verbs so that you can expand your vocabulary as you practice the pronunciation.

Regular Verbs

-Ar Verbs

cantar *to sing*

yo cantaré	*I will sing*	nosotros cantaremos	*we will sing*
tú cantarás	*you will sing*	vosotros cantaréis	*you will sing*
él cantará	*he will sing*	ellos cantarán	*they will sing*
ella cantará	*she will sing*	ellas cantarán	*they will sing*
Ud. cantará	*you will sing*	Uds. cantarán	*you will sing*

cobrar *to charge* (money)

yo cobraré	nosotros cobraremos
tú cobrarás	vosotros cobraréis
ella cobrará	ellas cobrarán

dar *to give*

yo daré	nosotros daremos
tú darás	vosotros daréis
él dará	ellos darán

estar *to be*

yo estaré	nosotros estaremos
tú estarás	vosotros estaréis
ella estará	ellas estarán

gozar *to enjoy*

yo gozaré	nosotros gozaremos
tú gozarás	vosotros gozaréis
ella gozará	ellas gozarán

marchar *to march*

yo marcharé	nosotros marcharemos
tú marcharás	vosotros marcharéis
él marchará	ellos marcharán

opinar *to opine, to give an opinion*

yo opinaré	nosotros opinaremos
tú opinarás	vosotros opinaréis
Ud. opinará	Uds. opinarán

patinar *to skate*

yo patinaré	nosotros patinaremos
tú patinarás	vosotros patinaréis
él patinará	ellos patinarán

pegar *to hit*

yo pegaré	nosotros pegaremos
tú pegarás	vosotros pegaréis
Ud. pegará	Uds. pegarán

regresar *to return*

yo regresaré	nosotros regresaremos
tú regresarás	vosotros regresaréis
él regresará	ellos regresarán

triunfar *to triumph*

yo triunfaré	nosotros triunfaremos
tú triunfarás	vosotros triunfaréis
Ud. triunfará	Uds. triunfarán

A Word About Pronunciation

When a word carries a written accent, you will stress that syllable: Make sure you pronounce the verbs in this way: **yo canta<u>ré</u>**, **tú canta<u>rás</u>**, **él canta<u>rá</u>**, **nosotros canta<u>re</u>mos**, **vosotros canta<u>réis</u>**, **ellos canta<u>rán</u>**. Practice pronouncing these verb forms aloud with confidence.

-Er Verbs

atender *to attend to, to serve*

yo atenderé	nosotros atenderemos
tú atenderás	vosotros atenderéis
ella atenderá	ellas atenderán

caer *to fall*

yo caeré	nosotros caeremos
tú caerás	vosotros caeréis
Ud. caerá	Uds. caerán

comer *to eat*

yo comeré	nosotros comeremos
tú comerás	vosotros comeréis
Ud. comerá	Uds. comerán

leer *to read*

yo leeré	nosotros leeremos
tú leerás	vosotros leeréis
Ud. leerá	Uds. leerán

merecer *to deserve*

yo mereceré	nosotros mereceremos
tú merecerás	vosotros mereceréis
él merecerá	ellos merecerán

responder *to respond*

yo responderé	nosotros responderemos
tú responderás	vosotros responderéis
ella responderá	ellas responderán

ser *to be*

yo seré	nosotros seremos
tú serás	vosotros seréis
ella será	ellas serán

vencer *to conquer, to vanquish*

yo venceré	nosotros venceremos
tú vencerás	vosotros venceréis
Ud. vencerá	Uds. vencerán

ver *to see*

yo veré	nosotros veremos
tú verás	vosotros veréis
él verá	ellos verán

-Ir Verbs

asistir *to attend*

yo asistiré	nosotros asistiremos
tú asistirás	vosotros asistiréis
Ud. asistirá	Uds. asistirán

cumplir *to carry out, to comply, to fulfill, to complete*

yo cumpliré	nosotros cumpliremos
tú cumplirás	vosotros cumpliréis
ella cumplirá	ellas cumplirán

compartir *to share*

yo compartiré	nosotros compartiremos
tú compartirás	vosotros compartiréis
él compartirá	ellos compartirán

corregir *to correct*

yo corregiré	nosotros corregiremos
tú corregirás	vosotros corregiréis
Ud. corregirá	Uds. corregirán

dirigir *to direct*

yo dirigiré	nosotros dirigiremos
tú dirigirás	vosotros dirigiréis
ella dirigirá	ellas dirigirán

inscribirse *to enroll, to register*

yo me inscribiré	nosotros nos inscribiremos
tú te inscribirás	vosotros os inscribiréis
él se inscribirá	ellos se inscribirán

ir *to go*

yo iré	nosotros iremos
tú irás	vosotros iréis
ella irá	ellas irán

vivir *to live*

yo viviré	nosotros viviremos
tú vivirás	vosotros viviréis
él vivirá	ellos vivirán

A Word About *-ir* Verbs with a Written Accent in the Infinitive

-Ir verbs that have a written accent in the infinitive, such as **oír** (*to hear*), **reír** (*to laugh*), and **sonreír** (*to smile*), lose the written accent in the stem in order to form the future: **oiré, reiré, sonreiré**.

Irregular Verbs

There are only 12 basic irregular verbs in the future tense. These verbs show a change in the stem, but the endings are the same as those you have just learned. Add **-é**, **-ás**, **-á**, **-emos**, **-éis**, **-án** to the irregular stem. Practice saying these verb forms aloud, and learn them so that you will be able to use the future tense freely.

caber *to fit* (one thing inside another)

yo **cabr**é	nosotros **cabr**emos
tú **cabr**ás	vosotros **cabr**éis
ella **cabr**á	ellas **cabr**án

decir *to say*

yo **dir**é	nosotros **dir**emos
tú **dir**ás	vosotros **dir**éis
Ud. **dir**á	Uds. **dir**án

hacer *to do, to make*

yo **har**é	nosotros **har**emos
tú **har**ás	vosotros **har**éis
él **har**á	ellos **har**án

poder *to be able, can*

yo **podr**é	nosotros **podr**emos
tú **podr**ás	vosotros **podr**éis
Ud. **podr**á	Uds. **podr**án

poner *to put*

yo **pondr**é	nosotros **pondr**emos
tú **pondr**ás	vosotros **pondr**éis
él **pondr**á	ellos **pondr**án

querer *to want*

yo **querr**é	nosotros **querr**emos
tú **querr**ás	vosotros **querr**éis
ella **querr**á	ellas **querr**án

saber *to know*

yo **sabr**é	nosotros **sabr**emos
tú **sabr**ás	vosotros **sabr**éis
Ud. **sabr**á	Uds. **sabr**án

salir *to leave, to go out*

yo **saldr**é	nosotros **saldr**emos
tú **saldr**ás	vosotros **saldr**éis
él **saldr**á	ellos **saldr**án

tener *to have*

yo **tendr**é	nosotros **tendr**emos
tú **tendr**ás	vosotros **tendr**éis
ella **tendr**á	ellas **tendr**án

valer *to be worth*

yo **valdr**é	nosotros **valdr**emos
tú **valdr**ás	vosotros **valdr**éis
Ud. **valdr**á	Uds. **valdr**án

Reminder

Valer is most frequently used in the third person.

¿Cuánto vale?	*How much is it worth?*
¿Cuánto valdrá?	*How much will it be worth?*

venir *to come*

yo **vendr**é	nosotros **vendr**emos
tú **vendr**ás	vosotros **vendr**éis
Ud. **vendr**á	Uds. **vendr**án

A Word About *haber*

Habrá means *there will be* and *will there be?* It is the future tense of the verb **haber**.

¿Habrá una fiesta al fin del año?	*Will there be a party at the end of the year?*
¿Habrá clases de literatura el próximo semestre?	*Will there be literature classes next semester?*
¿Habrá mucho que hacer mañana?	*Will there be a lot to do tomorrow?*

Compound forms of verbs are conjugated in the same way as the main verb.

decir
    contradecir *to contradict*   contra**dir**é, *etc.*

hacer
    deshacer *to undo*   des**har**é, *etc.*

poner
    componer *to compose*   com**pondr**é, *etc.*
    proponer *to propose*   pro**pondr**é, *etc.*

tener
    contener *to contain*   con**tendr**é, *etc.*
    detener *to detain*   de**tendr**é, *etc.*
    mantener *to maintain*   man**tendr**é, *etc.*
    retener *to retain*   re**tendr**é, *etc.*

venir
    prevenir *to prevent*   pre**vendr**é, *etc.*

Uses of the Future Tense

The future tense is used in both Spanish and English to express a future time. The simple future transmits more of a commitment or a strong decision than does the future periphrastic (**ir** + **a** + *infinitive*). The difference also exists in English: *I will arrive at 7 P.M.* is a little stronger in terms of commitment than *I am going to arrive at 7 P.M.*

¿A qué hora estarás en casa?	*At what time will you be home?*
Paula llegará más rápido por avión.	*Paula will arrive faster by plane.*
Yo haré la tarea para la semana que viene.	*I will do the homework for the coming week.*
Carlos vendrá a verme cuando quiera.	*Carlos will come to see me when he wants.*
El cantante cantará si le gusta la música.	*The singer will sing if he likes the music.*
¿Quién será el próximo presidente de los Estados Unidos?	*Who will be the next president of the United States?*

Exercise 10.1

Complete the following sentences with the correct future form of the verb in parentheses. All verbs in this exercise are regular.

1. Si Isabel va a Italia, yo _____ también. (ir)

2. Sara dice que _____ el martes. (llegar)

3. Yo te _____ mañana, si quieres. (ver)

4. El profesor sabe que nosotros _____ durante las vacaciones. (estudiar)

5. El amigo no _____ la pronunciación de Manuel. (corregir)

6. Los artistas piensan que la gente _____ sus pinturas. (comprar)

7. El hombre nos promete que _____ de fumar. (dejar)

8. Nadie me _____ a México; yo _____ solo. (acompañar/viajar)

9. ¿Dónde _____ tú más tarde? (estar)

10. Los periodistas izquierdistas dicen que _____. (triunfar)

11. Después de la escuela secundaria, los estudiantes _____ a la universidad. (asistir)

12. ¿Cuánto me _____ Ud. por este chaleco? (cobrar)

13. Nosotros _____. (vencer)

14. Si yo te hago una pregunta, ¿me _____? (responder)

 Exercise 10.2

Complete the following sentences with the correct future form of the verb in parentheses. All verbs in this exercise are irregular.

1. Yo lo _____. (hacer)

2. El novio piensa que ella _____ a verlo. (venir)

3. Él no _____. (salir)

4. Nosotros no le _____ nada a nadie. (decir)

5. ¿_____ tú ir de vacaciones en julio? (poder)

6. Si los padres no los vigilan, sus hijos _____ la ropa en el piso. (poner)

7. ¿Cuánto _____ esta chaqueta? (valer)

8. ¿Quién _____ las llaves? (tener)

9. El espía no sabe nada hoy, pero _____ mucho mañana. (saber)

10. ¿_____ mucha gente en el gimnasio el primero de enero? (haber)

 ## Exercise 10.3

Translate the following sentences into Spanish, using verbs from the list below. Use each verb only one time.

aprender, comprar, decir, fijarse, gustar, perderse, poder, practicar, quejarse, reírse, repetir, ser, tener cuidado

1. *If she is not careful, she will get lost.*

   _____

2. *If Jorge tells it to me, I will not repeat it to anyone.*

   _____

3. *If we practice, we will be able to learn a new language.*

   _____

4. *They will buy the house if they like the garden and the balcony.*

   _____

5. *If the play is funny, the audience will laugh.*

   _____

6. *He will never notice anything. He will never complain.*

   _____

Exercise 10.4

Rewrite the following sentences in the future tense. This exercise includes both regular and irregular verbs.

EXAMPLE   Como mucho el día de acción de gracias.

      Comeré mucho el día de acción de gracias.

1. Él viene a verme. _____

2. Tengo una cita con el dentista en febrero.

   _____

3. ¿Cuánto vale el carro? _____

4. ¿Qué me dices? _____

5. Salimos para México en julio. _____

6. Trabajo en un teatro. _____

7. Hay once estudiantes aquí. _____

8. Empezamos a estudiar. _____

9. El muchacho tiene éxito. _____

10. Los deportistas tienen sed. _____

11. ¿Cuánto me cobra Ud.? _____

12. Yo patino porque me gusta. _____

13. Ella no se mete en la vida de los otros.

    _____

14. El pueblo vence. _____

15. Triunfamos. _____

16. La muchacha cumple diez años el miércoles.

    _____

17. Olivia vive en Perú. _____

18. La maestra corrige la tarea. _____

19. Yo asisto a la universidad. _____

20. Elena sueña que te vio. _____

Exercise 10.5

Translate the following sentences into English.

1. Sabré más mañana de lo que sé hoy.

   _____

2. Tres sillas y ocho estudiantes no cabrán en el salón.

   _____

3. Los médicos no dormirán hasta las cuatro de la mañana.

   _____

4. Pronto volveré.

   _____

5. De vez en cuando, te visitaré en Brasil.

   _____

6. Si Uds. quieren ir de compras, yo los llevaré.

   _____

7. Si él se pone nervioso, hablará en voz baja.

   _____

8. Si corres mucho, podrás perder peso.

   _____

9. Si Ud. pierde sus llaves, ¿qué hará?

   _____

10. Ellos me dicen que Uds. se casarán el año que viene.

    _____

Expressing Doubt or Probability in the Present

The equivalent in English can be *I wonder* or *it is probably* to indicate doubt or probability. You will know from context whether the sentence or question expresses the simple future or probability in the present.

| ¿Qué hora será? | *I wonder what time it is.* |
| Serán las diez. | *It's probably ten o'clock.* |

¿Dónde estará Enrique?	*I wonder where Henry is.*
Estará en casa.	*He's probably at home.*
¿Quién será?	*I wonder who that is. /* *Who can that be?*
¿Cuántos años tendrán ellas?	*I wonder how old they are. /* *How old might they be?*
No vendrá hoy.	*He probably won't come today.*

Expressing the Future Using the Present Tense

- The present indicative is often used when there is another element in the sentence that indicates future time.

Ella canta mañana.	*She'll sing tomorrow.*
Bailamos el viernes.	*We'll dance on Friday.*

- The present tense, not the future, is used when asking for instructions.

¿Doblo aquí?	*Shall I turn here?*
¿Camino a la derecha?	*Shall I walk to the right?*

- The present tense, not the future, is used when you're asking for things. These are not actions that take place in the future; in these cases, *will* is a helping verb expressing a voluntary mood.

¿Me da el bolígrafo, por favor?	*Will you give me the pen, please?* (literally, *Do you give me the pen, please?*)
¿Me prestas tu carro?	*Will you lend me your car?* (literally, *Do you lend me your car?*)
¿Me llamas cuando llegues?	*Will you call me when you arrive?* (literally, *Do you call me when you arrive?*)
¿Le traes flores?	*Will you bring him flowers?* (literally, *Do you bring him flowers?*)
¿Nos dan Uds. regalos?	*Will you give us presents?* (literally, *Do you give us presents?*)

Exercise 10.6

Rewrite the following sentences to indicate probability.

EXAMPLE   El libro no cabe en mi bolsa.

        El libro no cabrá en mi bolsa.

1. ¿Tiene hambre el niño? _____
2. ¿Qué hace la mujer? _____
3. ¿Quién pone la mesa? _____
4. Ella sabe las direcciones. _____
5. ¿Cuánto vale este apartamento lujoso?

Placement of Reflexive, Indirect, and Direct Object Pronouns

Review object pronouns as you continue adding to your knowledge of tenses. The reflexive, indirect, and direct object pronouns have two possible positions when used with the future tense.

- Object pronouns can be placed directly before the conjugated verb.
- Object pronouns can be attached to an infinitive if one is used in the phrase or sentence.

Paula le dará direcciones.	*Paula will give you directions.*
Esta noche leeré un libro y después me acostaré.	*Tonight, I will read a book and then I'll go to bed.*
¿Quién me podrá contestar? ¿Quién podrá contestarme? }	*Who will be able to answer me?*
¿Lo podrás llamar más tarde? ¿Podrás llamarlo más tarde? }	*Will you be able to call him later?*

The Future Progressive Tense

The future progressive tense emphasizes action that will be in progress in the future. When you don't need to express action that will be in progress in the future, use the simple future tense.

Formation of the Future Progressive Tense

The future progressive is a compound tense. To form this tense, conjugate **estar** in the future and follow it with the gerund of the main verb.

yo estaré comiendo	*I will be eating*
tú estarás jugando	*you will be playing*
Ud. estará festejando	*you will be celebrating*
nosotros estaremos bebiendo	*we will be drinking*
vosotros estaréis bailando	*you will be dancing*
Uds. estarán celebrando	*you will be celebrating*

Uses of the Future Progressive Tense

The future progressive tense emphasizes action that will take place in the future: *I will be arriving by 10 o'clock*, for example. If you don't need to emphasize the action, use the simple future: *I will arrive by 10 o'clock*.

Estaré llegando a medianoche.	*I will be arriving at midnight.*
¿Cuándo estarás saliendo para el Canadá?	*When will you be leaving for Canada?*
Mi amigo estará escuchando música toda la mañana.	*My friend will be listening to music all morning.*
Estaremos leyendo su libro esta noche.	*We will be reading your book tonight.*
Los muchachos estarán jugando al tenis hasta las cinco cuando oscurezca.	*The children will be playing tennis until five o'clock when it gets dark.*

The Future Perfect Tense

In Spanish, as in English, the future perfect tense refers to an action that will be completed in the future before another action occurs or before some point of time in the future.

Formation of the Future Perfect Tense

The future perfect is a compound tense. To form this tense, conjugate **haber** in the future and follow it with the past participle of the main verb.

yo habré comido	*I will have eaten*
tú habrás cocinado	*you will have cooked*
Ud. habrá visto	*you will have seen*
nosotros habremos limpiado	*we will have cleaned*
vosotros habréis vuelto	*you will have returned*
Uds. habrán ido	*you will have gone*

Uses of the Future Perfect Tense

The future perfect tense expresses action that will have taken place by a specific time in the future.

La muchacha habrá leído el artículo para el viernes.	*The girl will have read the article by Friday.*
Yo habré visto esta película antes de que el grupo se reúna.	*I will have seen this film before the group meets.*
Las mujeres habrán terminado su conversación antes de preparar la cena.	*The women will have finished their conversation before preparing supper.*
Julia habrá bailado con este hombre tres veces antes de salir de la fiesta.	*Julia will have danced with this man three times before leaving the party.*
En agosto, la camarera habrá trabajado en el restaurante un año.	*In August, the waitress will have worked in the restaurant for a year.*

Exercise 10.7

Translate the following sentences into English.

1. ¿Adónde habrás ido después de salir de tu casa?

   _____

2. Habremos comprado nuestros tiquetes para el sábado.

   _____

3. Habré visto a los estudiantes antes de que viajen a México.

   _____

4. En un mes, habré vivido aquí por diez años.

   _____

5. ¿Habrás terminado tu trabajo para la semana que viene?

   _____

Reading Comprehension

El porvenir

"Volveré," dice el amante,
"comeré," dice el glotón,
"bailaré," dice el cojo,
"trabajaré," dice él sin profesión.

"Votaré," dice el ciudadano,
"me reiré," dice el juglar,
"dormiré," dice el insomne,
"te cuidaré," dice su mamá.

"Prometeré," dice el político,
"curaré" dice el doctor,
"recordaré" dice el amnésico,
"enseñaré" dice el profesor.

Y todos se encontrarán
Y todos se hablarán
Todos dirán la verdad y mentiras
Y todos se morirán.

Verbos

cuidar	*to take care of, to care for*
encontrarse	*to meet*
votar	*to vote*

Nombres

el amante	*the lover*
el amnésico	*the amnesiac*
el cojo	*the cripple, the lame person*
el glotón	*the glutton*
el insomne	*the insomniac*
el juglar	*the juggler*
el porvenir	*the future*

Preguntas

1. ¿Cuáles personas dicen la verdad?

   _____

2. ¿Cuáles mienten?

   _____

3. ¿Con quiénes se identifica Ud.?

   _____

11

The Conditional Tense

The conditional tense is used to describe actions that are uncertain in the future. Unlike the future tense, which expresses future certainty, the conditional expresses an action that would happen if another condition were met. This is a simple tense, in that it uses no helping verb in Spanish. It corresponds to the conditional tense in English, which uses *would* as an auxiliary verb: *I would go, but I don't have time,* for example.

Formation of the Conditional Tense

Most verbs are regular in the conditional tense. To form the conditional, use the infinitive as the stem and add the following endings to the infinitive: **-ía**, **-ías**, **-ía**, **-íamos**, **-íais**, **-ían**. These endings are used for all verbs, both regular and irregular, in the conditional tense. Practice pronouncing the following conditional verb forms aloud and be sure to stress the accented syllable.

 Pronunciation Reminder
Practice pronouncing the **d** with a soft **th** sound.

Regular Verbs

-*Ar* Verbs

ayudar *to help*	
yo ayudaría	nosotros ayudaríamos
tú ayudarías	vosotros ayudaríais
Ud. ayudaría	Uds. ayudarían

199

disfrutar *to enjoy*

yo disfrutaría	nosotros disfrutaríamos
tú disfrutarías	vosotros disfrutaríais
él disfrutaría	ellos disfrutarían

estar *to be*

yo estaría	nosotros estaríamos
tú estarías	vosotros estaríais
ella estaría	ellas estarían

felicitar *to congratulate*

yo felicitaría	nosotros felicitaríamos
tú felicitarías	vosotros felicitaríais
Ud. felicitaría	Uds. felicitarían

festejar *to feast, to celebrate*

yo festejaría	nosotros festejaríamos
tú festejarías	vosotros festejaríais
él festejaría	ellos festejarían

fracasar *to fail*

yo fracasaría	nosotros fracasaríamos
tú fracasarías	vosotros fracasaríais
Ud. fracasaría	Uds. fracasarían

llenar *to fill*

yo llenaría	nosotros llenaríamos
tú llenarías	vosotros llenaríais
ella llenaría	ellas llenarían

recordar *to remember*

yo recordaría	nosotros recordaríamos
tú recordarías	vosotros recordaríais
él recordaría	ellos recordarían

Pronunciation Reminder

The **r** at the beginning of a breath group is pronounced as an **rr** trill. Practice pronouncing these forms of **recordar** with the trilled **r**.

-Er Verbs

beber to drink

yo bebería	nosotros beberíamos
tú beberías	vosotros beberíais
Ud. bebería	Uds. beberían

conocer to know, to be acquainted with

yo conocería	nosotros conoceríamos
tú conocerías	vosotros conoceríais
él conocería	ellos conocerían

proteger to protect

yo protegería	nosotros protegeríamos
tú protegerías	vosotros protegeríais
ella protegería	ellas protegerían

ser to be

yo sería	nosotros seríamos
tú serías	vosotros seríais
él sería	ellos serían

traer to bring

yo traería	nosotros traeríamos
tú traerías	vosotros traeríais
ella traería	ellas traerían

volver to return

yo volvería	nosotros volveríamos
tú volverías	vosotros volveríais
Ud. volvería	Uds. volverían

-Ir Verbs

admitir to admit

yo admitiría	nosotros admitiríamos
tú admitirías	vosotros admitiríais
ella admitiría	ellas admitirían

dormir *to sleep*

yo dormiría	nosotros dormiríamos
tú dormirías	vosotros dormiríais
él dormiría	ellos dormirían

exigir *to demand*

yo exigiría	nosotros exigiríamos
tú exigirías	vosotros exigiríais
él exigiría	ellos exigirían

fingir *to pretend*

yo fingiría	nosotros fingiríamos
tú fingirías	vosotros fingiríais
Ud. fingiría	Uds. fingirían

Pronunciation Reminder

The **g** before an **i** is pronounced like the English **h** as in *hot*.

ir *to go*

yo iría	nosotros iríamos
tú irías	vosotros iríais
ella iría	ellas irían

medir *to measure*

yo mediría	nosotros mediríamos
tú medirías	vosotros mediríais
Ud. mediría	Uds. medirían

Irregular Verbs

There are 12 basic irregular verbs in the conditional tense. The conditional and future tenses have the same stems in their irregular verbs. Add **-ía**, **-ías**, **-ía**, **-íamos**, **-íais**, **-ían** to the irregular stem. Practice pronouncing these verb forms aloud, and learn them so that you will be able to use the conditional tense freely.

caber *to fit* (one thing inside another)

yo **cabría**	nosotros **cabríamos**
tú **cabrías**	vosotros **cabríais**
ella **cabría**	ellas **cabrían**

decir *to say, to tell*

yo **diría**	nosotros **diríamos**
tú **dirías**	vosotros **diríais**
Ud. **diría**	Uds. **dirían**

hacer *to do, to make*

yo **haría**	nosotros **haríamos**
tú **harías**	vosotros **haríais**
él **haría**	ellos **harían**

poder *to be able, can*

yo **podría**	nosotros **podríamos**
tú **podrías**	vosotros **podríais**
Ud. **podría**	Uds. **podrían**

poner *to put*

yo **pondría**	nosotros **pondríamos**
tú **pondrías**	vosotros **pondríais**
él **pondría**	ellos **pondrían**

querer *to want*

yo **querría**	nosotros **querríamos**
tú **querrías**	vosotros **querríais**
ella **querría**	ellas **querrían**

saber *to know*

yo **sabría**	nosotros **sabríamos**
tú **sabrías**	vosotros **sabríais**
Ud. **sabría**	Uds. **sabrían**

salir *to leave, to go out*

yo **saldría**	nosotros **saldríamos**
tú **saldrías**	vosotros **saldríais**
él **saldría**	ellos **saldrían**

tener *to have*

yo **tendría**	nosotros **tendríamos**
tú **tendrías**	vosotros **tendríais**
ella **tendría**	ellas **tendrían**

valer *to be worth*

yo **valdría**	nosotros **valdríamos**
tú **valdrías**	vosotros **valdríais**
Ud. **valdría**	Uds. **valdrían**

Reminder

As noted, **valer** is most often used in the third person:

¿Cuánto vale?	*How much is it worth?*
¿Cuánto valdría?	*How much would it be worth?*
Valdría la pena.	*It would be worth the trouble.*

venir *to come*

yo **vendría**	nosotros **vendríamos**
tú **vendrías**	vosotros **vendríais**
Ud. **vendría**	Uds. **vendrían**

A Word About *haber*

Habría means *there would be* and *would there be?* It is the conditional tense of the verb **haber**.

Sin estudiantes, no habría universidades.	*Without students, there would be no universities.*
¿Habría luz sin sol?	*Would there be light without the sun?*
¿Habría comida sin plantas?	*Would there be food without plants?*

Compound forms of verbs are conjugated in the same way as the main verb.

decir
    contradecir *to contradict*   contra**diría**, *etc.*

hacer
    deshacer *to undo*   des**haría**, *etc.*

poner

componer *to compose*	com**pondr**ía, *etc.*
proponer *to propose*	pro**pondr**ía, *etc.*

tener

contener *to contain*	con**tendr**ía, *etc.*
detener *to detain*	de**tendr**ía, *etc.*
mantener *to maintain*	man**tendr**ía, *etc.*
retener *to retain*	re**tendr**ía, *etc.*

venir

prevenir *to prevent*	pre**vendr**ía, *etc.*

Uses of the Conditional Tense

The conditional tense expresses action that is uncertain in the future. This tense corresponds to the English conditional tense: *I would go,* for example.

Nadie comería en este restaurante.	*No one would eat in this restaurant.*
Me gustaría ir al cine con mi amigo.	*I would like to go to the movies with my friend.*
¿Te gustaría ir conmigo?	*Would you like to go with me?*
Nos encantaría viajar a Perú.	*We would love to travel to Peru.*
Elena dijo que cerraría la maleta.	*Elena said that she would close the suitcase.*
Yo sabía que el mago no me diría nada.	*I knew that the magician wouldn't tell me anything.*
¿Gastarías todo en un día?	*Would you spend everything in one day?*

A Word About English *would*

In English, the translation of the Spanish imperfect tense sometimes uses the word *would* as a helping verb when expressing repeated action in the past. Following are examples of the imperfect tense:

Cuando Madeleine era niña, ella practicaba el piano cada día.	*When Madeleine was a child, she would practice the piano every day.*
El hombre viejo ponía sus dientes en agua cada noche antes de dormirse.	*The old man would put his teeth in water every night before falling asleep.*

Exercise 11.1

Complete the following sentences with the correct conditional form of the verb in parentheses.

1. Yo _____. (producir)

2. Nosotros lo _____. (hacer)

3. ¿Qué _____ Uds.? (decir)

4. Él _____ pero no quiere. (venir)

5. ¿Cuánto me _____ Ud. por mi libro? (dar)

6. Ellos _____ temprano. (acostarse)

7. Los niños y sus padres _____ pronto. (regresar)

8. ¿Por qué _____ Ud. tacones? (llevar)

9. ¿A Uds. les _____ salir esta noche? (gustar)

10. ¿_____ luz sin electricidad? (haber)

11. Yo _____ esa película. (ver)

12. Nosotros no _____ esta noche. (salir)

13. Laura dijo que _____ mañana. (llegar)

14. Yo sabía que ella _____. (entender)

15. ¿Quién _____ hacer tal cosa? (poder)

16. ¿Por qué _____ Samuel al teatro si siempre se duerme? (ir)

Placement of Reflexive, Indirect, and Direct Object Pronouns

The reflexive, indirect, and direct object pronouns have two possible positions when used with the conditional tense.

- Object pronouns can be placed directly before the conjugated verb.

- Object pronouns can be attached to an infinitive if one is used in the phrase or sentence.

Yo te prestaría mi carro, pero está en el taller de mecánico.	*I would lend my car to you, but it is in the shop.*
¿Te interesaría comprarlo?	*Would it interest you to buy it?*

¿Cuánto me cobraría por la flor?   *How much would you charge me*
                                    for the flower?

Enrique le daría las flores a su   *Henry would give flowers to his*
  novia, pero no tiene bastante   *girlfriend, but he doesn't have*
  dinero para comprárselas.   *enough money to buy them*
                                      for her.

Exercise 11.2

Rewrite the following sentences in the conditional tense. Be sure to include all necessary written accents. Pronounce your answers aloud.

EXAMPLE   Nadie duerme aquí. ___*Nadie dormiría aquí.*___

1. Yo la ayudo. _____

2. Ella va de compras. _____

3. ¿Miras tú televisión? _____

4. Ellos venden la comida. _____

5. Los mozos les dan la comida a los clientes.

   _____

6. Tenemos mucho que hacer. _____

7. El conductor maneja rápidamente. _____

8. ¿Cantas? _____

9. ¿Vienen Uds. a mi casa? _____

10. Yo lo hago. _____

11. No le digo nada. _____

12. Te cobro cien dólares. _____

13. Los niños no leen mucho. _____

14. Sé nadar. _____

15. Hay mucha gente en los trenes. _____

16. No caben más. _____

17. Le traigo las flores a su hermana. _____

18. Nos ponemos los zapatos. _____

19. ¿Puede Ud. acompañarme al bus? _____

20. ¿A Uds. les gusta ir al cine? _____

 Exercise 11.3

Complete the following sentences with the correct conditional form of the verb in parentheses.

1. Ella _____ tocar el piano, pero nunca practica. (poder)

2. La enfermera le prometió al paciente que él _____. (mejorarse)

3. Yo no _____ de la situación. (quejarse)

4. Nosotros no le _____ nada. (decir)

5. Enrique y su esposa sabían que sus hijos _____ en sus vacaciones. (divertirse)

6. Emanuel y su hermano nos aseguraron que todo _____ bien. (estar)

7. Los gemelos _____ una fiesta pero no es su cumpleaños. (tener)

8. La terapeuta física me dijo que no me _____ más los pies. (doler)

 Exercise 11.4

Translate the following sentences into Spanish.

1. *José would like to learn to swim, but he is afraid of the water.*

   _____

2. *I would not say anything to him, because I do not know him well.*

   _____

3. *Our Mexican friends would come to California to visit their family, but they prefer to travel to Europe this year.*

   _____

   _____

4. *Juan told me that he would give the book to you if you want to study it.*

_____

5. *We would go to Julia's party, but we don't know where she lives.*

_____

The conditional tense may be used to express speculation or conjecture in the past. The translation *I wonder or It was probably* indicates doubt or conjecture. You will know from context whether the sentence or question expresses the simple conditional or probability in the past.

¿Qué hora sería?	*I wonder what time it was.*
¿Dónde estaría el doctor?	*I wonder where the doctor was. / Where could the doctor have been?*
Estaría en el hospital.	*He was probably at the hospital.*
¿Cuántos años tendrían estas mujeres?	*I wonder how old these women were.*
¿Quién sería?	*Who could that have been? / I wonder who that was.*

The Conditional Progressive Tense

The conditional progressive tense expresses doubt about action in the future.

Formation of the Conditional Progressive Tense

The conditional progressive is a compound tense. To form this tense, conjugate **estar** in the conditional and follow it with the gerund of the main verb.

yo estaría limpiando	*I would be cleaning*
tú estarías pintando	*you would be painting*
Ud. estaría bailando	*you would be dancing*
nosotros estaríamos durmiendo	*we would be sleeping*
vosotros estaríais dibujando	*you would be drawing*
Uds. estarían escribiendo	*you would be writing*

Uses of the Conditional Progressive Tense

The conditional progressive tense expresses doubt in the future and emphasizes the action. When you don't need to emphasize the action, use the simple conditional. You'll find that the simple conditional is used more frequently in everyday speech.

¿Quién estaría haciendo ruido?	*Who would be making noise?*
Yo estaría tocando el piano,	*I would be playing the piano,*
pero me lesioné las manos.	*but I hurt my hands.*
Las parejas estarían bailando,	*The couples would be dancing,*
pero se cansaron.	*but they got tired.*

The Conditional Perfect Tense

The conditional perfect tense is used to express an action that would have taken place, but did not: *I would have paid you, but I left my money at home,* for example.

Formation of the Conditional Perfect Tense

The conditional perfect is a compound tense. To form this tense, conjugate the helping verb **haber** in the conditional tense and follow it with the past participle of the main verb.

yo habría ido	*I would have gone*
tú habrías salido	*you would have gone out*
él habría sonreído	*he would have smiled*
nosotros habríamos escrito	*we would have written*
vosotros habríais entrado	*you would have entered*
ellos habrían llamado	*they would have called*

Uses of the Conditional Perfect Tense

The conditional perfect tense, which is used to refer to an action that would have occurred but did not, is often followed by English *but*.

Nos habríamos quedado, pero	*We would have stayed, but*
no nos gustó la situación.	*we didn't like the situation.*

| Ella habría ido a España este mes, pero no tenía tiempo. | *She would have gone to Spain this month, but she didn't have time.* |
| Tú lo habrías podido hacer, pero se te pasó el deseo. | *You would have been able to do it, but you lost the desire.* |

Remember that reflexive, indirect, and direct object pronouns precede the verb form. The object pronouns are never attached to the past participle.

Yo **te** habría llamado, pero me dormí temprano.	*I would have called you, but I fell asleep early.*
El doctor **lo** habría ayudado, pero tenía miedo de un pleito.	*The doctor would have helped him, but he was afraid of a lawsuit.*
Los actores **le** habrían dado flores a su directora, pero costaban demasiado.	*The actors would have given flowers to their director, but they cost too much.*

The conditional perfect tense may also express speculation or conjecture in the past.

La gente honesta habría devuelto la cartera y el dinero.	*The honest people had probably returned the wallet and the money.*
Habrían sido las once cuando los muchachos llegaron.	*It must have been eleven o'clock when the children arrived.*
Habría sido noviembre cuando nos reunimos.	*It must have been November when we met.*

Exercise 11.5

Translate the following sentences into Spanish.

1. *He would have arrived on time, but he lost the directions.*

   _____

2. *We would not have told our secret to anyone.*

   _____

3. Juan and his companion would have gone to Mexico, but they decided to save their money for the following year.

_____

_____

4. Antonio and I would have traveled to Colombia, but the flight cost too much.

_____

5. Enrique would have been a good president, but he wanted to have more time to spend with his family.

_____

_____

6. Elvira would have returned the money that she found, but she gave it to her son.

_____

📖 Reading Comprehension

¿Qué haría Ud. en las siguientes situaciones?

Answer the following questions orally.

1. ¿Diría Ud. una mentira para proteger a su amigo?

2. ¿Compraría Ud. algo antes de verlo?

3. Si vas a un casino, ¿cuánto dinero apostarías antes de irte?

4. Ud. está en una clase de veinte estudiantes y todos están copiando excepto Ud. (Ellos reciben el examen de antemano y aprenden de memoria las respuestas sin saber nada. Ud. está estudiando.) ¿Le diría Ud. al maestro lo que está pasando en la clase?

5. Su hijo tiene catorce años y quiere jugar al fútbol americano para su escuela. Ud. sabe que es peligroso y que muchos niños se lesionan. ¿Lo dejaría jugar o firmaría el documento prohibiéndole que juegue?

6. Su mejor amigo está para casarse. Ud. está en un restaurante y ve a su prometida besar a otro hombre. ¿Se lo diría a su amigo?

7. Ud. encuentra una cantidad de dinero en las montañas con la identificación de una persona que se había muerto en un accidente. ¿Le devolvería Ud. el dinero a la familia?

8. ¿Viajaría Ud. solo?

9. ¿Tomaría Ud. crédito por un libro que no había escrito?

10. Su mejor amigo es pintor. ¿Le diría Ud. la verdad si a Ud. no le gusta su pintura?

Verbos

aprender de memoria	*to learn by heart, to memorize*
copiar	*to copy*
firmar	*to sign*
lesionarse	*to get hurt*

12

The Present Perfect Subjunctive

The present perfect subjunctive mood refers to the recent past and is translated as the present perfect in English: *the train has arrived,* for example.

Like all subjunctive moods, the present perfect subjunctive must be caused. The main clause must have a verb or expression that calls for the use of the subjunctive mood in the dependent clause. The present or future tense of certain verbs in the main clause will cause the present perfect subjunctive in the dependent clause.

Formation of the Present Perfect Subjunctive

The present perfect subjunctive is a compound verb form. To form the present perfect subjunctive, conjugate the present subjunctive of the helping verb **haber** and follow it with the past participle of the main verb.

yo haya hablado	*I have spoken*
tú hayas llegado	*you have arrived*
ella haya huido	*she has fled*
nosotros hayamos vendido	*we have sold*
vosotros hayáis leído	*you have read*
ellas hayan votado	*they have voted*

Uses of the Present Perfect Subjunctive

The present perfect subjunctive can be used to express a past action if the main clause is in the present or future tense. The main clause must contain

214

a verb or expression that causes the subjunctive in the dependent clause. The most common use is the present indicative in the main clause and the present perfect subjunctive in the dependent clause.

Yo sé	que el tren ha llegado.
I know (present indicative)	*that the train has arrived.* (present perfect)
Yo **dudo**	que el tren **haya** llegado.
I doubt (present indicative)	*that the train has arrived.* (present perfect subjunctive)
El maestro sabe	que los estudiantes han estudiado.
The teacher knows	*that the students have studied.*
El maestro **espera**	que los estudiantes **hayan** estudiado.
The teacher hopes	*that the students have studied.*

NOTE The English translation of the dependent clause is the same, whether the Spanish verb is in the indicative or the subjunctive mood.

- Main clause in the present, dependent clause in present perfect subjunctive

Me alegro de que Fernando **haya estado** bien.	*I am glad that Fernando has been well.*
Enrique duda que su amigo le **haya escrito**.	*Henry doubts that his friend has written to him.*
Yo lo siento que Uds. no **hayan ido** a España.	*I regret it that you have not gone to Spain.*
Irene no piensa que su vecino **se haya quejado** de ella.	*Irene doesn't think that her neighbor has complained about her.*
¿Esperas que le **hayamos dado** el dinero al dueño?	*Do you hope that we have given the money to the owner?*
Es probable que la mujer **haya parqueado** el carro.	*It is probable that the woman has parked the car.*
¿Conocen Uds. a alguien que **haya vivido** en Japón?	*Do you know anyone who has lived in Japan?*
Nos gusta que tú **hayas tenido** éxito.	*It pleases us that you have been successful.*
Me alegro de que Uds. **se hayan divertido**.	*I am glad that you have had a good time.*

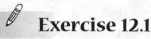 ## Exercise 12.1

Translate the following sentences into Spanish.

1. *Is it possible that they have fallen asleep?*

   _____

2. *It is probable that we have had a lot of opportunities.*

   _____

3. *We are glad that our two friends have met each other.*

   _____

4. *I'm sad that the hotel hasn't called to confirm my reservation.*

   _____

5. *José hopes that we have felt well.*

   _____

6. *The lawyer is glad that his clients have read the contract.*

   _____

7. *The engineers regret that the buildings have had problems.*

   _____

8. *The worker is sad that his boss has not called to find out where he is.*

   _____

 ## Exercise 12.2

Complete the following sentences with the correct present perfect subjunctive form of the verb in parentheses.

EXAMPLE   El hombre está triste de que su familia no lo _*haya visitado*_. (visitar)

1. Espero que Uds. _____ bien. (estar)

2. Nos alegramos mucho de que el bañero le _____ la vida a la nadadora. (salvar)

3. Miguel duda que nosotros _____ a subir la montaña. (atreverse)

4. ¿Conoces a alguien que _____ todas las obras de Shakespeare? (leer)

5. La rey quiere que su reina _____ feliz. (ser)

6. Los viajantes esperan que los trenes no _____. (demorarse)

7. Son las seis de la mañana. La mamá no piensa que sus hijos

   _____. (levantarse)

8. Son las once de la noche el sábado. Patricia espera que sus amigos

   _____ mucho en la fiesta. (divertirse)

9. Me alegro mucho de que Uds. _____ a la clase. (venir)

10. Es una lástima que el vaso _____. (romperse)

- Main clause in the future, dependent clause in the present perfect subjunctive

  If the verb in the main clause is either the future periphrastic (**ir** + **a** + *infinitive*) or the simple future, the present perfect subjunctive can be used in the dependent clause. This structure is used infrequently in everyday speech.

Será fantástico que todo el mundo **haya** leído este libro.	*It will be fantastic that everyone has read this book.*
Será importante que los chóferes **hayan aprendido** a manejar.	*It will be important that the drivers have learned to drive.*
El director esperará que los actores **hayan aprendido** el argumento.	*The director will hope that the actors have learned the script.*
Susana no irá a menos que su mejor amiga **haya ido**.	*Susan will not go unless her best friend has gone.*

📖 Reading Comprehension

La isla en el Caribe

Me alegro mucho de que mis amigos se hayan puesto tan contentos antes de mi gran viaje a verlos. Se llaman Samuel y Teresa y viven en una isla que se llama Saba.

Nos encontramos por primera vez en el Yucatán donde viajamos juntos.

Según ellos, Saba es el mejor sitio del mundo. Estoy muy emocionada de que ellos me hayan invitado a su hogar tan especial. Ella es francesa y él es de Inglaterra. Han pasado más de veinte años fuera de sus países. No sé por qué han escogido esta isla en el medio del Caribe. Nunca me han dado la razón y nadie sabe el porqué, excepto ellos.

Estoy contenta de que hayamos podido estar en contacto por tanto tiempo, comunicándonos por correo electrónico.

Arreglo mi maleta, pensando en lo que mis amigos me han dicho. Con cuidado, meto en ella bloqueador, anteojos de sol y camisas de algodón. Me dicen que llueve mucho, así que incluyo un paraguas pequeño y un impermeable. En caso de que haya sol, y esperándolo, traigo dos trajes de baño, una bata, sandalias y gafas para nadar. A ellos les gusta bucear, y a mí también. Dejo en casa mi abrigo, y escojo una chaqueta y un chaleco que compré en Guatemala. Me gusta llevar pantalones, pero voy a traer una falda también. No sé si necesitaré calcetines o botas, pero los traeré de todos modos.

Será mi primer viaje a la isla y mis amigos la describen como un paraíso, pero un paraíso sin muchas provisiones. Me piden que les lleve muchos víveres como nueces, queso, cereal y chocolate. Mi pobre maleta, cambiada a maletón, pesa mucho con toda la comida, pero llevaré todo, y con muchas ganas.

Me recogieron en el aeropuerto y fuimos a Saba a su hogar. Ellos se sentaron en el sofá. Samuel empezó a trabajar en la computadora; ella no hizo nada aquella primera noche.

Esta pareja que siempre hablaba, dejó de hablar.

Dormí bastante bien la primera noche a pesar de los insectos, reyes de la casa que andaban por toda la casa, y el sonido de la ranas más allá de mi ventana.

Samuel y Teresa, mis queridos amigos, no sé lo que les había pasado. Pasé mis vacaciones a solas. Ellos no se atrevían a salir de la casa, hasta sacar la basura. Samuel llegaba al lindero de la casa, suspiraba y volvía a la sala mientras Teresa cocinaba.

Por fin, me llevaron al aeropuerto, me dejaron allí, nos despedimos y nos separamos. Fue la última vez que los vi.

Verbos

atreverse (a)	*to dare (to)*
bucear	*to snorkel, to skin dive*
recoger	*to pick up*
suspirar	*to sigh*

Nombres

el abrigo	*the coat*
la bata	*the robe*
las botas	*the boots*
los calcetines	*the socks*
el chaleco	*the vest*
la chaqueta	*the jacket*
la falda	*the skirt*
el impermeable	*the raincoat*
el lindero	*the edge, the border*
el maletón	*the big suitcase*
la nuez, las nueces	*the nut, the nuts*
los pantalones	*the pants*
el paraguas	*the umbrella*
la rana	*the frog*
el rey	*the king*
el traje de baño	*the bathing suit*
la última vez	*the last time*

Expresiones

de todos modos	*anyway*
en caso de	*in case*
fuera de	*outside (of)*
más allá de (mi ventana)	*outside (my window)*
por fin	*at last*
por primera vez	*for the first time*

Preguntas

1. ¿Dónde está Saba?

   _____

2. ¿Cómo es la isla?

   _____

3. ¿Qué pone la persona en su maleta? ¿Por qué pesa tanto?

   _____

4. ¿Se llevaron bien?

   _____

5. ¿Van a verse de nuevo?

   _____

6. ¿La persona que viaja, es mujer u hombre?

   _____

13

The Imperfect Subjunctive

The imperfect subjunctive mood expresses past action. So far, you have studied the present subjunctive and the present perfect subjunctive. Next is the imperfect subjunctive. If the main clause begins in the past, it can cause the subjunctive in the past.

Remember that the subjunctive mood cannot exist alone. Another element in the sentence always causes it to be used. The imperfect subjunctive is used after the following elements:

- Certain impersonal expressions
- Certain verbs
- Certain conjunctions
- Certain dependent adjective clauses
- Certain expressions

Formation of the Imperfect Subjunctive

To form the imperfect subjunctive for all verbs, first drop the ending of the third-person singular of the preterit. What remains is the stem of the imperfect subjunctive for all forms.

Any irregularity in the stem of the preterit tense will have the same irregularity in the imperfect subjunctive.

Imperfect Subjunctive of -ar Verbs

To conjugate all but three **-ar** verbs in the imperfect subjunctive, begin with the third-person singular (**él**, **ella**, **Ud.**) of the preterit tense. Drop the preterit ending and add **-ara**, **-aras**, **-ara**, **-áramos**, **-arais**, **-aran** to the stem.

Infinitive	Third-Person Preterit	Imperfect Subjunctive	
bailar	bailó	yo bailara	nosotros bailáramos
		tú bailaras	vosotros bailarais
		ella bailara	ellas bailaran
cantar	cantó	yo cantara	nosotros cantáramos
		tú cantaras	vosotros cantarais
		él cantara	ellos cantaran
cerrar	cerró	yo cerrara	nosotros cerráramos
		tú cerraras	vosotros cerrarais
		Ud. cerrara	Uds. cerraran
recordar	recordó	yo recordara	nosotros recordáramos
		tú recordaras	vosotros recordarais
		él recordara	ellos recordaran

The only **-ar** verbs with different endings in the imperfect subjunctive are verbs that are irregular in the preterit: **andar**, **estar**, **dar**.

Imperfect Subjunctive of -er and -ir Verbs

To conjugate both **-er** and **-ir** verbs in the imperfect subjunctive, drop the ending from the third-person singular of the preterit to get the stem. Then add **-iera**, **-ieras**, **-iera**, **-iéramos**, **-ierais**, **-ieran** to the stem.

-Er Verbs

Infinitive	Third-Person Preterit	Imperfect Subjunctive	
beber	bebió	yo bebiera	nosotros bebiéramos
		tú bebieras	vosotros bebierais
		él bebiera	ellos bebieran
comer	comió	yo comiera	nosotros comiéramos
		tú comieras	vosotros comierais
		ella comiera	ellas comieran

Infinitive	Third-Person Preterit	Imperfect Subjunctive	
conocer	conoció	yo conociera	nosotros conociéramos
		tú conocieras	vosotros conocierais
		Ud. conociera	Uds. conocieran
entender	entendió	yo entendiera	nosotros entendiéramos
		tú entendieras	vosotros entendierais
		él entendiera	ellos entendieran
ver	vio	yo viera	nosotros viéramos
		tú vieras	vosotros vierais
		ella viera	ellas vieran
volver	volvió	yo volviera	nosotros volviéramos
		tú volvieras	vosotros volvierais
		él volviera	ellos volvieran

-Ir Verbs

Infinitive	Third-Person Preterit	Imperfect Subjunctive	
abrir	abrió	yo abriera	nosotros abriéramos
		tú abrieras	vosotros abrierais
		él abriera	ellos abrieran
escribir	escribió	yo escribiera	nosotros escribiéramos
		tú escribieras	vosotros escribierais
		ella escribiera	ellas escribieran
salir	salió	yo saliera	nosotros saliéramos
		tú salieras	vosotros salierais
		Ud. saliera	Uds. salieran
vivir	vivió	yo viviera	nosotros viviéramos
		tú vivieras	vosotros vivierais
		Ud. viviera	Uds. vivieran

-Ir verbs that are irregular in the third-person singular of the preterit show the same irregularity in the stem of the imperfect subjunctive.

Infinitive	Third-Person Preterit	Imperfect Subjunctive	
mentir	mintió	yo mintiera tú mintieras él mintiera	nosotros mintiéramos vosotros mintierais ellos mintieran
pedir	pidió	yo pidiera tú pidieras ella pidiera	nosotros pidiéramos vosotros pidierais ellas pidieran
seguir	siguió	yo siguiera tú siguieras ella siguiera	nosotros siguiéramos vosotros siguierais ellas siguieran
dormir	durmió	yo durmiera tú durmieras Ud. durmiera	nosotros durmiéramos vosotros durmierais Uds. durmieran
morirse	se murió	me muriera te murieras él se muriera	nos muriéramos os murierais ellos se murieran

A Word About Pronunciation

The stress in the imperfect subjunctive is on the second-to-last, or penultimate, syllable. As you practice, make sure you pronounce the verbs in this way: **yo cantara, tú cantaras, él cantara, nosotros cantáramos, vosotros cantarais, ellos cantaran**. If a word carries a written accent, stress the accented syllable: **nosotros cantáramos**. The more you practice, the more natural this sound becomes.

Irregular Stems in the Preterit

Verbs with irregular stems in the preterit have the same irregularity in the imperfect subjunctive. Drop the ending from the third-person singular and add **-iera**, **-ieras**, **-iera**, **-iéramos**, **-ierais**, **-ieran** to the stem.

Infinitive	Third-Person Preterit	Imperfect Subjunctive	
andar	anduvo	yo anduviera tú anduvieras él anduviera	nosotros anduviéramos vosotros anduvierais ellos anduvieran

Infinitive	Third-Person Preterit	Imperfect Subjunctive	
caber	cupo	yo cupiera	nosotros cupiéramos
		tú cupieras	vosotros cupierais
		ella cupiera	ellas cupieran
dar	dio	yo diera	nosotros diéramos
		tú dieras	vosotros dierais
		Ud. diera	Uds. dieran
estar	estuvo	yo estuviera	nosotros estuviéramos
		tú estuvieras	vosotros estuvierais
		Ud. estuviera	Uds. estuvieran
hacer	hizo	yo hiciera	nosotros hiciéramos
		tú hicieras	vosotros hicierais
		él hiciera	ellos hicieran
poder	pudo	yo pudiera	nosotros pudiéramos
		tú pudieras	vosotros pudierais
		ella pudiera	ellas pudieran
poner	puso	yo pusiera	nosotros pusiéramos
		tú pusieras	vosotros pusierais
		Ud. pusiera	Uds. pusieran
querer	quiso	yo quisiera	nosotros quisiéramos
		tú quisieras	vosotros quisierais
		él quisiera	ellos quisieran
saber	supo	yo supiera	nosotros supiéramos
		tú supieras	vosotros supierais
		ella supiera	ellas supieran
tener	tuvo	yo tuviera	nosotros tuviéramos
		tú tuvieras	vosotros tuvierais
		Ud. tuviera	Uds. tuvieran
venir	vino	yo viniera	nosotros viniéramos
		tú vinieras	vosotros vinierais
		él viniera	ellos vinieran

Irregular preterits whose stem ends in **-j** have **-eran**, not **-ieran**, in the third-person plural. Take a look at **decir**, **producir**, and **traer**.

Infinitive	Third-Person Preterit	Imperfect Subjunctive	
decir	dijo	yo dijera	nosotros dijéramos
		tú dijeras	vosotros dijerais
		ella dijera	ellas dijeran
producir	produjo	yo produjera	nosotros produjéramos
		tú produjeras	vosotros produjcrais
		Ud. produjera	Uds. produjeran
traer	trajo	yo trajera	nosotros trajéramos
		tú trajeras	vosotros trajerais
		él trajera	ellos trajeran

The conjugations for **ir** and **ser** are identical in the imperfect subjunctive. The meaning will be clarified in context.

Infinitive	Third-Person Preterit	Imperfect Subjunctive	
ser	fue	yo fuera	nosotros fuéramos
		tú fueras	vosotros fuerais
		Ud. fuera	Uds. fueran
ir	fue	yo fuera	nosotros fuéramos
		tú fueras	vosotros fuerais
		él fuera	ellos fueran

A Word About *haber*

Hubiera is the imperfect subjunctive form of **haber**, formed from the third-person singular of the preterit, **hubo**, meaning *there was, there were*.

Compound forms of verbs are conjugated in the same way as the main verb.

decir
    contradecir *to contradict*   yo contradijera, *etc.*

hacer
    deshacer *to undo*   yo deshiciera, *etc.*

poner

componer *to compose*	yo compusiera, *etc.*
proponer *to propose*	yo propusiera, *etc.*

tener

contener *to contain*	yo contuviera, *etc.*
detener *to detain*	yo detuviera, *etc.*
mantener *to maintain*	yo mantuviera, *etc.*

producir

conducir *to conduct*	yo condujera, *etc.*
traducir *to translate*	yo tradujera, *etc.*

traer

atraer *to attract*	yo atrajera, *etc.*
distraer *to distract*	yo distrajera, *etc.*

venir

prevenir *to prevent*	yo previniera, *etc.*

Uses of the Imperfect Subjunctive

When the main clause contains a verb or expression that causes the subjunctive in a dependent clause, the presence of an element in the main clause that begins in the past makes it mandatory to use the imperfect subjunctive in the dependent clause. You do not have to make any decisions, nor do you have a choice about whether or not to use it. The conditional can also cause the imperfect subjunctive in the dependent clause.

After Certain Impersonal Expressions

Certain impersonal expressions in the main clause will cause the subjunctive in the dependent clause.

If the impersonal expressions are in the preterit, the imperfect, or the conditional tense, they will cause the imperfect subjunctive in the dependent clause. Note the differences in the English translations for the dependent clauses below, depending on what is expressed by the verb in the main clause.

- Preterit

Fue una lástima que no **pudiéramos** ir a la fiesta.	*It was a shame that we were not able to go to the party.*
Fue importante que ella no **se enojara**.	*It was important that she not get angry.*
Fue posible que el hombre **colgara** el teléfono.	*It was possible that the man hung up the telephone.*

- Imperfect

Era probable que ella no **quisiera** ir al dentista.	*It was probable that she didn't want to go to the dentist.*
Era posible que el estudiante **supiera** la respuesta.	*It was possible that the student knew the answer.*
Era posible que Octavio la **conociera** en Madrid.	*It was possible that Octavio met her in Madrid.*

- Conditional

¿**Sería** posible que su esposo **tuviera** razón?	*Would it be possible that her husband was right?*
¿**Sería** posible que Isabel **se fuera**?	*Would it be possible that Isabel went away?*
¿**Sería** posible que **cocinaras** esta noche?	*Would it be possible for you to cook tonight?*
Sería necesario que la policía **capturara** el criminal.	*It would be necessary that the police force capture the criminal.*

Exercise 13.1

Complete the following sentences with the correct imperfect subjunctive form of the verb in parentheses, then translate the sentence.

EXAMPLES   Fue fantástico que nosotros ___*tuviéramos*___ éxito. (tener)
It was fantastic that we were successful.

Era imposible que Octavio ___*durmiera*___ bien anoche. (dormir)
It was impossible that Octavio slept well last night.

¿Sería posible que ellos me ___*vieran*___ en el teatro? (ver)
Would it be possible that they saw me in the theater?

1. Fue importante que Jaime me _____. (hablar)

2. Era una lástima que ella no _____ bien anoche. (sentirse)

3. ¿Fue posible que Uds. _____ a mi hermana? (conocer)

4. Fue necesario que nosotros _____ ejercicios. (hacer)

5. Era imposible que no _____ tráfico hoy. (haber)

6. Fue urgente que la ambulancia _____ dentro de cinco minutos. (llegar)

7. Era posible que nosotros le _____ un regalo a la maestra. (dar)

8. Fue dudoso que mi sobrina me _____ la verdad; fue posible que me _____. (decir/mentir)

9. Sería bueno que Uds. _____. (mejorarse)

10. Era probable que toda la clase _____. (graduarse)

11. Sería imposible que Sara _____ sin decirnos nada. (irse)

12. Fue bueno que nosotros la _____. (llamar)

13. Sería necesario que los turistas _____ mucha agua en las montañas. (tomar)

14. Sería dudoso que nosotros _____ a México este año. (viajar)

15. Fue posible que Beatriz e Isabel _____ en Italia. (quedarse)

After Certain Verbs

Review the verbs that cause the subjunctive mood in a dependent clause, namely, verbs that express wishes and preferences; verbs that express hope, regret and emotion; verbs that express orders; and verbs that express uncertainty. These verbs in the main clause will cause the subjunctive mood in the dependent clause. If the main clause is in the preterit, the imperfect, or the conditional, the dependent clause will be in the imperfect subjunctive.

- Preterit

  Yo **quise** que Ud. **cantara**.
  I wanted you to sing. (literally, *I wanted that you sang.*)

  Mi suegra **se alegró** de que yo la **visitara**.
  My mother-in-law was happy that I visited her.

  Tu amigo te **pidió** que lo **llamaras**.
  Your friend asked you to call him.

Los padres de Paula le **exigieron** que ella **compartiera** sus juguetes.	*Paula's parents demanded that she share her toys.*

- Imperfect

Yo **esperaba** que él **tuviera** tiempo.	*I hoped that he had time.*
Julieta **esperaba** que Romeo **viniera** a verla.	*Juliet hoped that Romeo would come to see her.*
Esperábamos que Uds. **pudieran** pasar sus vacaciones con nosotros.	*We were hoping that you would be able to spend your vacation with us.*

- Conditional

Los padres **desearían** que sus hijos **jugaran** en el parque.	*The parents would want their children to play in the park.*
¿A Ud. le **molestaría** que yo **fumara**?	*Would it bother you that I smoke?*
Yo **preferiría** que él no **viniera**.	*I would prefer that he not come.*

A Word About the English Translations

You can see that English translations of the imperfect subjunctive are not exact. Just remember that if you start out in either the past (preterit or imperfect) or the conditional in the main clause, the verb or impersonal expression will cause the imperfect subjunctive in the dependent clause.

Exercise 13.2

Translate the following sentences into English. In these sentences, the verb in the main clause is in the preterit and the verb in the dependent clause is in the imperfect subjunctive.

1. Quise que ellas me escribieran.

_____

2. Mi vecino prefirió que yo no le trajera nada.

_____

3. Nos alegramos de que él llegara temprano.

_____

4. Ella nos rogó que no nos fuéramos.

_____

5. Me alegré de que te mudaras a una casa.

_____

6. El dueño insistió en que pagáramos la renta.

_____

7. Yo le dije a mi amigo que me llamara.

_____

8. El turista le sugirió al taxista que no condujera tan rápido.

_____

Exercise 13.3

Complete the following sentences with the correct imperfect subjunctive form of the verb in parentheses. In these sentences, the verb in the main clause is in the preterit.

EXAMPLE   El abogado insistió en que la mujer __*fuera*__ a la corte. (ser)

1. Yo quise que Julio me _____ en español. (hablar)

2. Julio me aconsejó que yo _____ más. (estudiar)

3. Susana insistió en que su primo _____ con su hermano. (bailar)

4. Manuel no quiso que su esposa _____ en el cabaret. (cantar)

5. Me alegré de que Uds. _____ a la clase. (venir)

Exercise 13.4

Complete the following sentences with the correct imperfect subjunctive form of the verb in parentheses. In these sentences, the verb in the main clause is in the imperfect.

1. Ella quería que sus padres _____ en Nueva York. (quedarse)

2. La madre no quería que nosotros le _____ flores. (traer)

3. La doctora le aconsejaba al paciente que _____ menos. (comer)

4. El hombre le sugería que Ud. me _____ el libro. (prestar)

5. La mujer esperaba que nosotros la _____. (ayudar)

6. Los candidatos nos rogaban que _____ por ellos. (votar)

 ## Exercise 13.5

Complete the following sentences with the correct imperfect subjunctive form of the verb in parentheses. In these sentences, the verb in the main clause is in the conditional.

1. El dentista esperaría que sus pacientes _____ en su oficina a las nueve de la mañana. (estar)

2. Me gustaría que tú _____. (callarse)

3. Ella se alegraría de que nosotros lo _____. (hacer)

4. Te gustaría que yo te _____ al tren esta noche? (acompañar)

Exercise 13.6

Translate the following sentences into English.

1. El muchacho quería que sus padres le trajeran un regalo.

   _____

2. Los amigos de Miguel querían que él perdiera peso.

   _____

3. ¿Para qué querían Uds. que yo les prestara dinero?

   _____

4. Federico esperaba que Linda se casara con él.

   _____

5. La estudiante en España se alegró de que sus padres estuvieran orgullosos de ella.

   _____

6. Yo quise que ellos se quedaran conmigo.

   _____

7. Esperábamos que no fuera nada grave.

   _____

8. El marido no quería que su esposa se jubilara.

   _____

 ## Exercise 13.7

Complete the following sentences with either the infinitive or the correct imperfect subjunctive form of the verb in parentheses. Read the sentences and questions carefully.

EXAMPLE   El hombre flaco no quería __*comer*__ el helado. (comer)

1. Yo no quería _____ en el tren. Me gusta _____ en la ducha. (cantar/cantar)

2. Es importante _____ bien para _____ bien. (comer/vivir)

3. Fue importante que los doctores _____ a los pacientes. (cuidar)

4. El hombre esperaba que sus vecinos _____ de escuchar música en alto volumen. (dejar)

5. ¿Por qué me dijiste que yo te _____? (esperar)

6. Susana le pidió a su hijo que _____. (acostarse)

7. La mujer no quiso _____ en el ascensor. (bajar)

8. Antes de _____ a México, Antonio llamó a sus amigos. (viajar)

9. Yo no creía que _____ la verdad. (ser)

10. ¿Qué querías tú que yo te _____? (decir)

📖 Reading Comprehension

El barco económico

Lucía siempre tenía ganas de ir a las Islas Galápagos y quería que su buen amigo la acompañara, pero no quiso. Después de haberlo pensado bien, decidió ir sola, primero a Quito, capital de Ecuador. Ella conoció a mucha gente en la ciudad, exploró los vecindarios durante el día; por la noche volvía a su hotel que le costaba cinco dólares. Ella comía el desayuno en una cafetería, el almuerzo en otra, y cenaba en un buen restaurante en el centro. Esperaba que alguien pasara por allí, que la viera sentada, que entrara en el restaurante, y que hablara con ella. Esperaba que los dos se llevaran bien y que él quisiera ir con ella a la isla.

Al fin y al cabo, Lucía viajó a Guayaquil, la entrada de las islas, y la salida de los barcos y cruceros. En la agencia de viajes, le sugirieron que fuera en barco económico con un grupo pequeño de aventureros. "Costaría menos," dijo la agente, "y sería más divertido el viaje." La agente la convenció.

La mujer tomó la decisión, compró su pasaje de ida y vuelta para el próximo día, y después de una noche inquieta e indecisa, abordó el barco chiquito. Aquella primera noche, el barco salió, y entre las olas, la tormenta, y el huracán, los ocho pasajeros pasaron la noche mareados bajo las estrellas centelleantes del cielo.

Verbos

abordar	*to board*
convencer	*to convince*
llevarse (bien)	*to get along (well)*
tener ganas	*to desire*

Nombres

el huracán	*the hurricane*
las olas	*the waves*
la tormenta	*the storm*
el vecindario	*the neighborhood*

Adjetivos

centelleante	*twinkling*
inquieto	*unquiet, agitated*
mareado	*seasick*

Expresiones

al fin y al cabo	*after all*
e indecisa	*and indecisive* (When expressing *and* in Spanish, **e** replaces **y** before a word that begins with an emphasized **i-** or **hi-**.)
el pasaje de ida y vuelta	*round-trip ticket*

Preguntas

1. ¿Cuántos pasajeros hay en el barco económico?

   _____

2. ¿Adónde fue Lucía?

   _____

3. ¿A ella le gustó Quito?

   _____

4. ¿Quién habló con ella en el restaurante?

   _____

5. ¿Qué decidió hacer?

   _____

6. ¿Piensa Ud. que los pasajeros se van a divertir?

   _____

After Certain Conjunctions

The subjunctive form follows certain conjunctions if the main clause has a different subject from the dependent clause.

Ella les enseñó a sus estudiantes **para que** ellos **aprendieran**.	*The professor taught her students so that they learned.*
Antes de que él **fuera** a España, le vendimos su boleto.	*Before he went to Spain, we sold him his ticket.*
En caso de que ellos te **llamaran**, ¿qué les dirías?	*In case they called you, what would you say to them?*
A pesar de que Emil le **diera** flores, la mujer no aceptó su invitación.	*In spite of the fact that Emil gave her flowers, the woman didn't accept his invitation.*

| Yo no lo haría **sin que** Uds. me **ayudaran**. | *I wouldn't do it without your helping me.* |
| Yo te iba a esperar **hasta que** **llegaras**. | *I was going to wait for you until you arrived.* |

After Certain Dependent Adjective Clauses

The subjunctive mood is used in a dependent clause if the object or person described in the main clause of a sentence is indefinite or nonexistent. In the following examples, the objects and persons described in the main clause are not known.

¿Conoció Ud. a **alguien** que **supiera** hablar chino?	*Did you meet anyone who knew how to speak Chinese?*
Yo había buscado una **piscina** que **quedara** cerca de mi casa.	*I had looked for a pool that was located near my house.*
Nunca encontramos a **nadie** que siempre **tuviera** razón.	*We never found anyone who was always right.*

After Certain Expressions

- **ojalá**

  An interjection of Arabic origin, **ojalá** means *would to God that* or *may God grant that* and expresses great desire. It can also be translated as *I hope*.

Ojalá que fuera verdad.	*Would to God that it were true.*
Ojalá que Uds. vivieran aquí conmigo.	*Would to God that you lived here with me.*
Ojalá que pudiera hacerlo.	*I hope that you were able to do it.*

- **como si**

  A verb that follows **como si** (*as if*) will be in the imperfect subjunctive. The verb in the main clause can be in the present, the past, or the conditional.

| Ud. le trata como si **fuera** niño. | *You treat him as if he were a child.* |
| El hombre lo describe como si **estuviera** allí. | *The man describes it as if he were there.* |

Carla nos dio las direcciones como si **supiéramos** el camino.	*Carla gave us directions as if we knew the way.*
Los hombres nos saludaron como si nos **conocieran**.	*The men greeted us as if they knew us.*
Los hombres nos hablaban como si los **conociéramos**.	*The men spoke to us as if we knew them.*
Pietro hablaría como si **tuviera** razón.	*Pietro would speak as if he were right.*

- **quisiera**

  The verb **querer** can be used in the imperfect subjunctive in a main clause, where it is used to soften statements and questions. This form changes the translation of *I want,* for example, to *I would like.*

yo quisiera	nosotros quisiéramos
tú quisieras	vosotros quisierais
Ud. quisiera	Uds. quisieran

  Compare the meanings of the following pairs of sentences:

Quiero más café, por favor.	*I want more coffee, please.*
Quisiera más café, por favor.	*I would like more coffee, please.*
Queremos ir contigo al aeropuerto.	*We want to go with you to the airport.*
Quisiéramos ir contigo.	*We would like to go with you.*
¿Quieres pedir prestado mi libro?	*Do you want to borrow my book?*
¿Quisieras pedirlo prestado?	*Would you like to borrow it?*

- **pudiera**

  The imperfect subjunctive form of **poder** can be used independently in a main clause. It is used to soften statements, for example, **puedo** (*I can, I am able*) to **yo pudiera** (*I could, I would be able*).

yo pudiera	nosotros pudiéramos
tú pudieras	vosotros pudierais
ella pudiera	ellas pudieran

  Compare the meanings of the following pairs of sentences:

¿Puedes prestarme diez dólares?	*Can you lend me ten dollars?*
¿Pudieras prestarme diez dólares?	*Could you lend me ten dollars?*

¿Nos puede dar mil dólares?   *Can you give us a thousand dollars?*

¿Nos pudiera Ud. dar mil dólares?   *Could you give us a thousand dollars?*

Exercise 13.8

Complete the following sentences with either the infinitive or the correct imperfect subjunctive form of the verb in parentheses.

1. Sara habla sin _____ nada. (saber)

2. La mamá prendió las luces para que sus hijos _____ ver. (poder)

3. Él baila como si _____ un bailarín profesional. (ser)

4. Ojalá que ella _____ hoy. (venir)

5. ¿Había alguien que _____ todas las capitales de los Estados Unidos? (saber)

6. Dolores preparó la comida antes de _____. (ducharse)

7. Ella preparó la comida antes de que su hijo _____ para la escuela. (salir)

8. El niño no quiere _____ las manos antes de _____. (lavarse/comer)

9. Elena y su hermana viajan como si _____ mucho dinero. (tener)

10. Ojalá que Fernando nos _____ la verdad. (decir)

11. Isabel nos contó todo como si ella _____ allí. (estar)

12. Antes de _____ a España, él estudió por dos años. (ir)

13. Íbamos a jugar tenis hasta que _____ a llover. (empezar)

14. La enfermera no le daría medicina a la paciente a menos que ella la _____. (necesitar)

Exercise 13.9

Rewrite the following sentences in the past tense. Make sure you read the main clause carefully to see whether the subjunctive is necessary in the dependent clause.

EXAMPLES   Yo sé que el tren viene.   *Yo sabía que el tren venía.*

Yo dudo que el tren venga.   *Yo dudaba que el tren viniera.*

1. Laura quiere que su esposo la acompañe a Chile.

   _____

2. Es necesario que la gente no fume en los edificios.

   _____

3. Julia está contenta de que Uds. estén aquí.

   _____

4. Yo sé que su nieta quiere ir a la universidad.

   _____

5. Me alegro de que puedas correr en el maratón.

   _____

6. ¿Qué quieres que yo haga?

   _____

7. Raúl y yo esperamos que Uds. se encuentren bien.

   _____

8. ¿Es importante que el carpintero sepa lo que está haciendo?

   _____

9. Espero que el vuelo de mis amigos llegue a tiempo.

   _____

10. Los deportistas dudan que ganemos el partido.

    _____

11. Nuestros amigos nos ruegan que no subamos a la cumbre de la montaña.

    _____

12. Los entrenadores insisten en que la gente haga más ejercicio.

    _____

Exercise 13.10

Translate the following sentences into Spanish.

1. *It was necessary that she begin the lessons on time.*

   _____

2. *It was a pity that he didn't know how to express himself.*

   _____

3. *Would it be possible that they had already left the reunion?*

   _____

4. *Joann's children begged her not to smoke.*

   _____

5. *Would you like me to speak with your boss?*

   _____

6. *My brother doubted that I sang well yesterday.*

   _____

7. *My daughter's teacher suggested that I call her.*

   _____

8. *I wanted them to stay with me. They wanted me to go with them.*

   _____

9. *I would like to make a documentary that is about the Incas.*

   _____

10. *I want to take your photo, if you don't mind.*

    _____

After *si* in a Contrary-to-Fact *si*-clause

When you express the idea that an action would happen (conditional tense) *if* another action occurred in the past, the imperfect subjunctive is used in the clause that begins with **si**.

Si él tuviera más tiempo, me traería flores.	*If he had more time, he would bring me flowers.*

Si Ud. anduviera más rápido,
llegaría a tiempo.

*If you walked more quickly,
you would arrive on time.*

¿**Si yo** te **diera** un regalo,
lo aceptarías?

*If I gave you a present,
would you accept it?*

Si Ricardo bailara mejor,
su compañera estaría contenta.

*If Richard danced better,
his companion would be happy.*

A Word About the *si*-clause in the Present

A **si**-clause used with a present tense verb never causes the subjunctive. When you express the idea that an action will happen (future tense) *if* another action occurs in the present, the imperfect subjunctive is not used.

Si tú vas, yo iré también.

If you go, I will go too.

Si ellos vienen a verme, estaré
contenta.

*If they come to see me, I will be
happy.*

Si Lola quiere asistir a una
universidad, sus padres
pagarán el primer año.

*If Lola wants to attend a university,
her parents will pay the first year.*

In the following examples, a clause whose verb is in the conditional tense begins the sentence. Note that the imperfect subjunctive follows the word **si**. It doesn't matter whether the sentence begins with the conditional tense or the **si**-clause, the subjunctive always follows **si**.

Yo iría a la fiesta **si tú fueras**
también.

*I would go to the party if you
were going also.*

Mi hermano me vería más,
si viviera cerca.

*My brother would see me more
if he lived close by.*

Podríamos hacer la tarea
si tuviéramos más tiempo.

*We would be able to do the
homework if we had more time.*

Habría más gente en la playa
si hiciera calor.

*There would be more people
at the beach if it were hot.*

Iríamos a verla **si** nos **invitara**.

*We would go to see her if she
invited us.*

¿Me harías un préstamo **si yo
prometiera** devolvértelo?

*Would you give me a loan if I
promised to return it to you?*

Exercise 13.11

*Complete the following sentences with the correct form of the verbs in parentheses. Each sentence requires both the conditional and the imperfect subjunctive verb forms. Remember that the imperfect subjunctive follows the **si**-clause.*

EXAMPLES   ¿Qué __*haría*__ Ud. si sus amigos le __*dijeran*__ una mentira? (hacer/decir)

Si no __*hubiera*__ tráfico, __*podríamos*__ salir más tarde. (haber/poder)

1. Si Fernando _____ más alto, _____ deportista. (ser/ser)

2. Si a María le _____ bailar, _____ a fiestas. (gustar/ir)

3. Si nosotros le _____ cartas, nuestro amigo nos

   _____. (escribir/responder)

4. Si yo _____ mejor, yo _____ reírme. (sentirse/poder)

5. Los artistas _____ más dinero, si _____

   sus pinturas. (ganar/vender)

6. Los médicos dicen que los insomnes _____ mejor

   si _____ a la misma hora cada noche. (dormir/acostarse).

7. Nosotros _____ con soltura si _____ todos los verbos. (hablar/saber)

8. La muchacha no _____ frío si _____ la chaqueta. (tener/ponerse)

9. El niño no _____ tanto si no le _____ el estómago. (llorar/doler)

10. Yo no _____ si Ud. _____ que yo

    _____. (irse/querer/quedarse)

If the sentence or question includes the word **si** in a sentence that is not contrary-to-fact, but rather is simply a statement, the subjunctive is not used.

Si yo **he dicho** algo indiscreto,   *If I have said something*
    lo siento.   *indiscreet, I am sorry.*

| Si ellos **han completado** el curso, los felicito. | *If they have completed the course, I congratulate them.* |
| Si Jaime **estaba** aquí, no lo vimos. | *If James was here, we didn't see him.* |

📖 Reading Comprehension

Xochicalco
(The place of the flowers)

Si Leonora pudiera viajar al pasado, ella viajaría al décimo siglo para averiguar por qué casi todos los centros de los mayas se habían desaparecido acerca del año 900 A.D. Nadie sabe la causa, según ella. Pienso que ella habría sido una buena arqueóloga por su curiosidad, pero me dijo que jamás le gustaba la idea de excavar la tierra, ni con máquinas, ni con las manos. Prefiere andar por las ruinas, sintiendo como era la vida en la edad de los mayas.

¿Has oído de Xochicalco, cerca de Cuernavaca, México? Supongo que no. Es poco conocido, pero magnífico, dice ella. La estructura principal se llama 'la serpiente emplumada' y ella se quedaba horas mirándola, tratando de entender lo que significa el arte del templo.

Me contó que quería subir la pirámide de Quetzalcóatl, pero no pudo. Un guía la vio intentar y la mostró como se hace. En vez de ascender recto, como hace casi toda la gente, él le dijo que subiera y bajara zigzagueando. De esta manera, escaló rápida y fácilmente.

¿Has oído de Ceibal en Guatemala? Por fin, Leonora fue con otro fanático de los mayas y estaba muy feliz con su compañero. Viajaron por barco por el Río Pasión. Me habría gustado acompañarla también, pero ella no pensaba en mí. De todos modos, ella y su amigo se enteraron que Ceibal, poblado en 900 B.C. y abandonado en 900 A.D., habría podido ser el centro de la civilización maya. En un sitio bien escondido, vieron estatuas de hombres negros y otras que parecían ser judíos. Estoy seguro que se divirtieron mucho.

Leonora quería que yo te recomendara otros sitios fantásticos para explorar. En el Yucatán, sería una maravilla que visitaras las ruinas de Tulum en la costa de México, o Chitzén Itzá entre Cancún y Mérida, Uxmal donde se ve estatuas de Chac, el dios de la lluvia, o Tikal, en Guatemala, una de las más grandes de todas. Y si vas, no te olvides de mí y el secreto del zigzag.

Verbos

averiguar	*to find out, to verify*
enterarse	*to become informed*
escalar	*to climb*
excavar	*to excavate, to dig*
suponer	*to suppose*
zigzaguear	*to zigzag*

Preguntas

1. ¿Es hombre o mujer el narrador/la narradora?

   _____

2. ¿Cuántas personas hay en el cuento?

   _____

3. ¿Cuántas ruinas menciona la persona principal?

   _____

4. De las ruinas mencionadas en esta narración, ¿cuál es la más antigua?

   _____

14

The Past Perfect Subjunctive

The past perfect subjunctive, also called the pluperfect subjunctive, is often translated the same as the indicative past perfect tense in English, for example, *I had eaten*. Like all subjunctives, this form must be caused by a verb or expression that causes the use of the subjunctive mood in the dependent clause.

Formation of the Past Perfect Subjunctive

The past perfect subjunctive is a compound verb form. To form the past perfect subjunctive, use the imperfect subjunctive of the helping verb **haber** and follow it with the past participle of the main verb.

yo hubiera contestado	*I had answered*
tú hubieras hablado	*you had spoken*
ella hubiera escrito	*she had written*
nosotros hubiéramos ido	*we had gone*
vosotros hubierais estudiado	*you had studied*
ellas hubieran votado	*they had voted*

Uses of the Past Perfect Subjunctive

The past perfect subjunctive expresses action that happened before another action occurred. As you know, the subjunctive mood cannot exist alone. An element in the main clause causes the subjunctive in the dependent clause.

After Certain Verbs

Certain verbs cause the subjunctive in a dependent clause. If the verb in the main clause is in the past (imperfect or preterit), these verbs can cause the past perfect subjunctive in the dependent clause.

Yo **esperaba**	que el avión **hubiera** llegado.
I hoped (imperfect)	*that the plane had arrived.*
	(past perfect subjunctive)

Rosario **quería**	que hubiéramos pagado la cuenta.
Rosario wanted	*that we had paid the bill.*
(imperfect)	(past perfect subjunctive)

Me **alegré**	de que ella **hubiera** vuelto.
I was glad (preterit)	*that she had returned.* (past perfect subjunctive)

Ella dudaba que sus amigos hubieran tenido razón.	*She doubted that her friends had been right.*
Yo no creía que el alcalde te hubiera reconocido.	*I didn't believe that the mayor had recognized you.*
El niño temía que su madre se hubiera ido.	*The child feared that his mother had gone.*
Lo sentimos que Uds. no se hubieran sentido bien.	*We were sorry that you had not felt well.*

After Certain Impersonal Expressions

Certain impersonal expressions in the main clause cause the subjunctive in a dependent clause. If these expressions are in the past, they can cause the past perfect subjunctive in the dependent clause.

Fue **posible** que los niños se **hubieran** dormido.	*It was possible that the children had fallen asleep.*
Era importante que yo hubiera asistido a la conferencia en México.	*It was important that I had attended the conference in Mexico.*

• After **ojalá**

The past perfect subjunctive is used to express a contrary-to-fact wish in the past with **ojalá**.

Ojalá que yo hubiera sabido.	*I wish that I had known. / Would to God that I had known.*

Ojalá que la hubiéramos encontrado.	*Would to God that we had found her.*
Ojalá que ellos se hubieran quedado.	*Would to God that they had stayed.*

- **quisiera**

  The use of the imperfect subjunctive of **querer**, most often **quisiera**, in the main clause can cause the past perfect subjunctive in the dependent clause.

La niña quisiera que su mamá le hubiera dado un caballo para su cumpleaños.	*The child wished that her mother had given her a horse for her birthday.*
Ellos quisieran que el hotel hubiera tenido una piscina.	*They wished that the hotel had had a swimming pool.*
¿Quisieras tú que yo te hubiera dicho la verdad?	*Did you wish that I had told you the truth?*

Exercise 14.1

Complete the following sentences with the correct past perfect subjunctive form of the verb in parentheses. In these sentences, the main clause is in the imperfect or preterit. Note the element that causes the use of this mood.

EXAMPLE   Era importante que nosotros __hubiéramos recibido__ el cheque. (recibir)

1. Jorge no estaba seguro que nosotros _____ la cuenta. (pagar)

2. Ella esperaba que nosotros _____ una cita con su hija. (hacer)

3. Yo no podía creer que mi amigo _____ tal cosa. (decir)

4. No había nadie en la fiesta que _____ por todo el mundo. (viajar)

5. La princesa nunca creía que su príncipe _____. (venir)

6. Deseábamos que no _____ tanto. (llover)

7. Elena se alegró mucho de que Uds. _____. (mejorarse)

8. Sus parientes sintieron mucho que Irene y Gustavo no

_____. (casarse)

9. Roberto dudaba que nosotros _____ todo el dinero.
(gastar)

10. Yo no pensaba que las flores _____. (vivir)

Exercise 14.2

Translate the following sentences into English.

1. Ojalá que no se lo hubiéramos dicho.

_____

2. Ojalá que Uds. hubieran estado bien.

_____

3. Ojalá que hubiéramos ido de vacaciones.

_____

4. Fue necesario que el carpintero lo hubiera construido.

_____

5. Fue urgente que nosotros hubiéramos llevado al hombre enfermo al hospital.

_____

6. Era una lástima que nadie hubiera estado en el teatro.

_____

7. Esperábamos que todo el mundo se hubiera aprovechado de la situación.

_____

8. Los porteros dudaban que los inquilinos nuevos hubieran pintado las paredes.

_____

9. El abogado no pensaba que sus clientes hubieran ganado.

_____

10. Fue posible que los ladrones hubieran robado el banco.

_____

The Contrary-to-Fact Conditional *si*-clause in the Past

When you express the idea that an action would have happened (conditional perfect tense) *if* another action had occurred in the past, the past perfect subjunctive follows the clause that begins with **si**.

Review the conditional perfect tense:

yo habría hecho	*I would have done*
tú habrías comido	*you would have eaten*
ella habría hablado	*she would have spoken*
nosotros habríamos escrito	*we would have written*
vosotros habríais cocinado	*you would have cooked*
ellas habrían contestado	*they would have answered*

The **si**-clause expresses the idea that something would have happened if something else had happened. Remember that the subjunctive form follows **si**.

Si yo **hubiera** tenido más tiempo, yo habría ido a verlo.	*If I had had more time, I would have gone to see him.*
Si Paulo **hubiera seguido** las direcciones, él habría llegado a tiempo.	*If Paul had followed the directions, he would have arrived on time.*
Ella habría sabido la respuesta **si hubiera leído** el cuento.	*She would have known the answer if she had read the short story.*
Habríamos mirado la película **si hubiéramos podido** hallar la grabación.	*We would have watched the movie if we had been able to find the tape.*

A Word About the *si*-clause

In everyday speech, the perfect conditional (for example, **habría hecho**) is sometimes replaced by the past perfect subjunctive (**hubiera hecho**). In these sentences, when a **si**-clause is present, both clauses will contain the same tense—the past perfect subjunctive.

Compare the following sentences to the ones you have just studied. Note that the English translations are the same. Both forms are correct.

Si él **hubiera tenido** más tiempo, yo **habría ido** a verlo.	*If he had had more time, I would have gone to see him.*
Si él **hubiera tenido** más tiempo, yo **hubiera ido** a verlo.	*If he had had more time, I would have gone to see him.*

Si Paulo **hubiera seguido** las direcciones, él **habría llegado** a tiempo.	*If Paul had followed the directions, he would have arrived on time.*
Si Paulo **hubiera seguido** las direcciones, él **hubiera llegado** a tiempo.	*If Paul had followed the directions, he would have arrived on time.*
Carmen **habría sabido** la respuesta si **hubiera leído** el cuento.	*Carmen would have known the answer if she had read the story.*
Carmen **hubiera sabido** la respuesta si **hubiera leído** el cuento.	*Carmen would have known the answer if she had read the story.*
Si Ana **hubiera puesto** las gafas en la mesa, ella las **habría encontrado**.	*If Ana had put the eyeglasses on the table, she would have found them.*
Si Ana **hubiera puesto** las gafas en la mesa, ella las **hubiera encontrado**.	*If Ana had put the eyeglasses on the table, she would have found them.*

Exercise 14.3

Review the conditional perfect tense, then translate the following sentences into Spanish. Remember that object pronouns are placed directly before the verb form and are never attached to the past participle.

EXAMPLE   *We would have eaten.*   Habríamos comido.

1. *I would have gone.* _____

2. *You would have eaten.* _____

3. *We would have laughed.* _____

4. *They would have told you.* _____

5. *The teachers would have taught.* _____

6. *Marisa would have been happy.* _____

7. *Hillary would have been president.* _____

8. *It would have been possible.* _____

9. *The women would have learned it.* _____

10. *The men would have left.* _____

Exercise 14.4

Translate the following sentences into Spanish. These sentences include a contrary-to-fact **si**-*clause.*

EXAMPLE   *We would have eaten in the restaurant if we had gone there before.*

Habríamos comido en el restaurante si hubiéramos ido

allá antes.

1. *I would have gone to the party if I had not been afraid.*

   _____

2. *You (Ud.) would have eaten the fish if we had cooked it at home.*

   _____

3. *We would have laughed if the movie had been funny.*

   _____

4. *They would have told you the truth if you (tú) had wanted to know it.*

   _____

5. *The teachers would have taught if the students had arrived.*

   _____

6. *Marisa would have been happy if she had known how to skate.*

   _____

7. *Hillary would have been president if more people had voted for her.*

   _____

8. *It would have been possible that they had seen me.*

   _____

9. *The women would have learned it if they had bought the book.*

   _____

10. *The men would have left the house if they had had somewhere to go.*

   _____

Reference Chart:
Sequence of Tenses with the Subjunctive Mood

If the verb in the main clause is in the present or future, the verb in the dependent clause can be in the present subjunctive.

Present and Future		Present Subjunctive
PRESENT INDICATIVE	Ud. espera	que su amiga llame.
PRESENT PERFECT	Ud. ha esperado	que su amiga llame.
PRESENT PROGRESSIVE	Ud. está esperando	que su amiga llame.
SIMPLE FUTURE	Ud. esperará	que su amiga llame.
FUTURE PERIPHRASTIC	Ud. va a esperar	que su amiga llame.
IMPERATIVE	Espere (Ud.)	que su amiga llame.

If the verb in the main clause is in the present or future, the verb in the dependent clause can be in the present perfect subjunctive, depending on the meaning you want to express.

Present and Future		Present Perfect Subjunctive
PRESENT INDICATIVE	Yo espero	que Sara haya llamado.
PRESENT PERFECT	He esperado	que ella haya llamado.
PRESENT PROGRESSIVE	Estoy esperando	que Juan haya llamado.
SIMPLE FUTURE	Esperaré	que ellos hayan llamado.
FUTURE PERIPHRASTIC	Voy a esperar	que tú hayas llamado.
IMPERATIVE	Espere (Ud.)	que él haya llamado.

If the verb in the main clause is in the past (imperfect or preterit) or conditional, the verb in the dependent clause can be in the imperfect subjunctive.

Past and Conditional		Imperfect Subjunctive
IMPERFECT	Ud. insistía	que él cantara.
PRETERIT	Ud. insistió	que el cantante cantara.
PAST PERFECT	Ud. había insistido	que el cantante cantara.
PAST PROGRESSIVE	Ud. estaba insistiendo	que ellos cantaran.
	Ud. estuvo insistiendo	que ellos cantaran.
CONDITIONAL	Ud. insistiría	que cantáramos.
PERFECT CONDITIONAL	Ud. habría insistido	que la cantante cantara.

If the verb in the main clause is in the past (imperfect or preterit) or conditional, the verb in the dependent clause can be in the past perfect subjunctive.

Past and Conditional		Past Perfect Subjunctive
IMPERFECT	Ud. insistía	que la bailarina hubiera bailado.
PRETERIT	Ud. insistió	que el bailarín hubiera bailado.
PAST PERFECT	Ud. había insistido	que ellos hubieran bailado.
PAST PROGRESSIVE	Ud. estaba insistiendo	que todos hubieran bailado.
	Ud. estuvo insistiendo	que todos hubieran bailado.
CONDITIONAL	Ud. insistiría	que hubiéramos bailado.
PERFECT CONDITIONAL	Ud. habría insistido	que yo hubiera bailado.

 Exercise 14.5

Complete the following sentences with the correct present subjunctive form of the verb in parentheses. The verb in the main clause is in the present tense.

EXAMPLE   Te digo que _te cuides_. (cuidarse)

1. Espero que Uds. _____ bien. (estar)

2. Nos alegramos mucho de que el hombre _____ en el maratón. (correr)

3. El cocinero espera que te _____ su comida. (gustar)

4. Te digo que no _____. (quejarse)

5. Es imposible que nosotros _____ todo. (saber)

6. Dudamos que los inquilinos le _____ al dueño. (ganar)

7. Ojalá que los huéspedes _____. (venir)

8. ¿Hay alguien aquí que _____ cien dólares? (tener)

9. Espero que Uds. _____ bien. (sentirse)

10. La pareja sugiere que los invitados _____ bien. (vestirse)

Exercise 14.6

Complete the following sentences with the correct present subjunctive form of the verb in parentheses. The verb in the main clause is in the imperative.

1. Dile al niño que _____. (acostarse)

2. Dígale al taxista que nos _____ a nuestro destino. (llevar)

3. Pídele al hombre malo que _____. (irse)

4. Aconséjenles a los acusados que _____ un buen abogado. (conseguir)

5. Deja que ellos _____. (entrar)

6. No permitas que los niños _____. (caerse)

Exercise 14.7

*Complete the following sentences with the correct present subjunctive form of the verb in parentheses. The verb in the main clause is in the simple future or future periphrastic (**ir** + **a** + infinitive).*

1. ¿Será imposible que los adolescentes _____ a sus padres? (escuchar)

2. Susana no irá a menos que su mejor amigo _____. (ir)

3. Voy a pedir que la gente no _____ más. (fumar)

4. Margarita insistirá que su compañero _____ el oficio de la casa. (hacer)

5. El juego no se acabará hasta que la mujer gorda _____. (cantar)

Exercise 14.8

Complete the following sentences with the correct present subjunctive form of the verb in parentheses. The verb in the main clause is in the present perfect.

1. Yo he querido que Uds. _____ a mi novio. (conocer)

2. ¿Has deseado que tu familia _____ viajar contigo? (poder)

3. Le hemos dicho a la juventud que _____ ocho horas cada noche. (dormir)

4. Juana les ha sugerido a sus padres que no _____ tanto. (trabajar)

5. Las dos familias han esperado siempre que sus hijos _____ felices. (ser)

6. ¿Quién se ha alegrado de que sus enemigos _____ éxito? (tener)

7. Ha sido difícil que la gente _____ construir una casa nueva. (lograr)

8. Ha sido bueno que nosotros _____ todo. (aprender)

Exercise 14.9

Complete the following sentences with the correct imperfect subjunctive form of the verb in parentheses. The verb in the main clause is in the preterit.

1. Fue necesario que los bomberos _____ en la casa quemada. (entrar)

2. El soldado dudó que _____ mucho peligro. (haber)

3. Mandé que el camarero me _____ la cuenta. (traer)

4. Ella salió sin que nosotros _____. (fijarse)

5. Yo te rogué que _____ a mi lado. (sentarse)

6. El dueño mandó que nosotros _____ del edificio en seguida. (salir)

Exercise 14.10

Complete the following sentences with the correct imperfect subjunctive form of the verb in parentheses. The verb in the main clause is in the imperfect.

1. Julia esperaba que su amigo _____. (mejorarse)

2. Ellos temían que Ud. no _____. (regresar)

3. Los profesores se alegraban de que a sus alumnos les _____ su clase. (encantar)

4. Estábamos contentos de que Miguel le _____ el anillo. (dar)

5. José lo sentía que nosotros no _____. (animarse)

6. Yo no creía que tú me _____. (ver)

 ## Exercise 14.11

Complete the following sentences with the correct imperfect subjunctive form of the verb in parentheses. The verb in the main clause is in the conditional.

1. ¿Sería posible que la guerra no _____? (empezar)

2. ¿Sería posible que la gente poderosa _____ de la guerra? (desistir)

3. Sería probable que los turistas de la ciudad _____ en el campo. (perderse)

4. Ella lo haría si _____ necesario. (ser)

5. La mujer viajaría si _____ caminar. (poder)

6. El hombre tocaría el violín como si _____ en el concierto. (estar)

7. ¿Te gustaría que nosotros _____ con tu jefe? (hablar)

8. Yo iría a Bolivia si yo _____ bien el español. (saber)

9. ¿Qué haría Ud. si su mejor amigo no le _____ nada? (decir)

10. ¿Cambiarías tu manera de vivir si tú _____ mucho dinero? (ganar)

Exercise 14.12

Translate the following sentences into English.

1. El autor leyó el artículo para que pudiéramos entenderlo.

   _____

2. Antes de que su novia fuera a España, Federico estudió el español por dos años.

   _____

3. Íbamos a jugar al tenis hasta que empezara a llover.

_____

4. El doctor sabía que al paciente se le había hinchado la rodilla.

_____

5. Elena aprendería a hablar español, pero no le gusta estudiar.

_____

6. Fue necesario que el mejor arquitecto diseñara el museo.

_____

7. No sería posible que sucediera tal desastre.

_____

8. El juez esperó que los testigos hubieran visto todo.

_____

9. Los turistas llegarían a las dos si los trenes no se demoraran tanto.

_____

10. Yo hubiera ido de vacaciones con ella si ella me hubiera invitado.

_____

11. ¿Le habrías hecho el favor si Andrés te hubiera pedido?

_____

12. ¿Sería posible que Uds. aprendieran y entendieran todas las lecciones?

_____

📖 Reading Comprehension

Su punto de vista

Lo confieso: no pienso mucho en la comida. Si yo hubiera sido mejor cocinera, si hubiera tenido el talento para combinar ingredientes, tal vez yo hubiera podido disfrutar más las celebraciones de glotonería.

Era un día nublado de noviembre. Lo recuerdo bien. Yo vivía con cuatro mujeres en un apartamento grande y alegre, de colores exuberantes. Cada noviembre hacíamos planes para el día de acción de gracias. Mi compañera de cuarto cocinaba un pavo de dieciocho libras y se despertaba durante la noche para lardearlo. Otra amiga horneaba un pastel de calabaza. Un amigo que vivía cerca traía verduras, frutas y queso. Para la gente a quien no le gustaba el pavo, cocinábamos jamón, chuletas, pescado, pollo asado y pato. Invitábamos a todos nuestros amigos. A las cinco de la tarde, empezábamos nuestra cena con la bebida tradicional—el ponche de huevo. Aquella noche, dejé mi plato de cebollas y judías verdes y me fui.

Huí a un restaurante y cené sola, pero no me importó. Por lo menos, no me tocó comer pavo. Hubo muchas tentaciones como mejillones en vino blanco, camarones y langosta en salsa verde y calamares fritos. Ofrecieron una ensalada con manzanas, nueces y pasas, aceitunas y tomates. Para el plato fuerte, ordené la paella para dos porque lleva mariscos, guisantes y chorizo. Después de descansar un rato, comí el flan de España y el helado de fresas. Bebí agua mineral; no tomé ni vino, ni cerveza, ni champaña, ni licor y no me emborraché. Volví a casa; mis amigos estuvieron contentos de verme, les había gustado mi plato de verduras y todos se acostaron agradecidos.

Verbos

combinar	*to combine*
emborracharse	*to get drunk*
hornear	*to bake*
lardear	*to baste*
ordenar	*to order*
tocarle (a uno)	*to have to*

Nombres

la aceituna	*the olive*
los calamares	*the squid*
los camarones	*the shrimp*
la cebolla	*the onion*
el chorizo	*the sausage*
la chuleta	*the pork chop*
la glotonería	*gluttony*
los guisantes	*the peas*
el jamón	*the ham*
la judía verde	*the string bean*
la langosta	*the lobster*
la libra	*the pound*
la manzana	*the apple*
el marisco	*the shellfish*

el mejillón	*the mussel*
la nuez, las nueces	*the nut, the nuts*
la paella	*the traditional rice dish of Spain*
la pasa	*the raisin*
el pastel de calabaza	*the pumpkin pie*
el pato	*the duck*
el pavo	*the turkey*
el pescado	*the fish*
el plato fuerte	*the main course*
el pollo asado	*the roast chicken*
el ponche de huevo	*the eggnog*
el queso	*the cheese*
las verduras	*the vegetables*

Adjetivo

| nublado | *cloudy* |

Expresiones

| tal vez | *perhaps* |
| un rato | *a little while* |

Preguntas

Answer the following questions orally.

1. ¿Es hombre o mujer la persona principal del cuento?

2. ¿Están enfadadas con ella sus compañeras de cuarto?

3. ¿Te gusta celebrar el día de acción de gracias?

4. ¿Cuál es tu comida favorita?

5. ¿Te molesta comer solo/sola?

6. ¿Cocinas bien?

15

Idioms

A **modismo** is a word or phrase that does not translate exactly into English.
Modismos are idioms; they are not slang.

Idioms with Prepositions

a fuerza de	*by dint of*
a la derecha	*to the right*
a la izquierda	*to the left*
a la vez	*at the same time*
a lo lejos	*in the distance*
a lo mejor	*probably*
a pie	*on foot*
a principios de	*at the beginning of*
a solas	*alone*
a través de	*across*
al aire libre	*in the open air*
al mismo tiempo	*at the same time*
al principio	*at the beginning, early on*
al revés	*inside out*
de buen humor	*in a good mood*
de buena gana	*willingly*
de día	*by day*
de esta manera	*in this way*
de hoy en adelante	*from now on*
de mal humor	*in a bad mood*
de mala gana	*unwillingly*

de ninguna manera	*by no means*
de noche	*by night*
de nuevo	*again*
de pie	*standing*
de pronto	*suddenly*
de repente	*suddenly*
de todos modos	*anyway*
¿de veras?	*really?*
derecho	*straight ahead*
día/semana/mes/año de por medio	*every other day/week/month/year*
en cambio	*on the other hand*
en cuanto a	*in regard to*
en efecto	*in fact, as a matter of fact*
en seguida	*right away*
por ninguna parte	*nowhere, not anywhere*
por todas partes	*everywhere*
recto	*straight ahead*

 ## Exercise 15.1

Translate the following sentences into English.

1. Al principio, todo era maravilloso.

   _____

2. Te pusiste la camisa al revés.

   _____

3. A fuerza del estudio, ella aprendió bien la historia.

   _____

4. Fuimos a Madrid a pie.

   _____

5. No me hables ahora; estoy de mal genio.

   _____

6. Ellos no encontraron sus llaves por ninguna parte.

   _____

7. No sé qué hacer en cuanto a sus problemas.

_____

8. De día trabajo, de noche duermo.

_____

9. Si queremos llegar a tiempo, tenemos que ir a la derecha.

_____

10. La muchacha puede escuchar música y estudiar a la vez.

_____

11. Pienso estar en México a principios de julio.

_____

12. Él me prestó su carro de mala gana.

_____

13. Les gusta cenar al aire libre.

_____

14. En efecto, Pablo lo supo ayer pero no me dijo nada.

_____

15. Un barco nos llevó a través del río.

_____

16. Estoy de muy buen humor hoy.

_____

17. Ud. debe caminar a la izquierda.

_____

18. A lo mejor, Enrique y Salomé vendrán la semana que viene.

_____

19. Lo hacemos de buena gana.

_____

20. El hombre prefiere caminar derecho.

_____

21. A lo lejos, la veo venir.

_____

22. Me gusta descansar. A mi amiga en cambio le gusta trabajar.

_____

23. Les digo que lo hagan de esta manera.

   _____

24. Escribo guiones para la televisión. ¿De veras?

   _____

25. Miguel no tiene mucho dinero, pero decidió viajar de todos modos.

   _____

26. Tú no tuviste éxito la primera vez, pero trataste de nuevo.

   _____

27. De hoy en adelante, vamos a correr cada día.

   _____

28. Asistimos a las clases día de por medio.

   _____

29. De repente, empezó a llover.

   _____

30. Se ve lo bueno y lo malo por todas partes.

   _____

Idioms with Verbs

With *tener*

tener _____ años	*to be _____ years old*
tener calor	*to be hot*
tener celos	*to be jealous*
tener cuidado	*to be careful*
tener dolor de (cabeza)	*to have a (head)ache*
tener envidia	*to be envious*
tener éxito	*to be successful, to have success*
tener frío	*to be cold*
tener ganas de	*to want, to desire*
tener hambre	*to be hungry*
tener la culpa	*to take the blame, to be at fault*
tener la palabra	*to have the floor*
tener lugar	*to take place*
tener mala cara	*to look bad*
tener miedo de	*to be afraid of, to have fear of*

tener mucho/poco/algo/ nada que hacer	*to have a lot/a little/something/ nothing to do*
tener por	*to take someone for, to consider someone to be*
tener prisa	*to be in a hurry*
tener que ver con	*to have to do with*
tener rabia	*to be in a rage, to be very angry*
tener razón	*to be right*
tener sed	*to be thirsty*
tener sueño	*to be sleepy*
tener suerte	*to be lucky*
tener vergüenza	*to be ashamed*

With *dar*

dar a	*to lead to* (places)
dar con	*to run into*
dar de comer	*to feed*
dar gritos	*to shout*
dar la cara	*to face*
dar la hora	*to strike the hour*
dar las gracias	*to give thanks*
dar un abrazo	*to give a hug, to embrace*
dar un paseo	*to take a walk*
dar una vuelta	*to take a walk*
darse cuenta de	*to realize*
darse la mano	*to shake hands*
darse por vencido	*to give up*
darse prisa	*to hurry*

With *echar*

echar de menos	*to miss* (a person or place)
echar flores	*to flatter*
echar la culpa	*to blame*
echarse a llorar	*to burst out crying*

With *hacer*

hace buen/mal tiempo	*it's good/bad weather*
hace calor	*it's hot/warm*
hace frío	*it's cold*
hace viento	*it's windy*

hacer caso a	*to pay attention to*
hacer daño a	*to harm*
hacer el bien/el mal	*to do good/bad*
hacer falta	*to be lacking*
hacer un papel	*to play a part*
hacer un viajc	*to take a trip*
hacerse + *profession*	*to become*
hacerse daño	*to hurt oneself*
hacerse tarde	*to become late*

With *hay*

hay cupo	*there is space*
hay que	*it is necessary*

With *llevar*

llevar a cabo	*to carry out* (a project, for example)
llevar la contraria	*to take the opposite point of view*
llevarse (algo)	*to carry (something) away*
llevarse bien/mal con	*to get along well/badly with*

With *meter*

meter la pata	*to put one's foot in one's mouth*
meter las narices	*to snoop around*
meterse en donde no le llaman	*to meddle*

With *poner*

poner a alguien por las nubes	*to heap praise on someone*
poner en claro	*to make clear*
poner en duda	*to put in doubt*
poner en ridículo	*to make look ridiculous*
poner las cartas sobre la mesa	*to put the cards on the table*
poner pleito	*to sue*
ponerse a	*to start to*

With *quedar*

quedar boquiabierto	*to be left astonished*
quedar en	*to agree on*
quedarse con	*to keep*
quedarse con el día y la noche	*to be left penniless*

With *tomar*

tomar en serio	*to take seriously*
tomarle el pelo	*to pull someone's leg*
tomárselo con calma	*to take it easy*

Exercise 15.2

Match each of the following sentences with the idiom that best describes it.

1. _____ Es agosto en Nueva York.
2. _____ Estamos cansados.
3. _____ Él no se equivoca.
4. _____ No hay agua en el desierto.
5. _____ No hice nada malo.
6. _____ A mi amigo le gusta apostar.

a. No tiene mucha suerte.
b. No tengo la culpa.
c. Tenemos calor.
d. Siempre tiene razón.
e. Los animales tienen sed.
f. Tenemos sueño.

Exercise 15.3

Translate the following sentences into English.

1. Cristina le hace caso a su maestro porque le agrada.

   _____

2. Elisa se lleva bien con su suegra.

   _____

3. Al niño le gustaba dar de comer a los pájaros en el parque.

   _____

4. El hotel da a la plaza.

   _____

5. Guillermo se hizo abogado.

   _____

6. Hace mucho tiempo que la visitante no ve a su patria. La extraña mucho y quiere darles un abrazo a todos sus amigos.

   _____

   _____

7. Me gustó el chaleco guatemalteco; le di doscientos pesos al vendedor y me lo llevé.

   _____

8. Me di cuenta de que todo no estaba bien.

   _____

9. La niña se echó a llorar.

   _____

10. Los mariscos me hacen daño.

   _____

Time Expressions

Present

The idea of how long someone has been doing something can be expressed by three different Spanish constructions, all using the simple present tense. The English translation is expressed best by the present perfect tense. The action begins in the past and continues into the present.

All three constructions below, shown with their literal translations, express the following question in the present:

How long has your professor been writing her book?

1. ¿Cuánto tiempo lleva su profesora escribiendo su libro?

   How much time does the professor carry writing her book?

2. ¿Desde cuándo escribe ella su libro?

   Since when does she write her book?

3. ¿Cuánto tiempo hace que ella escribe su libro?

   How much time does it make that she writes her book?

The same three constructions, shown with their literal translations, express the following statement in the present:

She has been writing her book for four years.

1. La autora lleva cuatro años escribiendo su libro.

   The author carries four years writing her book.

2. Ella escribe su libro desde hace cuatro años.

   She writes her book since it makes four years.

3. Hace cuatro años que ella escribe su libro.

   It makes four years that she writes her book.

Past

To express how long someone had been doing something, Spanish uses the imperfect tense. The English translation of this construction is expressed best by the past perfect tense. The action was continuing in the past when something else happened.

The constructions below, shown with their literal translations, express the following question in the past:

How long had Lorena been waiting for the bus when it arrived?

1. ¿Cuánto tiempo llevaba Lorena esperando el bus cuando llegó?

   How much time was Lorena carrying waiting for the bus when it arrived?

2. ¿Desde cuándo esperaba ella el bus cuando llegó?

   Since when was she waiting for the bus when it arrived?

3. ¿Cuánto tiempo hacía que ella esperaba el bus cuando llegó?

   How much time did it make that she was waiting for the bus when it arrived?

The constructions below, shown with their literal translations, express the following statement in the past:

She had been waiting for 30 minutes when the bus arrived.

1. Lorena llevaba media hora esperando cuando el bus llegó.

   Lorena carried a half hour waiting when the bus arrived.

2. Ella esperaba desde hacía media hora cuando el bus llegó.

   She was waiting since it made a half hour when the bus arrived.

3. Hacía media hora que ella
   esperaba cuando el bus llegó.

   *It made a half hour that she
   was waiting when the bus
   arrived.*

Exercise 15.4

Translate the following sentences into Spanish, using the present tense and one of the forms of expressing "how long." Try to practice all three possible forms as you complete the exercise.

EXAMPLES   How long has Jaime lived in the United States?

¿Cuánto tiempo hace que Jaime vive en los Estados Unidos?

OR *¿Desde cuándo vive Jaime en los Estados Unidos?*

OR *¿Cuánto tiempo lleva Jaime viviendo en los Estados Unidos?*

1. How long has the child been watching television?

   _____

2. How long has Adam been sleeping?

   _____

3. How long have you been wearing glasses?

   _____

4. How long have Isabel and Carlos been waiting?

   _____

5. How long have they been friends?

   _____

6. He has been sleeping for eight hours.

   _____

7. I've been wearing glasses for two years.

   _____

8. They have been waiting for 15 minutes.

   _____

Exercise 15.5

Translate the following sentences into English.

1. ¿Cuánto tiempo hacía que Ud. estaba en Chile cuando tuvo que salir?

   _____

2. ¿Desde cuándo nadaban los niños cuando el bañero llegó?

   _____

3. ¿Cuánto tiempo llevaba Antonio leyendo cuando se durmió?

   _____

4. Hacía dos meses que yo estaba en Paraguay cuando decidí volver a casa.

   _____

5. El hombre frustrado esperaba el tren desde hace veinte minutos.

   _____

6. Llevábamos quince meses viviendo en Paris.

   _____

Reading Comprehension

El fin del juego

Queridos lectores,

   Espero que a Uds. les haya gustado el libro. Ha sido un buen viaje y me alegro de que Uds. hayan llegado hasta el fin. Les dejo con una parte interesante de la historia de Sócrates en la cual él explica por qué no le va a molestar el fin de su vida.

   Ahora, me despido de Uds. y les deseo todo lo mejor.

Hasta el próximo,

La autora

La defensa de Sócrates
escrito por Platón

La asamblea vota por la inocencia o la culpabilidad de Sócrates. Lo condena a la pena de muerte. Lo siguiente es la respuesta de Sócrates ante la asamblea, antes de que se lo lleve a la cárcel.

SÓCRATES La gente dirá que Uds. condenan a muerte a Sócrates, un hombre sabio. Dirán que soy sabio si lo soy o no. Si Uds. hubieran esperado por un rato, sus deseos hubieran sido realizados en el camino de la naturaleza. Pueden ver que soy un hombre viejo.

Me gustaría discutir con Uds., los cuales me han absuelto, lo que ha pasado. Concédanme, les suplico, un momento de atención, porque nada impide que conversemos juntos, puesto que queda tiempo. Quiero decirles, como amigos, lo que acaba de sucederme, y explicarles lo que significa. Sí, jueces míos, me ha sucedido hoy una cosa maravillosa.

Nos engañamos todos sin duda si creemos que la muerte es un mal. Una prueba evidente de ello es que si yo hubiera de realizar hoy algún bien, el dios* no hubiera dejado de advertírmelo como acostumbra.

La muerte es un tránsito del alma de un lugar a otro. ¿Qué mayor ventaja puede presentar la muerte? Si la muerte es una cosa semejante, la llamo con razón un bien; porque entonces el tiempo todo entero, no es más que una larga noche.

Pero si la muerte es un tránsito de un lugar a otro, y si, según se dice, allá en un lugar está el paradero de todos los que han vivido, ¿qué mayor bien se puede imaginar, jueces míos? ¿Qué transporte de alegría no tendría yo cuando me encontrara con los héroes de la antigüedad, que han sido las víctimas de la injusticia? ¿Qué placer el poder comparar mis aventuras con las suyas? Pero aún sería un placer más grande para mí pasar allí los días, interrogando y examinando a todos estos personajes, para distinguir los que son verdaderamente sabios de los que creen serlo y no lo son. ¿Hay alguno, jueces míos, que no diera todo lo que tiene en el mundo por examinar al que condujo un ejército contra Troya, u Odiseo o Sísifo, y tantos otros, hombres y mujeres, cuya conversación y examen serían una felicidad inexplicable?

Ésta es la razón, jueces míos, para que nunca pierdan las esperanzas aún después de la tumba, fundadas en esta verdad: que no hay ningún mal para el hombre de bien, ni durante la vida, ni después de su muerte; y que los dioses tienen siempre cuidado de cuanto tiene relación con él; porque lo que en este momento me sucede a mí no es obra de azar, y estoy convencido de que el mejor partido para mí es morir ahora y liberarme de todos los disgustos de esta vida.

La hora de partir ha llegado, y nos vamos cada cual por su camino— yo, a morir, y Uds. a vivir. Solo dios sabe cual es mejor.

---

*Sócrates siempre decía que tenía un dios familiar, un dios personal y divino que le hacía advertencias desde su niñez. En cuanto a su juicio, esta voz no le había dicho nada.

Verbos

absolver	*to absolve*
acabar de + *infinitive*	*to have just* (+ infinitive)
acostumbrar	*to be accustomed*
advertir	*to warn*
conceder	*to concede*
engañarse	*to deceive oneself*
fundar	*to found*
impedir	*to impede*
realizar	*to fulfill*
significar	*to mean, to signify*
suplicar	*to beg*

Nombres

el azar	*chance*
el ejército	*the army*
la esperanza	*the hope*
el héroe	*the hero*
el paradero	*the place, the destination*
la tumba	*the tomb, the grave*

Expresiones

en cuanto a	*in regard to*
puesto que	*since*

Preguntas

1. ¿Cuál es la actitud de Sócrates ante la muerte?

2. ¿Cuál es la diferencia entre su dios personal y los dioses del estado?

3. ¿Qué espera hacer después de la muerte?

4. ¿Por qué quiere hablar con los jueces?

5. ¿Qué significa "no hay ningún mal para un hombre de bien, ni durante la vida, ni después de la muerte"? ¿Está Ud. de acuerdo con esta filosofía de Sócrates?

Appendix

List of Verbs

A

abordar *to board*
abrazar *to embrace*
abrir *to open*
absolver *to absolve*
acabar de (hacer algo) *to have just (done something)*
acabarse *to use up*
acercarse *to approach, to near*
aclarar *to clarify*
acompañar *to accompany*
aconsejar *to advise*
acordarse *to remember*
acostarse *to go to bed*
acostumbrar *to be accustomed*
actuar *to act*
acusar *to accuse*
adivinar *to guess*
admitir *to admit*
advertir *to warn*
agotar *to exhaust, to use up*
agradar *to be pleasing*
agradecer *to thank*
aguantar *to tolerate*
ahorrar *to save* (money)
alcanzar *to reach, to overtake*
almorzar *to have lunch*
alquilar *to rent*
alzar *to lift*

amar *to love*
amenazar *to threaten*
añadir *to add*
andar *to stroll, to walk*
animarse *to cheer up*
añorar *to yearn, to miss*
anular *to annul*
anunciar *to announce*
apagar *to turn off*
aparecer *to appear*
apartarse *to separate*
apostar *to bet*
apoyar *to support*
apreciar *to appreciate*
aprender *to learn*
apresurarse *to hurry*
apretar *to squeeze, to tighten*
aprobar *to pass* (a test)
arrancar *to pull out, to root out*
arreglar *to arrange, to fix*
arreglarse *to get dressed up, to get ready*
arriesgar *to risk*
asegurar *to assure*
asistir (a) *to attend, to be present at*
asustarse *to become scared*
atender *to attend to, to serve*
aterrizar *to land*
atraer *to attract*
atravesar *to cross*

273

atreverse (a) *to dare to*
averiguar *to check out, to find out*
ayudar *to help*

B

bailar *to dance*
bajar *to descend*
bajarse de *to get off* (a bus)
barrer *to sweep*
basar *to base*
beber *to drink*
bendecir *to bless*
besar *to kiss*
borrar *to erase*
bostezar *to yawn*
botar *to throw away*
brillar *to shine*
brindar *to drink a toast*
broncear *to tan*
bucear *to dive, to snorkel*
buscar *to look for*

C

caber *to fit* (one thing inside another)
caer *to fall*
caerse *to fall down*
calentar *to warm*
callarse *to be quiet*
calmarse *to calm down*
cambiar *to change*
cambiar de idea *to change one's mind*
cantar *to sing*
captar *to grasp the meaning of* (a word)
capturar *to capture*
cargar *to load*
casarse *to get married*
castigar *to punish*
celebrar *to celebrate*
cenar *to dine*
cepillarse *to brush* (one's teeth)
cerrar *to close*
charlar *to chat*
cobrar *to charge* (money)

cocinar *to cook*
coger *to catch, to grab*
colgar *to hang up* (a picture)
colocar *to put, to place*
combinar *to combine*
comenzar *to begin*
comer *to eat*
comparar *to compare*
compartir *to share*
competir *to compete*
componer *to compose*
comprar *to buy*
comunicar *to communicate*
conceder *to concede*
condenar *to condemn*
conducir *to drive*
confesar *to confess*
confirmar *to confirm*
conocer *to know, to be acquainted*
conseguir *to obtain*
construir *to build*
contar *to count, to tell a story*
contar con *to rely on*
contener *to contain*
contestar *to answer*
continuar *to continue*
contradecir *to contradict*
contribuir *to contribute*
convertir *to convert*
copiar *to copy*
corregir *to correct*
correr *to run*
corromper *to corrupt*
coser *to sew*
costar *to cost*
crear *to create*
crecer *to grow*
creer *to believe*
cruzar *to cross*
cubrir *to cover*
cuidar *to take care of*
cuidarse *to take of oneself*
cumplir *to complete, to comply*

D

dar *to give*
dar una vuelta *to take a walk*
darse cuenta (de) *to realize*
decepcionar *to disappoint*
decidir *to decide*
decir *to say, to tell*
defenderse *to defend oneself*
dejar *to allow, to leave* (something behind)
dejar de (hacer algo) *to stop (doing something)*
demorarse *to delay*
depender (de) *to depend (on)*
desaparecer *to disappear*
desayunarse *to have breakfast*
descansar *to rest*
describir *to describe*
descubrir *to discover*
desear *to desire*
desesperarse *to despair*
deshacer *to undo*
desistir *to desist*
despedirse (de) *to take one's leave (of)*
despertarse *to wake up*
destruir *to destroy*
detener *to detain*
detenerse *to stop*
devolver *to return* (an object)
dibujar *to draw*
dirigir *to direct*
disculparse *to apologize, to excuse oneself*
diseñar *to design*
disfrutar *to enjoy*
disolver *to dissolve*
distinguir *to distinguish*
distraer *to distract*
divertirse *to have a good time*
dividir *to divide*
divorciarse *to divorce*
doblar *to turn*
doler *to hurt*

dormir *to sleep*
dormirse *to fall asleep*
ducharse *to take a shower*
dudar *to doubt*
durar *to last*

E

echar *to give off, to throw* (multiple meanings)
elegir *to elect*
emborracharse *to get drunk*
empezar *to begin*
empujar *to push*
enamorarse *to fall in love*
encantar *to enchant*
encontrar *to find*
encontrarse (con) *to meet*
enfadarse *to get angry*
enfermarse *to become sick*
engañarse *to deceive oneself*
engordarse *to get fat*
enojarse *to get angry*
ensayar *to rehearse*
enseñar *to teach*
entender *to understand*
enterarse *to become informed*
entrar (en) *to enter*
entregar *to deliver, to hand in*
envejecer *to grow old*
enviar *to send*
envolver *to wrap*
equivocarse *to make a mistake*
escalar *to climb, to scale*
escapar *to escape*
escoger *to choose*
esconderse *to hide oneself*
escribir *to write*
escuchar *to listen to*
espantar *to scare, to frighten*
esperar *to wait for, to hope*
esquiar *to ski*
establecer *to establish*
estacionar *to park*

estar *to be*
estornudar *to sneeze*
exagerar *to exaggerate*
examinar *to examine*
excavar *to excavate, to dig*
exigir *to demand*
explicar *to explain*
explicarse *to explain oneself*
explorar *to explore*
expresarse *to express oneself*
extrañar *to miss* (a person or place)

F

felicitar *to congratulate*
festejar *to feast, to celebrate*
fijarse *to notice*
fingir *to pretend*
firmar *to sign*
fracasar *to fail*
fregar *to wash up* (plates), *to scrub,
   to scour*
freír *to fry*
fumar *to smoke*
fundar *to found*

G

ganar *to win*
gastar *to spend money*
gemir *to groan*
girar *to turn, to rotate*
gobernar *to govern*
gozar *to enjoy*
grabar *to record, to tape*
graduarse *to graduate*
gritar *to yell*
gustar *to be pleasing*

H

hacer *to do, to make*
hallar *to find*
hervir *to boil*
hinchar *to swell*
hincharse *to swell up*

hornear *to bake*
huir *to flee*

I

ignorar *not to know, not to pay attention*
imaginar *to imagine*
imaginarse *to imagine*
impedir *to impede*
implorar *to implore*
importar *to be important to*
inscribirse *to enroll, to register*
insistir *to insist*
inspirar *to inspire*
intentar *to intend*
interrumpir *to interrupt*
introducir *to insert*
investigar *to investigate*
ir *to go*
irse *to go away*

J

jubilarse *to retire*
jugar *to play* (a game)
juntar *to unite, to join*
jurar *to swear*

L

ladrar *to bark*
lastimarse *to hurt oneself*
lavarse *to wash oneself*
leer *to read*
lesionarse *to injure oneself*
levantarse *to get up*
liberar *to liberate*
limpiar *to clean*
llamar *to call*
llamarse *to call oneself, to be called*
llegar *to arrive*
llenar *to fill*
llevar *to carry, to wear*
llevarse (bien) *to get along (well)*
llorar *to cry*
llover *to rain*

lloviznar *to drizzle*
lograr *to attain*
luchar *to struggle, to fight*
lucir *to light up*

M

madrugar *to get up early*
maltratar *to mistreat*
mandar *to order, to send*
manejar *to drive*
mantener *to maintain*
maquillarse *to put on makeup*
marcar *to dial, to mark*
marchar *to march*
mascar *to chew*
masticar *to chew*
matar *to kill*
medir *to measure*
mejorarse *to get better*
mencionar *to mention*
mentir *to lie*
merecer *to deserve*
meter *to put inside*
meterse *to meddle, to interfere*
mezclar *to mix*
mirar *to look at, to watch*
mojarse *to get wet*
molestar *to annoy, to bother*
morder *to bite*
morir *to die*
morirse *to die*
mostrar *to show*
mover *to move*
moverse *to move oneself*
mudarse *to move* (from one place to another)
murmurar *to mumble*

N

nacer *to be born*
nadar *to swim*
necesitar *to need*
negar *to deny*

nevar *to snow*
notar *to note*

O

obedecer *to obey*
observar *to observe*
ocurrir *to occur*
ocurrirse *to get an idea, to occur to*
ofrecer *to offer*
oír *to hear*
oler *to smell*
olvidar *to forget*
olvidarse *to forget*
operar *to operate*
opinar *to opine, to have an opinion*
oponer *to oppose*
optar *to opt*
ordenar *to order*
oscurecer *to grow dark*

P

pagar *to pay*
parar *to stop*
pararse *to stand up*
parecer *to seem*
parquear *to park*
partir *to leave*
pasar *to pass, to spend* (time)
pasear *to take a walk, to stroll*
patinar *to skate*
pedir *to request*
pegar *to hit*
peinarse *to brush* (one's hair)
pelear *to fight*
pensar *to think*
pensar de *to think of, to opine*
pensar en *to think about*
perder *to lose*
perderse *to become lost, to lose*
perdonar *to pardon*
permitir *to permit*
pertenecer *to belong to*
picar *to sting*

pintar *to paint*
pisar *to step on, to tread on*
planchar *to iron*
poder *to be able, can*
poner *to put*
ponerse *to put on* (clothes), *to become* (emotion)
ponerse a *to begin*
portarse *to behave*
poseer *to possess*
preferir *to prefer*
preguntar *to ask a question*
preguntarse *to wonder*
prender *to turn on*
preocuparse (por) *to worry (about)*
preparar *to prepare*
presentar *to introduce, to present*
prestar *to lend*
prevenir *to prevent*
probar *to taste, to test*
probarse *to try on*
producir *to produce*
prohibir *to prohibit, to forbid*
prometer *to promise*
proponer *to propose*
proteger *to protect*
publicar *to publish*
pudrir *to rot*
pulir *to polish*

Q

quedarse *to stay, to remain*
quejarse *to complain*
quemar *to burn*
quemarse *to burn oneself*
querer *to want*
quitarse *to take off* (clothes)

R

realizar *to fulfill*
rebajar *to lower, to reduce*
recibir *to receive*
recoger *to pick up*

reconocer *to recognize*
recordar *to remember*
recuperarse *to recuperate*
reducir *to reduce*
referir *to refer*
regalar *to give a gift*
regresar *to return*
reírse *to laugh*
relatar *to relate a story*
renunciar *to renounce*
repetir *to repeat*
reportar *to report*
rescatar *to save, to rescue*
resolver *to resolve*
respirar *to breathe*
responder *to respond*
resultar *to result*
retener *to retain*
retirarse *to retire*
reunirse *to meet*
rezar *to pray*
robar *to rob*
rogar *to beg*
romper *to break*

S

saber *to know, to know how*
sacar *to take out*
salir *to leave, to exit, to go out*
salirle (bien) *to come out (well)*
saltar *to jump*
saludar *to greet*
salvar *to save* (a life)
satisfacer *to satisfy*
secar *to dry*
seguir *to follow, to continue*
sembrar *to sow*
sentarse *to sit down*
sentir *to regret*
sentirse *to feel* (an emotion)
separarse *to separate*
servir *to serve*
significar *to mean, to signify*

sollozar *to sob*
soltar *to loosen, to let go*
sonar *to sound*
soñar (con) *to dream (about)*
sonreír *to smile*
sorprender *to surprise*
sospechar *to suspect*
subir *to go up, to ascend*
subrayar *to underline*
suceder *to happen, to occur*
sufrir *to suffer*
sugerir *to suggest*
suplicar *to beg*
suponer *to suppose*
suspirar *to sigh*

T

tapar *to cover up, to plug up*
temblar *to tremble*
temer *to fear*
tener *to have*
tentar *to tempt*
terminar *to finish*
tirar *to throw*
tocar *to touch, to play* (an instrument)
tocarle a alguien *to be someone's turn*
tomar *to take*
torcer *to twist*
trabajar *to work*
traducir *to translate*
traer *to bring*
tragar *to swallow*
tranquilizarse *to calm down*
tratar *to treat*

tratar de (hacer algo) *to try to (do something)*
tratarse (de) *to be about*
triunfar *to triumph*
tronar *to thunder*
trotar *to trot*

U

usar *to use*

V

vacilar *to hesitate*
vagar *to wander*
valer *to be worth*
velar *to watch over, to stay awake*
vencer *to conquer, to vanquish*
vender *to sell*
venir *to come*
ver *to see*
vestirse *to get dressed*
viajar *to travel*
vigilar *to watch over, to guard*
visitar *to visit*
vivir *to live*
volar *to fly*
volver *to return*
votar *to vote*

Y

yacer *to lie down*

Z

zigzaguear *to zigzag*
zumbar *to buzz*

Answer Key

Chapter 1
Ser and *Estar* and the Present Tense

1.1   1. están (location)   2. está, está (health, health)   3. están (health)   4. están (location)   5. está (location)   6. está, está (changing mood, changing mood)   7. están (changing mood)   8. estoy (changing mood)   9. está (location)   10. está (location)

1.2   1. El rió está cerca de mi casa.   2. Australia está lejos de los Estados Unidos.   3. La flor blanca está encima de la mesa.   4. Los niños están juntos a sus padres.   5. La escuela está entre la iglesia y el banco.   6. La casa de Julia está detrás del correo.   7. Paula está aquí con sus hermanos.   8. Sus/Tus zapatos están debajo de mi silla.   9. Nuestro problema está bajo control.   10. Los parientes de Elena están en España. Sus maletas están en los Estados Unidos.

1.3   1. es, es (profession, point of origin)   2. son, es (profession, profession)   3. son (point of origin)   4. son (description)   5. es (description)   6. somos (identification)   7. son (material)   8. son (point of origin)   9. soy, es (point of origin, point of origin)   10. es (possession)   11. Eres (profession)   12. son (description)   13. es (point of origin)   14. es (profession)   15. Es (impersonal expression)

1.4   1. es 2. es 3. son 4. son 5. somos 6. está 7. estoy 8. está 9. estamos 10. Estás 11. están

1.5   1. soy 2. están 3. están 4. eres 5. es 6. están 7. están, estamos 8. es, están 9. está 10. son 11. están, es 12. está, está 13. es 14. están, están, son 15. está 16. está 17. es 18. Son 19. es 20. es

1.6   1. Los dentistas están en sus oficinas.   2. Todo el mundo está enfermo. Hasta los doctores están enfermos.   3. La sopa está caliente. La comida está deliciosa/sabrosa.   4. Es necesario estudiar.   5. ¿Es posible aprender todo?

1.7   1. está 2. Ser, ser 3. es 4. están 5. estoy 6. eres 7. es, Son 8. es 9. Son, es 10. Es 11. es 12. ser 13. estar 14. está 15. está 16. está 17. es 18. está 19. están 20. es 21. está 22. estar 23. está, está 24. están 25. soy 26. es 27. está, está 28. está 29. estamos 30. es

Chapter 2
Ser and *Estar* in the Preterit and Imperfect Tenses

2.1   1. fue   2. fui   3. estuvimos   4. estuvo   5. estuvieron   6. estuvo   7. estuvieron
8. Fue   9. estuvo   10. estuvieron   11. estuve   12. estuvimos

2.2   1. Yo era de Venezuela.   2. Ellos eran de España.   3. ¿Qué hora era?
4. Nosotros estábamos bien.   5. Mi jardín era el más hermoso de la ciudad.
6. Los tres amigos estaban aquí.   7. Yo no estaba cansada.   8. Éramos cantantes.
9. ¿Dónde estabas?   10. Yo estaba en la casa con mi hermana.

2.3   1. fui   2. estuvimos   3. era   4. estuvo   5. fue   6. fue, fui   7. era   8. era   9. Eran
10. era   11. era   12. estuvo/fue   13. estuvimos   14. Era/Fue   15. Era/Fue

2.4   1. compraste   2. traje   3. Era, tenía   4. Empezó, cerré / Empezaba, cerraba
5. cruzaba, llamó   6. estuvieron   7. andábamos, vimos   8. cobró, cobró
9. escribimos, recibieron   10. caminaba, me di cuenta de, sabía, estaba.
11. conoció   12. se divertían   13. iba   14. llegaron, se quedaron

Chapter 3
The Present Progressive Tense

3.1   1. hablando   2. besando   3. andando   4. viajando   5. limpiando   6. cenando
7. sacando   8. bebiendo   9. comiendo   10. aprendiendo   11. agradeciendo
12. escogiendo   13. viendo   14. abriendo   15. asistiendo   16. insistiendo
17. permitiendo   18. prohibiendo   19. creyendo   20. leyendo   21. trayendo
22. huyendo   23. oyendo   24. sirviendo   25. pidiendo   26. corrigiendo
27. repitiendo   28. siguiendo   29. durmiendo   30. muriendo   31. diciendo
32. haciendo

3.2   1. está corrigiendo   2. estamos sacando   3. estoy estudiando   4. estamos haciendo
5. están preparando   6. estás diciendo   7. está nevando   8. están durmiendo
9. están escribiendo   10. están hablando   11. estás friendo   12. está comiendo

3.3   1. leyendo   2. sabe   3. tocando   4. conocer   5. tener, quiere   6. almuerzan, salen
7. devolver   8. graduarse, hacer

3.4   1. está repitiendo   2. están siguiendo   3. estamos leyendo   4. están haciendo
5. están almorzando   6. estoy hirviendo   7. está siguiendo   8. están esperando

3.5   1. ¿Les están hablando las mujeres a los hombres?   2. ¿Qué me estás diciendo (tú)? /
¿Qué estás diciéndome? / ¿Qué me está diciendo (Ud.)?   3. ¿Puede Ud. repetir
la pregunta? Los estudiantes no le está prestando atención. / Los estudiantes no está
haciéndole caso.   4. Sabemos que él está buscando una idea. La necesita para escribir
un cuento.   5. ¿Qué está pasando?   6. El abogado fantástico está soñando con un viaje
a Italia.

3.6   *Answers will vary.*

3.7   1. quiere   2. viene   3. sabe, sabe   4. estoy pensando   5. podemos   6. llamando
7. sonríe   8. juegan   9. está confesando   10. despertarse   11. van   12. haciendo

3.8   1. We are going to María's house because she is preparing chicken with rice.   2. The waiter
is serving us our meal.   3. The nannies are taking care of a lot of children in the park.
4. It is 8 o'clock at night and it is already late, but the man keeps reading his favorite book.

He keeps reading it until 11 o'clock.   5. The girl is swimming in the pool, because her parents think that it is dangerous to swim in the ocean.   6. The children are putting the plates in the oven. They are putting them in the oven to annoy their parents.   7. Why are you lying to her/him?   8. Who is laughing?   9. The elephant has been living in the zoo for five years.   10. We keep learning Spanish.

3.9   1. ¿Por qué está llorando la gente?   2. Está lloviendo.   3. ¿Estás mirando televisión ahora? / ¿Está (Ud.) mirando televisión ahora?   4. ¿Por qué están riéndose las muchachas? / ¿Por qué se están riendo las muchachas?   5. Nos toca a nosotros. Estamos usando las computadoras ahora.   6. Teresa está esperando el tren, pero está perdiendo paciencia.   7. ¿En qué estás pensando? / ¿En qué está pensando?   8. Estamos tratando de dormirnos.

Chapter 4
The Past Progressive Tenses

4.1   1. Yo estaba limpiando la casa.   2. Rosa seguía comiendo.   3. Pablo les estaba vendiendo medicina a sus amigos.   4. Estábamos aprendiendo a bailar.   5. ¿Por qué me estaba mintiendo ella? / ¿Por qué estaba mintiéndome?   6. ¿Qué estaba Ud. haciendo? / ¿Qué estaba haciendo Ud.?   7. ¿Quién estaba durmiendo en el tren?   8. Todo el mundo estaba saliendo para las salidas.   9. Los muchachos y las muchachas estaban tirando la pelota.   10. Los políticos estaban empezando su campaña electoral.

4.2   1. We were having a good time until the play began.   2. Did you want to feed the birds in the park?   3. We knew that we were going to be successful.   4. The women were celebrating their retirement until 11 o'clock at night.   5. I was getting acquainted with Mexico, little by little.   6. Our professor was teaching for an hour yesterday.   7. We were working when our friends arrived.   8. What were you talking about?   9. She wasn't listening to me.   10. The waiter wasn't serving us the meal.   11. The teachers were repeating the instructions until we understood.   12. Why were you looking for them for so long when you knew that your friends were hiding?   13. We were dancing last night until midnight.   14. Nobody was walking around here.

4.3   1. esperaron   2. dijo   3. trajeron   4. se cayeron   5. di   6. pudo   7. fuimos   8. gustó   9. viste   10. conoció

4.4   1. era   2. tenían   3. quería   4. estudiaba   5. jugaba   6. escribía   7. estaba, se quejaba   8. ponía

4.5   1. le/les/te   2. les   3. le   4. me   5. te/le/les   6. nos

4.6   1. Julia looks for her sister. She is looking for her.   2. We take care of the babies. We take care of them.   3. The two brothers/siblings help their family. The family appreciates their help.   4. The gardener looks at the birds. He looks at them fly.   5. The students greet their teacher. They greet her every day.   6. Why are you calling me today? Why are you calling me at home?   7. Manuel visits the woman in Peru. He wants to marry her in the spring.   8. All the tourists are waiting for the train. It doesn't bother them to wait for it because it is cool out.

4.7   1. I swear it to you.   2. I put on my gloves. I put them on.   3. The indigenous woman doesn't sell water to us; she gives it to us.   4. I like the shellfish in this restaurant. The waiter serves them to me with pleasure.   5. Ana brings dessert to her friends. She brings it to them.

4.8   1. ¿Les dice la verdad a sus amigos? Se la decimos. / ¿Les dices la verdad a tus amigos? Te la decimos.   2. Siempre le escribo cartas. Se las estoy escribiendo ahora. / Siempre le escribo cartas. Estoy escribiéndoselas ahora.   3. Irene le da regalos a su hijo cada Navidad. Este año, va a dárselos el día de su cumpleaños. / Irene le da regalos a su hijo cada Navidad. Este año, se los va a dar el día de su cumpleaños.   4. Le mostramos la nueva zapatería a mi amiga. Ella mira los tacones, pero no nos los compra.   5. A veces, la gente no entiende lo que decimos. A veces tenemos que explicárselo.   6. Enrique les lee un cuento a sus hijos cada noche a las ocho. Se lo está leyendo ahora. / Enrique les lee un cuento a sus hijos cada noche a las ocho. Está leyéndoselo ahora.

4.9   1. Michael couldn't enter his house because he lost his keys.   2. The spoon fell and I got angry.   3. Careful! The glasses are going to fall. We broke two already.   4. It didn't occur to me to work yesterday.   5. You couldn't prepare the garlic soup last night. You ran out of garlic.   6. I forgot to do my homework.

Chapter 5
The Present Subjunctive

5.1   1. vengan   2. diga   3. haga   4. conozcan   5. durmamos   6. sepa   7. tomemos   8. se levanten   9. llegue   10. me quede   11. esté   12. dé   13. vayas   14. sean   15. lean   16. tenga   17. traigamos   18. se sientan

5.2   1. diga   2. pague   3. se sientan   4. deje de llorar   5. expliquemos   6. tenga   7. dé   8. sepa   9. haya   10. vayan   11. sea   12. hagamos   13. esté   14. bese

5.3   *Answers will vary. Some possible answers are shown.*   1. Yo dudo que a mis padres les guste viajar.   2. Lo siento que mi amigo tenga malos sueños.   3. Es posible que ella no se divierta mucho.   4. Él duda que seamos buenos estudiantes.   5. Ella teme que no volvamos a los Estados Unidos.   6. Yo le pido que Sara me traiga flores a mi casa.   7. Dudo que Ud. conozca a mi tío.   8. Es una lástima que mi hermano y yo no nos veamos mucho.   9. ¿Es posible que no haya clase los lunes?   10. No creo que Carla sea de Polonia.

5.4   1. tengan   2. tienen   3. visite   4. traigamos   5. ame   6. corrijamos   7. están   8. se queja   9. se quede   10. se van   11. baile   12. vea   13. estén   14. sepan   15. es   16. haga

5.5   1. antes de que, visite   2. Después de que, me bañe   3. a menos que, vayan   4. luego que, tenga   5. para que, sepan   6. luego que, terminen   7. Antes de que, venga   8. para que, puedas   9. hasta que, lleguen   10. En caso de que, tengan   11. para que, estén   12. a pesar de que, tengan   13. sin que, invite   14. después de que, se vayan   15. Cuando, pueda   16. cuando, nos reunamos / cuando, nos encontremos   17. Cuando, vuelvan / Cuando, regresen   18. cuando, aprenda

5.6   1. se enfermen   2. descansemos   3. llegue   4. se quejen   5. cocine   6. duermas   7. haya   8. tenga   9. esté   10. quiera   11. acompañe   12. sea   13. venga   14. hable

5.7   1. estén   2. pique   3. obtenga   4. conozca   5. sepa   6. ganen   7. vengan   8. preste   9. aprendan   10. ensayen

5.8   1. abramos   2. te vayas   3. perdone   4. nade   5. llegue

5.9   1. escuchen   2. fume   3. se pierda   4. diga, tome   5. cante

Chapter 6
Commands

6.1   1. Take your medicine and call the doctor in the morning.   2. Continue to the right, please.   3. Close the door, please, and open the window.   4. Run to the store and buy milk.   5. Prepare the meal tonight and afterward, take out the garbage, please.
6. Read *Don Quixote* for the class and write your opinion about the main theme.
7. Eat more fruits and vegetables.   8. Count on me.

6.2   1. apaga   2. comparte   3. decide   4. devuelve   5. dobla   6. mira   7. oye
8. regresa   9. termina   10. tira

6.3   1. Di   2. Sé   3. Lee   4. Escribe   5. Ten   6. Pon   7. Ven   8. Haz   9. Trae   10. Espera

6.4   1. fíjate   2. anímate   3. cállate   4. arréglate   5. muévete   6. vete   7. quédate
8. párate   9. cepíllate   10. vístete   11. diviértete   12. duérmete

6.5   1. Do me a favor.   2. Tell us the truth.   3. Go away.   4. Put on your socks.
5. Leave now.   6. Be a good dog.   7. Be careful.   8. Come here.

6.6   1. corre, no corras   2. camina, no camines   3. bebe, no bebas   4. sigue, no sigas
5. repite, no repitas   6. habla, no hables   7. mira, no mires   8. rompe, no rompas
9. vende, no vendas   10. abre, no abras   11. sube, no subas   12. empieza, no empieces
13. miente, no mientas   14. sal, no salgas   15. pon, no pongas   16. toca, no toques

6.7   1. No comas la ensalada en Guatemala. No la comas.   2. No corras; otro tren viene.
3. No me digas el secreto. No me lo digas.   4. No lo hagas.   5. No lo toques.
6. No tengas miedo.   7. No le prestes dinero a ella. No se lo prestes.   8. No vengas tarde al desfile.   9. No nos des malas noticias.   10. No le traigas dulces al niño. No se los traigas.   11. No te vayas.   12. No te preocupes.   13. No me esperes.   14. No tengas envidia.

6.8   1. Don't swim in this lake.   2. Don't walk in the mud.   3. Don't go to bed late.
4. Don't give it to us.   5. Don't leave the dirty plates on the table.   6. Don't work so much.
7. Don't come to class on Monday.   8. Don't arrive late.

6.9   1. diga, no diga   2. haga, no haga   3. trabaje, no trabaje   4. entre, no entre
5. lea, no lea   6. espere, no espere   7. beba, no beba

6.10   1. quédense, no se queden   2. siéntense, no se sienten   3. levántense, no se levanten
4. acuéstense, no se acuesten   5. duérmanse, no se duerman

6.11   1. digamos   2. empecemos   3. sigamos   4. vámonos   5. despertémonos   6. juguemos
7. esperemos   8. entremos   9. tomemos   10. crucemos   11. durmámonos
12. almorcemos   13. comamos   14. descansemos   15. volvamos

6.12   1. No lo toques.   2. No me lo digas.   3. No lo hagas.   4. Ayúdeme.   5. Dele el libro.
6. Déselo.   7. No se lo dé.   8. Bésame.   9. Siéntense Uds., por favor.   10. Empecemos.
11. Espérennos.   12. Vayan a la derecha.   13. Ten cuidado.   14. Llene este formulario, por favor.   15. No bebas tanto.   16. Saca la basura.   17. No se vaya.   18. No se preocupen.   19. Sigamos las direcciones.   20. Maneje más despacio, por favor.
21. Quédense por favor.   22. Llámame.   23. No compre nada.   24. No se rían.
25. Vamos.

6.13   1. se quede   2. diga   3. comer   4. se mejoren   5. busco   6. gusta   7. venga   8. sea
       9. quiere   10. visite   11. llega   12. hagan   13. compremos   14. estar, estés   15. ir
       16. gusta   17. guste   18. llame   19. esté   20. sepa   21. eres   22. vaya   23. tenga
       24. haya

Chapter 7
Nouns, Articles, Adjectives, and Pronouns

7.1   1. el, X   2. X, la   3. los, la   4. el   5. las   6. las   7. X, la   8. la, las   9. la

7.2   1. mis   2. sus   3. sus   4. sus   5. su   6. su   7. su   8. nuestra   9. nuestra   10. su

7.3   1. mío   2. suyo/tuyo, mío   3. suyos   4. suyas   5. mías   6. nuestra   7. mío   8. suyos

7.4   1. el nuestro   2. los suyos / los tuyos   3. la suya, la suya / la tuya   4. la mía
       5. los nuestros   6. la mía   7. el nuestro   8. el suyo

7.5   1. mío   2. suyos/tuyos   3. nuestros   4. suyos   5. suya   6. suya

7.6   1. el suyo / el tuyo   2. el suyo   3. el mío   4. los nuestros   5. la tuya   6. los suyos

7.7   1. lo que   2. que   3. que   4. que   5. quienes   6. que   7. Lo que   8. quien
       9. quienes   10. lo que   11. que   12. quien   13. cuya   14. cuyos

7.8   1. Rita sold the house that I liked.   2. What you said was true.   3. I don't know if this
       well-known man, who studies philosophy, wants to go to Greece with his friends.

7.9   1. quien   2. que   3. que / la que / la cual   4. la cual   5. las que / las cuales   6. que
       7. quien   8. que   9. que   10. quien / quienes   11. la cual

7.10   1. X   2. el   3. al   4. la   5. Al   6. lo   7. lo   8. la   9. X   10. lo   11. los   12. la
       13. la   14. las   15. Lo   16. la   17. al   18. el   19. los   20. X   21. X

7.11   1. la cual   2. quien   3. el cual   4. cuyo   5. cuya   6. los cuales   7. quienes   8. cuyas
       9. las cuales   10. cuyos

7.12   1. el viejo   2. el blanco   3. el grande

Chapter 8
The Present Perfect Tense

8.1   1. jugado   2. buscado   3. conocido   4. entrado   5. devuelto   6. sido   7. estado
       8. dado   9. visto   10. escrito   11. roto   12. tenido   13. querido   14. hecho
       15. dicho   16. ido   17. abierto   18. cerrado   19. muerto   20. amado

8.2   1. sido   2. tenido   3. podido   4. estado   5. querido   6. sabido   7. dicho   8. dado
       9. vuelto   10. puesto   11. hecho   12. llegado   13. he dormido   14. has roto
       15. ha abierto   16. hemos estado   17. habéis escrito   18. han visto

8.3   1. ha traído   2. hemos recibido   3. han llamado   4. han prestado   5. has amado
       6. han vuelto   7. se ha muerto   8. se han ido   9. han hecho   10. han hablado
       11. han viajado   12. he visto   13. he podido   14. se han acostado   15. nos hemos mudado

8.4   1. haber   2. hemos   3. han   4. haber   5. hemos   6. ha   7. han   8. haber   9. Han
       10. han

8.5   1. He cruzado la calle a la escuela.   2. Jamás he entrado en la clase.   3. Mis compañeros han entrado también.   4. Le hemos dicho "hola" al profesor.   5. Nos hemos sentado. 6. He escrito con lápiz.   7. Mis amigos han usado una computadora antes.   8. Hemos contestado las preguntas.   9. Hemos almorzado juntos.   10. Nos hemos despedido del profesor.   11. Hemos ido en bus a casa.   12. Les hemos saludado a nuestros padres al llegar a casa.

8.6   1. ¿Cómo has estado? / ¿Cómo ha estado? / ¿Cómo han estado?   2. ¿Adónde han ido todas las flores?   3. ¿Quién acaba de llamar?   4. ¿Qué has hecho? / ¿Qué ha hecho?   5. Hemos mandado/enviado el documento.   6. ¿Se han desayunado ellos hoy?   7. He prendido el horno, y he metido el pollo. Tengo que cocinarlo por una hora.   8. Ya no hace calor porque los estudiantes han abierto todas las ventanas en el salón.   9. Los exterminadores han matado todas las cucarachas.   10. Laura y su hija acaba de llegar a Italia.

Chapter 9
The Past Perfect Tense

9.1   1. Los niños pensaban/pensaron que sus padres habían salido.   2. Ya había puesto la mesa cuando mi familia llegó.   3. Roberto fue a un país que él nunca había visitado antes. 4. Mis colegas me dijeron que ellos habían terminado su trabajo.

9.2   1. The professor knew that I had studied.   2. The child thought that her dog had returned.   3. They said that they had returned the books to the library.   4. We believed that our friends had written to us.   5. We were sure that the young people had been successful / had had success.   6. We thought that the thieves had been in the bank. 7. The police believed that we had seen them.   8. We told the detectives that we had not been good witnesses.

9.3   1. ido   2. esperado, ver   3. descansado, cenar   4. jubilarse, pagado   5. dado, salir 6. dicho, perdido

9.4   1. quemada   2. rota   3. muerto   4. hecha   5. expresadas   6. dormido   7. querido 8. vendidos   9. compradas   10. pasado   11. resueltos   12. alquilado   13. escondido 14. entregadas   15. grabada

9.5   1. está cerrada   2. está abierta   3. está escrita   4. está construida   5. está hecha 6. están muertas   7. están fritos   8. están resueltos

9.6   1. Cerrada   2. herido, preocupados   3. nublado   4. arreglado   5. separada, dividido

9.7   1. Los antropólogos hallaron los vasos.   2. Un dictador ha gobernado el país. 3. El maestro enseñó la clase.   4. La víctima reconoció al criminal.   5. Los padres ofrecieron los regalos.   6. Catarina había planchado las camisas.   7. Los inquilinos apagaron las luces.   8. Se dice que Colón descubrió las Américas en 1492.

Chapter 10
The Future Tense

10.1   1. iré   2. llegará   3. veré   4. estudiaremos   5. corregirá   6. comprará   7. dejará 8. acompañará, viajaré   9. estarás   10. triunfarán   11. asistirán   12. cobrará 13. venceremos   14. responderás

10.2   1. haré   2. vendrá   3. saldrá   4. diremos   5. podrás   6. pondrán   7. valdrá 8. tendrá   9. sabrá   10. Habrá

10.3 1. Si ella no tiene cuidado, se perderá. 2. Si Jorge me lo dice, yo no se lo repetiré a nadie. 3. Si practicamos, podremos aprender un idioma nuevo. 4. Ellos comprarán la casa si les gustan el jardín y el balcón. 5. Si la obra de teatro es chistosa/divertida, el público se reirá. 6. Él nunca se fijará en nada. No se quejará jamás.

10.4 1. Él vendrá a verme. 2. Tendré una cita con el dentista en febrero. 3. ¿Cuánto valdrá el carro? 4. ¿Qué me dirás? 5. Saldremos para México en julio. 6. Trabajaré en un teatro. 7. Habrá once estudiantes aquí. 8. Empezaremos a estudiar. 9. El muchacho tendrá éxito. 10. Los deportistas tendrán sed. 11. ¿Cuánto me cobrará Ud.? 12. Yo patinaré porque me gusta. 13. Ella no se meterá en la vida de los otros. 14. El pueblo vencerá. 15. Triunfaremos. 16. La muchacha cumplirá diez años el miércoles. 17. Olivia vivirá en Perú. 18. La maestra corregirá la tarea. 19. Yo asistiré a la universidad. 20. Elena soñará que te vio. / Elena sueña que te verá.

10.5 1. I will know more tomorrow than what I know today. 2. Three chairs and eight students will not fit in the classroom. 3. The doctors will not sleep until four o'clock in the morning. 4. I will return soon. 5. From time to time, I will visit you in Brazil. 6. If you want to go shopping, I will take you. 7. If he becomes nervous, he will speak softly. 8. If you run a lot, you will be able to lose weight. 9. If you lose your keys, what will you do? 10. They tell me that you will get married next year.

10.6 1. ¿Tendrá hambre el niño? 2. ¿Qué hará la mujer? 3. ¿Quién pondrá la mesa? 4. Ella sabrá las direcciones. 5. ¿Cuánto valdrá este apartamento lujoso?

10.7 1. Where will you have gone after leaving your house? 2. We will have bought our tickets for Saturday. 3. I will have seen the students before they travel to Mexico. 4. In one month, I will have lived here for 10 years. 5. Will you have finished your work for the coming week?

Chapter 11
The Conditional Tense

11.1 1. produciría 2. haríamos 3. dirían 4. vendría 5. daría 6. se acostarían 7. regresarían 8. llevaría 9. gustaría 10. Habría 11. vería 12. saldríamos 13. llegaría 14. entendería 15. podría 16. iría

11.2 1. Yo la ayudaría. 2. Ella iría de compras. 3. ¿Mirarías tú televisión? 4. Ellos venderían la comida. 5. Los mozos les darían la comida a los clientes. 6. Tendríamos mucho que hacer. 7. El conductor manejaría rápidamente. 8. ¿Cantarías? 9. ¿Vendrían Uds. a mi casa? 10. Yo lo haría. 11. No le diría nada. 12. Te cobraría cien dólares. 13. Los niños no leerían mucho. 14. Sabría nadar. 15. Habría mucha gente en los trenes. 16. No cabrían más. 17. Le traería las flores a su hermana. 18. Nos pondríamos los zapatos. 19. Podría Ud. acompañarme al bus? 20. ¿A Uds. les gustaría ir al cine?

11.3 1. podría 2. se mejoraría 3. me quejaría 4. diríamos 5. se divertirían 6. estaría 7. tendrían 8. dolerían

11.4 1. A José le gustaría nadar, pero tiene miedo del agua. 2. Yo no le diría nada porque no lo conozco bien. 3. Nuestros amigos mexicanos vendrían a California a visitar a su familia, pero prefieren viajar a Europa este año. 4. Juan me dijo que le daría el libro si quiere estudiarlo. / Juan me dijo que le daría el libro si lo quiere estudiar. / Juan me dijo que te daría el libro si quieres estudiarlo. / Juan me dijo que te daría el libro si lo quieres estudiar. 5. Iríamos a la fiesta de Julia, pero no sabemos dónde vive.

11.5   1. Él habría llegado a tiempo, pero se le perdieron las direcciones.   2. No le habríamos dicho nuestro secreto a nadie.   3. Juan y su compañero habrían ido a México, pero decidieron ahorrar su dinero para el año entrante.   4. Antonio y yo habríamos viajado a Colombia, pero el vuelo costó demasiado.   5. Enrique habría sido un buen presidente, pero quería tener más tiempo para pasar con su familia.   6. Elvira habría devuelto el dinero que halló, pero se lo dio a su hijo.

Chapter 12
The Present Perfect Subjunctive

12.1   1. ¿Es posible que ellos se hayan dormido?   2. Es probable que hayamos tenido muchas oportunidades.   3. Estamos alegres de que nuestros dos amigos se hayan conocido.
4. Estoy triste de que el hotel no me haya llamado para confirmar mi reservación.
5. José espera que nosotros nos hayamos sentido bien.   6. El abogado se alegra de que sus clientes hayan leído el contrato.   7. Los ingenieros lo sienten que los edificios hayan tenido problemas.   8. El trabajador está triste de que su jefe no lo haya llamado para averiguar donde está.

12.2   1. hayan estado   2. haya salvado   3. nos hayamos atrevido   4. haya leído   5. haya sido
6. se hayan demorado   7. se hayan levantado   8. se hayan divertido   9. hayan venido
10. se haya roto

Chapter 13
The Imperfect Subjunctive

13.1   1. hablara: It was important that James speak to me.   2. se sintiera: It was a shame that she didn't feel well last night.   3. conocieran: Was it possible that you knew my sister?
4. hiciéramos: It was necessary that we do exercises.   5. hubiera: It was impossible that there was no traffic today.   6. llegara: It was urgent that the ambulance arrive within five minutes.   7. diéramos: It was possible that we gave a present to the teacher.
8. dijera, mintiera: It was doubtful that my niece told me the truth; it was possible that she lied to me.   9. se mejoraran: It would be good that you get better.   10. se graduara: It was probable that the whole class graduated.   11. se fuera: It would be impossible that Sara left without saying anything to us.   12. llamáramos: It was good that we called her.
13. tomaran: It would be necessary that the tourists drink a lot of water in the mountains.
14. viajáramos: It would be doubtful that we travel to Mexico this year.   15. se quedaran: It was possible that Beatriz and Isabel stayed in Italy.

13.2   1. I wanted them to write to me.   2. My neighbor preferred that I bring nothing to him.
3. We were glad that he arrived early.   4. She begged us not to go.   5. I was glad that you moved to a house.   6. The owner insisted that we pay the rent.   7. I told my friend to call me.   8. The tourist suggested to the cab driver that he not drive so fast.

13.3   1. hablara   2. estudiara   3. bailara   4. cantara   5. vinieran

13.4   1. se quedaran   2. trajéramos   3. comiera   4. prestara   5. ayudáramos   6. votáramos

13.5   1. estuvieran   2. te callaras   3. hiciéramos   4. acompañara

13.6   1. The child wanted his parents to bring him a present.   2. Michael's friends wanted him to lose weight.   3. Why did you want me to lend you money?   4. Fred hoped that Linda would marry him.   5. The student in Spain was glad that her parents were proud of her. 6. I wanted them to stay with me.   7. We hoped that it was nothing serious. 8. The husband did not want his wife to retire.

13.7   1. cantar, cantar   2. comer, vivir   3. cuidaran   4. dejaran   5. esperara   6. se acostara 7. bajar   8. viajar   9. fuera   10. dijera

13.8   1. saber   2. pudieran   3. fuera   4. viniera   5. supiera   6. ducharse   7. saliera 8. lavarse, comer   9. tuvieran   10. dijera   11. estuviera   12. ir   13. empezara 14. necesitara

13.9   1. Laura quería/quiso que su esposo la acompañara a Chile.   2. Era/Fue necesario que la gente no fumara en los restaurantes.   3. Julia estaba/estuvo contenta de que Uds. estuvieran aquí.   4. Yo sabía que su nieta quería ir a la universidad.   5. Me alegré de que pudieras correr en el maratón.   6. ¿Qué querías que yo hiciera?   7. Raúl y yo esperábamos/esperamos que Uds. se encontraran bien.   8. Era/Fue importante que el carpintero supiera lo que estaba haciendo.   9. Esperaba/Esperé que el vuelo de mis amigos llegara a tiempo.   10. Los deportistas dudaban/dudaron que ganáramos el partido. 11. Nuestros amigos nos rogaban/rogaron que no subiéramos a la cumbre de la montaña. 12. Los entrenadores insistían/insistieron que la gente hiciera más ejercicio.

13.10   1. Era/Fue necesario que ella empezara las lecciones a tiempo.   2. Era/Fue una lástima que él no supiera expresarse.   3. ¿Sería posible que ellos ya hubieran salido de la reunión? 4. Los hijos de Juana le rogaban/rogaron que no fumara.   5. ¿Quisieras que yo hablara con tu jefe?   6. Mi hermano dudó que yo cantara bien ayer.   7. La maestra de mi hija sugirió que yo la llamara.   8. Yo quería que ellos se quedaran conmigo. Ellos querían que yo fuera con ellos.   9. Me gustaría hacer un documental que se trata de los inca.   10. Yo quiero tomar su foto, si no le molesta.

13.11   1. fuera, sería   2. gustara, iría   3. escribiéramos, respondería   4. me sintiera, podría 5. ganarían, vendieran   6. dormirían, se acostaran   7. hablaríamos, supiéramos 8. tendría, se pusiera   9. lloraría, doliera   10. me iría, quisiera, me quedara

Chapter 14
The Past Perfect Subjunctive

14.1   1. hubiéramos pagado   2. hubiéramos hecho   3. hubiera dicho   4. hubiera viajado 5. hubiera venido   6. hubiera llovido   7. se hubieran mejorado   8. se hubieran casado 9. hubiéramos gastado   10. hubieran vivido

14.2   1. I wish / Would to God that we had not said it to him/you/her.   2. I wish that you had been well.   3. I wish that we had gone on vacation.   4. It was necessary that the carpenter construct it. / It was necessary for the carpenter to have constructed it.   5. It was urgent that we take the sick man to the hospital.   6. It was a pity that no one had been in the theater.   7. We hoped that everyone had taken advantage of the situation. 8. The doormen doubted that the new tenants had painted the walls.   9. The lawyer didn't think that his clients had won.   10. It was possible that the thieves had robbed the bank.

14.3   1. Yo habría ido.   2. Tú habrías comido. / Ud. habría comido. / Uds. habrían comido. 3. Nos habríamos reído.   4. Ellos le habrían dicho.   5. Los maestros habrían enseñado. 6. Marisa habría estado contenta.   7. Hillary habría sido presidente.   8. Habría sido posible.   9. Las mujeres lo habrían aprendido.   10. Los hombres habrían salido.

14.4　　1. Yo habría ido a la fiesta si yo no hubiera tenido miedo.　2. Ud. habría comido el pescado si lo hubiéramos cocinado en casa.　3. Nos habríamos reído si la película hubiera sido chistosa/divertida.　4. Ellos te habrían dicho la verdad si tú la hubieras querido saber. / Ellos te habrían dicho la verdad si tú hubieras querido saberla.　5. Los maestros habrían enseñado si los estudiantes hubieran llegado.　6. Marisa habría estado contenta si hubiera sabido patinar.　7. Hillary habría sido presidente si más gente hubiera votado por ella.　8. Habría sido posible que me hubieran visto.　9. Las mujeres lo habrían aprendido si hubieran comprado el libro.　10. Los hombres habrían salido de la casa si hubieran tenido adonde ir.

14.5　　1. estén　2. corra　3. guste　4. te quejes　5. sepamos　6. ganen　7. vengan　8. tenga　9. se sientan　10. se vistan

14.6　　1. se acueste　2. lleve　3. se vaya　4. consigan　5. entren　6. se caigan

14.7　　1. escuchen　2. vaya　3. fume　4. haga　5. cante

14.8　　1. conozcan　2. pueda　3. duerma　4. trabajen　5. sean　6. tengan　7. logre　8. aprendamos

14.9　　1. entraran　2. hubiera　3. trajera　4. nos fijáramos　5. te sentaras　6. saliéramos

14.10　　1. se mejorara　2. regresara　3. encantara　4. diera　5. nos animáramos　6. vieras

14.11　　1. empezara　2. desistiera　3. se perdieran　4. fuera　5. pudiera　6. estuviera　7. habláramos　8. supiera　9. dijera　10. ganaras

14.12　　1. The author read the article so that we could understand it.　2. Before his girlfriend went to Spain, Fred studied Spanish for two years.　3. We were going to play tennis until it began to rain.　4. The doctor knew that his patient's knee had swollen.　5. Elena would learn to speak Spanish, but she doesn't like to study.　6. It was necessary for the best architect to design the museum.　7. It wouldn't be possible for such a disaster to occur.　8. The judge hoped that the witnesses had seen everything.　9. The tourists would arrive a two o'clock if the trains weren't so delayed.　10. I would have gone on vacation with her if she had invited me.　11. Would you have done him the favor if Andrew had asked you?　12. Would it be possible that you learned and understood all the lessons?

Chapter 15
Idioms

15.1　　1. At the beginning, everything was wonderful.　2. You put on your blouse inside out. 3. By dint of study, she learned history well.　4. We went to Madrid on foot. 5. Don't speak to me now; I'm in a bad mood.　6. They didn't find their keys anywhere. 7. I don't know what to do in regard to your/his/her/their problems.　8. By day, I work; by night, I sleep.　9. If we want to arrive on time, we have to go to the right.　10. The girl can / is able to listen to music and study at the same time.　11. I think I'll be in Mexico at the beginning of July.　12. He lent me his car unwillingly.　13. They like to dine in the open air.　14. In fact, Paul found out yesterday but said nothing to me.　15. A boat carried us across the river.　16. I am in a very good mood today.　17. You should walk to the left. 18. Probably Henry and Salome will come next week.　19. We do it willingly. 20. The man prefers to walk straight ahead.　21. In the distance, I see her coming. 22. I like to rest. On the other hand, my friend likes to work.　23. I tell them to do it in this way.　24. I write scripts for television. Really?　25. Michael doesn't have a lot of money, but he decided to travel anyway.   26. You weren't successful the first time, but you tried again.   27. From now on, we are going to run every day.   28. We attend class every other day.   29. Suddenly, it began to rain.   30. One sees the good and the bad everywhere.

15.2   1. c   2. f   3. d   4. e   5. b   6. a

15.3   1. The girl pays attention to her teacher because she likes him.   2. Elisa gets along well with her mother-in-law.   3. The boy liked to feed the birds in the park.   4. The hotel faces the plaza.   5. Bill became a lawyer.   6. The visitor hasn't seen her homeland for a long time. She misses it a lot and wants to give all her friends a hug.   7. I liked the Guatemalan vest; I gave 200 pesos to the seller and carried it away.   8. I realized that everything was not all right.   9. The child burst out crying.   10. Shellfish harms me.

15.4   *Answers will vary. Some possible answers are shown.*   1. ¿Cuánto tiempo hace que el muchacho mira televisión?   2. ¿Desde cuándo duerme Adam?   3. ¿Cuánto tiempo lleva Ud. llevando gafas?   4. ¿Cuánto tiempo hace que Isabel y Carlos esperan?   5. ¿Desde cuándo son amigos ellos?   6. Hace ocho horas que él duerme.   7. Llevo dos años llevando gafas.   8. Hace quince minutos que ellos esperan.

15.5   1. How long had you been in Chile when you had to leave?   2. How long had the children been swimming when the lifeguard arrived?   3. How long had Tony been reading when he fell asleep?   4. I had been in Paraguay for two months when I decided to return home.   5. The frustrated man had been waiting for the train for 20 minutes.   6. We had been living in Paris for 15 months.

Index

An italic page number refers to a tense conjugation
of the verb.

abrir, *223*
acabar de, 165
acompañar, *33*
Adjectives
  demonstrative, 144
  possessive
    long-form, 132–34
    short-form, 130–31
  used as nouns, 149
admitir, *201*
andar, *31, 224*
apagar, *76*
Articles, 125–30, 137–38
  definite, 125, 126–30
  inclusion and omission of
    with nouns, 125, 126–30
    after **ser**, 137–38
  indefinite, 126
asistir, *184*
atender, *183*
ayudar, *29, 199*

bailar, *71, 222*
beber, *201, 222*
buscar, *76*

caber, *31, 186, 203, 225*
caer, *183*
cantar, *29, 71, 181, 222*
cerrar, *71, 222*

cobrar, *182*
comenzar, *76*
comer, *30, 72, 183, 222*
Commands, 97–111
  affirmative **tú**
    formation of, 98
    placement of object pronouns with, 100–101
    review, 104
  affirmative **Ud.**
    formation of, 107
    placement of object pronouns with, 108–9
    review, 110
  affirmative **Uds.**
    formation of, 108
    placement of object pronouns with, 108–9
    review, 110
  affirmative **vosotros**
    formation of, 118
    use of, 118, 119
  favor de + infinitive, 110
  hacer el favor de + infinitive, 111
  negative **tú**
    formation of, 102–3
    placement of object pronouns with, 103–4
    review, 104
  negative **Ud.**
    formation of, 107–8
    placement of object pronouns with, 109
    review, 110
  negative **Uds.**
    formation of, 108
    placement of object pronouns with, 109
    review, 110

negative **vosotros**
  formation of, 118–19
  use of, 118, 119
with nosotros
  formation of, 115–17
  placement of object pronouns with, 115–16
  puede Ud. + infinitive, 111
  tener la bondad de + infinitive, 110
como, 91
como si, 236
compartir, *30, 185*
Conditional perfect tense
  formation of, 210
  uses of, 210–11
Conditional progressive tense
  formation of, 209
  uses of, 210
Conditional tense
  formation of
    -ar verbs, 199–200
    -er verbs, 201
    -ir verbs, 201–2
    irregular verbs, 202–5
  placement of object pronouns with, 206–7
  uses of, 205, 209
conocer, *73, 201, 223*
corregir, *185*
cuando, 87
cumplir, *184*
cuyo, cuya, cuyos, cuyas, 140

dar, *32, 33, 75, 182, 225*
  in idioms, 264
de
  compared with **dé** (subjunctive form), 75
  contraction with **el**, 10
  uses of
    to express possession, 10
    to form compound nouns, 129
decir, *32, 34, 73, 186, 203, 226*
Definite articles, 125, 126–30
Demonstrative pronouns, 144–45
descubrir, *30*
Direct object pronouns. *See* Pronouns, object
dirigir, *185*
disfrutar, *200*
dormir, *31, 72, 202, 224*
Double object pronouns. *See* Pronouns, object

echar, in idioms, 264
el cual, la cual, los cuales, las cuales, 142–43

el de, la de, los de, las de, 150
el que, la que, los que, las que, 142
empezar, *76*
entender, *30, 223*
escribir, *223*
escuchar, used with the gerund or infinitive, 53
estar, *3, 22, 25, 32, 75, 182, 200, 225*
  common expressions with, 15
  uses of
    to express a personal opinion, 4, 16, 17, 24, 26
    to form progressive tenses, 41, 45, 58–59
    to indicate a changing mood or condition,
      4, 22, 26
    to indicate health status, 4, 22, 25
    to indicate location, 3, 22, 25
exigir, *202*
explicar, *76*

felicitar, *200*
festejar, *200*
fingir, *202*
fracasar, *200*
Future perfect tense
  formation of, 196
  uses of, 197
Future progressive tense
  formation of, 195
  uses of, 195
Future tense
  expressed by **ir** + **a** + infinitive, 46
  formation of
    -ar verbs, 181–83
    -er verbs, 183–84
    -ir verbs, 184–85
    irregular verbs, 186–88
  placement of object pronouns with, 194
  uses of, 188, 192–93

Gerund
  formation of, 41–44, 53
    -ar verbs, 41
    -er verbs, 42
    -ir verbs, 42
    irregular verbs, 43–44
    orthographic changes in, 42–43
  uses of
    to form the imperfect progressive tense,
      58–60
    to form the present progressive tense,
      41, 45
    without a helping verb, 53

Gerund, uses of (*continued*)
    with **ir**, 52
    with **llevar**, 52
    with **seguir**, 52
    verbs not used in gerund form, 53, 59–60,
        59–60
gozar, *182*
gustar, with the definite article, 127

haber, *33, 34, 75, 187, 204, 226*
    without the definite article, 127
    in idioms, 265
    in the infinitive with a past participle after a
        preposition, 161–62, 168
hablar, without the definite article, 127
hacer, *32, 73, 186, 203*
    in idioms, 264–65
hay. *See* **haber**

Idioms, 260–69
    with prepositions, 260–61
    with verbs, 263–66
      dar, 264
      echar, 264
      hacer, 264–65
      hay, 265
      llevar, 265
      meter, 265
      poner, 265
      quedar, 265
      tener, 263–64
      tomar, 266
Imperfect progressive tense
    formation of, 58–59
    uses of, 59–60
Imperfect subjunctive, 221–43
    formation of
      -ar verbs, 222
      -er verbs, 222–23
      -ir verbs, 223–24
      irregular verbs, 224–26
    in sequence of tenses, 252
    translation of, 230
    uses of, 221, 227
      after certain conjunctions, 235–36
      after certain dependent adjective clauses,
        236
      after certain expressions, 236–38
      after certain impersonal expressions, 227–28
      after certain verbs, 229–30
      after **si** in a contrary-to-fact **si**-clause, 240–41

Imperfect tense, 25–36
    compared to the preterit tense, 27, 35–36
    of irregular verbs, 35
    of regular verbs, 33–35
    uses of, 25
      to express English *would*, 205
      to replace the past progressive tenses, 58
Indefinite articles, 126
Indirect object pronouns. *See* Pronouns, object
inscribirse, *185*
ir, *32, 35, 75, 185, 202, 226*
    + **a** + infinitive (future periphrastic), 46, 91, 92,
      217

leer, *183*
llegar, *76*
llenar, *200*
llevar, in idioms, 265
lo
    + adjective, 147
    expressions with, 147
lo que, 140–41

marchar, *182*
medir, *202*
mentir, *31, 72, 224*
merecer, *184*
meter, in idioms, 265
mirar, used with the gerund or infinitive, 53
morirse, *224*

no, position of, before **estar**, 45
Nouns, 125–30
    abstract, 128
    adjectives used as, 149
    in apposition, 129–30
    inclusion and omission of articles with, 125,
      126–30
    neuter **lo** + adjective, 147
    pronouns used as, 150

oír, used with the gerund or infinitive, 53
ojalá, 89, 236, 246–47
opinar, *182*

Passive voice, 176–77
Past participles
    formation of, 154–57
    uses of
      as an adjective with **estar**, 172–74
      in formation of the past perfect tense, 167–68

in formation of the present perfect tense, 157–58
with the infinitive **haber** after a preposition, 161–62, 168
in the passive voice with **ser**, 176–77
Past perfect subjunctive, 243–53
formation of, 245
in sequence of tenses, 253
uses of, 245–53
after certain impersonal expressions, 246–47
after certain verbs, 246
after **si** in a contrary-to-fact conditional **si**-clause, 249–50
Past perfect tense, 167–68
formation of, 167
placement of object pronouns with, 168
uses of, 167–68
Past progressive tenses, 58–62. *See also* Imperfect progressive tense; Preterit progressive tense
uses of, 58
patinar, *182*
pedir, *31, 72, 224*
pegar, *182*
pensar, *29, 71*
poder, *32, 34, 72, 186, 203, 225*
poner, *32, 73, 186, 203, 225*
in idioms, 265
por, used with the passive voice, 176–77
Possession, expressing, 10
Possessive pronouns, 135–37
Prepositions
in idioms, 260–61
+ infinitive, 47
position of, 9
Present perfect subjunctive, 214–17. *See also* Past participle
formation of, 214
in sequence of tenses, 252
uses of, 214–15, 217
Present perfect tense, 154–62. *See also* Past participle
formation of, 157–58
placement of object pronouns with, 160–61
uses of, 159–62
Present progressive tense, 40–47
English translation of, 46
formation of, 41, 45. *See also* gerund
uses of, 40–41, 45, 92
Present subjunctive
formation of, 70–77
-**ar** verbs, 71

-**er** verbs, 72–74
-**ir** verbs, 72–75
irregular verbs, 75
verbs with orthographic changes, 76
in sequence of tenses, 252
uses of, 70
after **acaso, quizás**, or **tal vez**, 89
after **aunque**, 90
after certain conjunctions, 85–87
in certain dependent adjective clauses, 89
after certain impersonal expressions, 77–78
after certain tenses, 91–92
after certain verbs, 79–83
after **como**, 91
after compounds of -**quiera**, 90
after **cuando**, 87
after **ojalá**, 89
after **por más que** and **por mucho que**, 89
Present tense
of **estar**, 3
expressing the future, 193
of **ser**, 8
uses of, 40, 53, 111
Preterit progressive tense
formation of, 61
uses of, 61–62
Preterit tense, 21–36
compared to the imperfect tense, 27, 35–36
of irregular verbs, 31–33
of regular verbs, 29–31
-**ar** verbs, 29
-**er** verbs, 30
-**ir** verbs, 30–31
uses of, 21
producir, *32, 226*
Progressive tenses. *See* Past progressive tenses; Present progressive tense
Pronouns
demonstrative, 144–45
object
direct, 48–50
double, 49–50
indirect, 48–50
placement of, 48–50, 100–101, 103–4, 160–61, 162, 194
reflexive, 48–50
possessive, 135–37
relative, 139–41
subject, 3, 4, 45, 48
used as nouns, 150

Pronunciation
  of **d**, 155, 199
  of future tense forms, 183
  of imperfect subjunctive forms, 224
  of imperfect tense forms, 34
  of past participles, 155
  of present subjunctive forms, 77
  of preterit tense forms, 30
  of trilled **r**, 200
proteger, *201*
pudiera, 237–38

que (conjunction), 77
que (pronoun), 139
quedar, in idioms, 265
querer, *32, 34, 72, 186, 203, 225*
quien, 139–41
quisiera, 237, 247

Reading comprehension
  El apartamento, 165
  El barco económico, 234
  El conde Lucanor, 178
  La defensa de Sócrates, 270
  Lo fatal, 152
  El hospital, 67–68
  La isla en el Caribe, 218–19
  El juicio, 94
  Machu Picchu, 19
  Los maderos de San Juan, 151
  Marianela, 38
  Mi viaje, 146
  La Noche de Brujas, 121–22
  La parada del bus, 56
  Perdida en Nicaragua, 113–14
  El porvenir, 197
  ¿Qué haría Ud. en las siguientes situaciones? 212
  Recordando Nicaragua, 171
  Su punto de vista, 257–58
  El sueño, 170
  Xochicalco, 243
recordar, *29, 71, 200, 222*
Reflexive pronouns. *See* Pronouns, object
regresar, *183*
Relative pronouns, 139–41
responder, *184*

saber, *32, 34, 75, 187, 203, 225*
salir, *31, 73, 187, 203, 223*

seguir, *224*
  used with the gerund or infinitive, 53, 59, 62
sentirse, *34*
Sequence of tenses, 252–53
ser, *8, 23, 26, 33, 35, 75, 184, 201, 226*
  common expressions with, 15
  uses of
    to describe someone or something, 8, 16, 17, 23, 24, 26
    to express possession/ownership, 9–10
    to express what something is made of, 9
    to express where an event takes place, 10
    to identify someone or something, 9, 23, 27
    in impersonal expressions, 11
    to indicate point of origin, 9, 26
    to indicate profession, 8, 23
    to tell time, 11, 27
si-clauses, 249
Subject pronouns, 3, 4, 45, 48
Subjunctive mood. *See individual subjunctive tenses*

tener, *32, 34, 73, 187, 204, 225*
  in idioms, 263–64
Time expressions, 267–69
tocar, *76*
tomar, in idioms, 266
trabajar, *33*
traer, *32, 73, 201, 226*
triunfar, *183*

valer, *187, 204*
vencer, *184*
venir, *32, 34, 73, 187, 204, 225*
  used with the gerund, 59, 62
ver, *30, 31, 35, 72, 184, 223*
  used with the gerund or infinitive, 53
Verb tenses. *See individual verb tenses*
vivir, *72,185, 223*
Vocabulary, key
  adjectives, 6
    of time, 21
  adverbs
    of direction, 5
    of location, 5
    of time, 21
  interrogative words, 5
  prepositions of location, 5–6
volver, *201, 223*